Fostering Spirituality in the Workplace

A Leader's Guide to Sustainability

Priscilla Berry

First published in 2013 by
Business Expert Press, LLC
222 East 46th Street, New York, NY 10017
www.businessexpertpress.com

ISBN-13: 978-1-60649-652-7 (paperback)
ISBN-13: 978-1-60649-653-4 (e-book)

Business Expert Press Principles of Responsible Management (PRME)
collection

Collection ISSN: Forthcoming (print)
Collection ISSN: Forthcoming (electronic)

Cover and interior design by Exeter Premedia Services Private Ltd.,
Chennai, India

First edition: 2013

10 9 8 7 6 5 4 3 2 1

Printed in the United States of America.

Writing a book is always a journey, and this text has proven no exception. It would not have been possible without the support of and real help in data mining, editing, and writing from my friend Amy Cavanaugh. It was wonderful, Amy, having a psychic on my sofa. More gratitude to you than you will ever know. My daughter Catherine provided energy and encouragement. In addition, my inspiration always comes from my students, many of whom I can still see their faces.

There is no greater calling than to teach, and teaching is the greatest part of anyone's legacy. I have learned more from my students than they have learned from me. My passion for learning and teaching comes from my Mom, thanks Mom.

In conversations about this book, all my friends said they could not wait to buy my book; I hope they keep their promise.

If one body like the United Nations, or one organization like the World Justice Project, or one movement like the Clinton Initiative can continue to bring a voice for world peace and freedom from oppression now by realizing the innate dignity of man, there is hope. If this book causes one corporation to rethink its strategy and seek its spiritual core or if one leader realizes the necessity to incorporate spirituality in the workplace, the synergy will be amazing.

Love you all,

pb

Abstract

This book explores historical data, analyzes current events from the world stage, and delivers a worldview that challenges some existing paradigms in business. As we are living business history, the book draws from the epic economic, environmental, and cultural shifts in our collective consciousness. The impact of these deep and rapid changes on companies, employees, and the global economy cannot be underestimated and future world leaders must be prepared to lead in a manner that is socially responsible, ethical, and profitable. A corporation with a business model that polarizes or operates solely in the interest of its shareholders is unsustainable. Current benchmarks are unrealistic tools for businesses to rely upon as measures of future success. The mindset of profitability at any cost is causing us to grapple with a historically unprecedented world crisis, which threatens civilization, as we know it. A widespread erosion of ethics and responsible behavior in the business world has resulted from a failure of society and institutions of higher education to instill and teach moral principles.

In response, this short read begins a vital conversation by introducing some thought paradigms that will challenge current business practices, create a vision for the future, and provide a road map to navigate this uncharted territory.

Those in a position of power and influence must stage an immediate revolution or we will be crushed by what we have created. This is not a doomsday prophecy, rather a statement of patterns that have been quantified by scientists, economists, and educators. Readers of this book will be ignited and transformed by a compelling personal and professional call to action resulting in the realignment of corporate values and operations. Just as great tribal leaders historically came together, business leaders must set their intention on protecting the human and capital resources of their corporations for the higher good of society and the world.

Graduate business students and corporate leaders are made aware in this book how we are now operating in a business environment that has forever changed. It outlines specific action that students must understand and corporate leaders must take now to end the economic and moral decline in this first part of the 21st century.

Keywords

corporate social responsibility, the UN compact, leadership, corporate governance, sustainability, ethics, integrity, the Euro zone, fiscal crisis.

Contents

Foreword

"The truth is in the story" and Dr. Berry has a fascinating story to relate. Here is a remarkable educator who recognizes the influence of world events, and has suggestions for adapting to a very different and challenging environment. The author is highly sensitive to the daily change in communications, and this should alert every reader. We must awaken to reality.

From losing our "moral compass" to finding our "global selves", we travel an amazing road with the author. Each chapter reveals our own journey, and we become sensitive to the fact we have concentrated on our mind and body, with little reference to our spirit. Here is a masterful description of what has happened in our society. This author addresses this sensitive subject with brilliance.

All of us learn from this amazing story, whether the reader is the corporate leader or a business major in a college. The book is a great "read."

Dr. Francis B. Kinne

About Dr. Kinne

The first woman president of a Florida university, Francis Bartlett Kinne became president of Jacksonville University in 1979. Two months after becoming President, she created the JU Davis College of Business and established the School of Nursing. After leading the University for 10 years, she became Chancellor Emeritus in 1994.

Dr. Kinne is the author of Iowa Girl: *The President Wears a Skirt* c. 2000.

Preface

The Truth Is in the Story

Southerners share their wisdom through storytelling. I am a southern girl and these are my stories...the stories I have lived, the stories I have read, the stories that were told to me, the stories that form the fabric of my life and the life of the world. It is, after all, the story that is the core of life; without the story, we have nothing. We do not grow or move forward in any manner unless the story is told...the story of who we are, the story of what we do, the story of why we do the things we do. Countries, corporations, and communities need the stories and corporate leaders need now to be the storytellers. We must never allow ourselves to be so distracted that we fail to hear the story, because without the story, we do not have our souls or the wisdom and vision to find our way forward. We do not grow or move forward in any manner unless the story is told. We can be the master of our fate, the captain of our destiny, but only if we listen to and repeat the story.[1]

We do not grow or move forward in any manner unless the story is told.

Our Global Selves

It does not matter who you are or where you are in the world; you are impacted now by world events and the actions taken by other people who, in the past, were seemingly not connected to you. It is not possible for us or for any developed economy to disaggregate from world events. Being uninformed or ignorant of the world does not take you out of it. In every community, corporation, and country, the people who survive will have one quality in common: the capacity to change and adapt. The course we are on is not sustainable, and civilizations and peoples have faced this in the past. The survivors are those who adapt; this is the highest and most evolved characteristic of the human species; and only the species who adapt will live to tell the tale!

Darwin's Evolution

Fostering Spirituality in the Workplace is about the world's Darwinist obsession with monetary success, which has come at a greater cost than we as a community, or corporation, or country are aware. The outcome of the survival of the fittest today, or that process of natural selection, which produces the fit, is that neither the world that it produced nor the leaders now seem so fit. The world of social selection is more, in a true Darwinian interpretation, the world of adaptability, and less Cain and Abel. However, the Cain and Abel model persists. Our greed causes us to kill. We have continued to work with old models, and think, in our naivetés, that ethical lapses or crimes are acceptable and tolerated in corporate and governmental leadership, and that through gaining the competitive edge, at any costs, we win. We have a whole generation or more of leaders whose culture has grown out of prestigious business schools based solely on Milton Friedman, who wrote many times that it was the sole responsibility of business to produce profit and that nothing else should be considered by the corporation.[2]

> *Corporate and business culture, and all aspects of culture for that matter, have been laboring under the same outmoded paradigm that has tended to stifle innovation and creativity in medicine.*
>
> Dr. Larry Malerba

Larry Malerba is a holistic physician, educator, and the author of *Green Medicine: Challenging the Assumptions of Conventional Health Care.*[3] Dr. Malerba writes articles for *Huffington Post, Natural News,* and the American Holistic Medical Association. The physician recently corresponded with me about my book and its thesis and this is how the concepts of *Fostering Spirituality in the Workplace* resonate within his work:

Corporate and business culture, and all aspects of culture for that matter, have been laboring under the same outmoded paradigm that has tended to stifle innovation and creativity in medicine. Western civilization's left-brain, analytical, and materialistic mode of perceiving and understanding tends to value

competition over cooperation, the quantitative at the expense of
the qualitative, and the status of the part over the well-being of
the whole, and quick fixes rather than processes that promote
genuine healing.[4]

While Darwinian survival of the fittest may apply in some limited
sense to lower life forms, it is a sign of skewed values and stunted awareness in human endeavors. The popular notion of unlimited growth is a
delusion. Modern capitalism's single-minded and slavish dedication to
profit and the bottom line is a destructive force that fails in the long run
to recognize the interconnectedness of all things on all levels.

To neglect any one aspect is to bring potential harm to the general
well-being of the whole. The same principles of green health and healing that are being nurtured in the alternative medical movement can be
applied to all aspects of corporate culture. This ultimately entails a
broader holistic perspective that respects personal choice, embraces the
diversity of individual human potential, is grounded in ecological consciousness and spiritual awareness, and balances the needs of body,
heart, mind, and soul" (Personal communication with Dr. Malerba). As
we move Darwin through his evolution, we must absorb the holistic
view that shows how we are all connected and become conscious of our
spiritual nature.

Religion and Spirituality

The time is at hand for Corporate Leadership, the world over, to articulate the path to wholeness, which is achieved through infusing spirituality into the life of their workplace. To underscore how religion has
failed in its mission to connect man to the higher-order thinking of spirituality, a new survey by the Pew Research Center's Forum on Religion &
Public Life, conducted jointly with the PBS television program
Religion & Ethics NewsWeekly, *Nones on the Rise,* released ☉ October
10, 2012, confirms this reality with the numbers. "One-fifth of the
U.S. public—and a third of adults under 30—are religiously unaffiliated
today, the highest percentages ever in Pew Research Center polling.
Many of the country's 46 million unaffiliated adults report they are

religious or spiritual in some way. Two-thirds of them say they believe in God (68%). More than half say they often feel a deep connection with nature and the earth (58%), while more than a third classify themselves as 'spiritual' but not 'religious' (37%), and one-in-five (21%) say they pray every day. In addition, most religiously unaffiliated Americans think that churches and other religious institutions benefit society by strengthening community bonds and aiding the poor."[5]

> *Everyone has a spirit including the agnostics, the atheist, and those who have gravitated away from religion, now referred to as "nones."*

The majority of people in the Pew Survey seemed to conclude that religion had lost its appeal, and they saw the religious institutions as being too caught-up with the same things as the secular world: money, power, politics, and increasing the separation of their practice of religion by their list of rules.[6]

Everyone has a spirit including the agnostics, the atheist, and those who have gravitated away from religion, now referred to as "nones." Obviously, cultivation of the human spirit is not always found in organized religion. Too often, the assumption that religion is a precursor to the spiritual proves inaccurate. We see clearly in the Pew Research Survey that the two are distinct in the minds of most people.

Note about the chapters: An International Insight, Discussion Questions, an Exercise, Supplemental Readings, and a Case Study are included in each chapter.

Many of the accounts in the narrative have date stamps ( ) to give the reader some idea of timing on the world stage for what is discussed and how it is a prognostication of what is/must come to pass in order for us to change our unsustainable course.

Here We Go!

Redefining the Community

Communities must become small cells acting locally to remain aware and create unity that makes the space they inhabit safe and secure for their children and the elderly. They do so by investing time and accepting as real and valuable the fact that "I am my brother's keeper" (Genesis, 4:9, KJV).[1] The homeless must become the responsibility of the community, not of a far-removed government agency. Some of this is already in place in our communities. For example, churches have a corporate structure living within communities; they have strong and organized systems of ingathering and distribution, and they listen to the need and meet the need.

John Donne, a 17th-century English poet, expresses the connectivity clearly:

> No man is an island,
> Entire of itself.
> Each is a piece of the continent,
> A part of the main.
> If a clod be washed away by the sea,
> Europe is the less.
> As well as if a promontory were.
> As well as if a manor of thine own
> Or of thine friends were.
> Each man's death diminishes me,
> For I am involved in mankind.
> Therefore, send not to know
> For whom the bell tolls,
> It tolls for thee.[2]

Change Is Coming, Ready or Not

No current world event can be discussed without integrating the events on 9/11 and its aftermath. At the time, it seemed an incomprehensible tragedy and now 11 years later, we know it went world over to the core of who we are and what we believe about ourselves. The attack also changed the paradigm of US domestic and multinational corporations, in that the destruction was directed to the US financial center and to the US military power. The corporate structure was seen as completely vulnerable for the first time. It did challenge the United States to consider retreating from the world stage, as many suggest may be the answer, to end the hatred that seems directed at US institutions and what is perceived as US Imperialism or hegemony.

Just as isolation and retreat are not a solution for survival, so war is not the answer.

Just as isolation and retreat are not a solution for survival, so war is not the answer. As a country and as a world, we must understand how the entire industrialized world was forever changed by the events of 9/11.

A group of 19, by number, militants, by designation, an extremist group of al-Qaeda commandeered four US airliners and, on a predetermined suicide mission spurred via their Islamic religion, flew two planes into the World Trade Center in New York. A third plane was flown into the Pentagon in Washington D.C., and courageous passengers brought down a fourth plane in a field outside Pennsylvania, intended for the United States Capital Building. This tragedy is often referred to just as 9/11 and has become a code word that triggers strong emotion in the US and fear world over. The attacks killed over 3,000 people in New York City and D.C. , and included in that number are more than 400 police officers and firefighters. The combat initiatives that were triggered by the terrorist attacks defined the presidency of George W. Bush.[3]

Just as many of us remember where we were when John Kennedy was shot and killed,[4] we also now remember where we were when 9/11 occurred. I was sitting next to George Stavridis; it was strange because we were in a gym, and one never sits in the gym. However, I always took every opportunity to talk with George, or at least exchange hearty quips with him; he was a master of one-liners. Occasionally, he would let me help tie the strings of his boxing gloves. George was staying fit—once a Marine, always a Marine. I am not sure of his age at the time, early to middle 70s maybe, but his dark eyes always flashed with a passion and thrill for life. As we sat that morning, the small TV in the gym began running the horror show, and when the plane hit the Pentagon, George grabbed my hand. "My son works in that building," he said. I was terror struck, and will remember the fear on George's face until the day I die. "What can we do?" he asked. My reply now seems so weak, but I said, "We will call the Red Cross; they will be the first responders. And we can pray." We did place the call and, of course, we prayed; all that could be done at that point was to collect information. George heard from his son, Jim, by the end of the day. At that time, it seemed an eternity had passed. George's son, Jim, was in the Pentagon, and Jim recalled that, when the plane struck, he was in his office on the 4th floor. His office was on the side of the building where the plane hit and about 150 feet away from the point of impact. The plane hit the 2nd floor or Jim would not be alive today. Jim, Admiral James G. Stavridis, Supreme Allied Commander, Europe and Commander United States European Command, says: "War is not the way, but a strong military is an imperative in today's world."[5]

We cannot walk blindly into some naïve "kum bah yah" notion that a single vision, shared by some, will automatically be embraced as the solution to the problems that beset us now. We cannot stop our push or fail to give our strong voice to the vision for peace and freedom for all.

We cannot walk blindly into some naïve "kum bah yah" notion that a single vision, shared by some, will automatically be embraced as the solution to the problems that beset us now. We cannot stop our push or fail to give our strong voice to the vision.

Admiral Stavridis was honored with a Freedom Award on behalf of all NATO troops at the Atlantic Council Freedom's Challenge dinner and awards ceremony held in Berlin in November 2009 in celebration of the 20th anniversary of the fall of the Berlin Wall. Secretary of State, Hillary Clinton, delivered the keynote address and Admiral Stavridis, in his acceptance of the award, quoted Carl Schurz, a German political leader who said: "If you want to be free, there is but one way,—it is to guarantee an equally full measure of liberty to all your neighbors. There is no other way."[6]

George was proud of his son, and a grateful nation thanks Admiral Stavridis for his service. Jim was spared on 9/11, and George died just 11 days after the 9/11 attack, yet another casualty of that tragic day in our history, one can only speculate the numbers of lives lost that are not in the final totals and not written on the wall. This is just one of thousands of stories that the world must never forget.

I am so moved today as I write on ☉ September 11, 2012, 11 years after 9/11, to hear General Martin E. Dempsey, chairman of the Joint Chiefs of Staff, as he represented the US military in such a strong and steadfast manner, and noted that in the numbers who died, there were individuals from 90 different countries.[7] The population of the United States is not a homogeneous grouping; the foreign-born in the United States number almost 40 million and of the foreign-born, 17 million are naturalized and 22 are noncitizens (US Census Bureau, 2012). A prayer was offered to begin the ceremony with a strong affirmation for the goal of continuing liberty for all and praying for the strength and courage to be "not weary in well doing" and to persevere. Interestingly, this ceremony comes 5 days after the Democratic Convention that augured over the language of the position for God on the platform.[8] On this day in September, President Obama seemed clear about the role of God as he spoke to the families and friends of those who died when he spoke of the message from Scripture that tells us to not be overcome by evil, but to overcome evil with good.[9] The *American Spectator* carried an article by Aaron Goldstein who writes, somewhat critical of the president's remarks, "It's all well and good to spend the anniversary of the September 11th attacks painting a mural celebrating our diversity. But if we want to overcome evil with good, we have to do four things. First, we must acknowledge there is evil. Second, we must understand the ideology behind this evil and in this particular case this involves understanding its religious and political components. Third, we must be prepared to confront and defeat this evil. Fourth, even if we triumph over the man responsible for bringing about this evil, it doesn't mean the evil dies with him."[10]

Liberty and Leadership

This idea of liberty for all is not new, but is one that speaks of a real understanding of leadership. Do read a bit about King Cyrus (Kourosh), 580–530 BC, the conqueror and creator of the Persian Empire and see how he conducted himself as the leader to his conquered subjects. Persia's first and only humanist, while in power, Cyrus the Great saved Jews and released them from Babylonian slavery. He was the only ancient ruler who refused to enslave, so unlike others who wield power, especially many of the more recent shameful dictators who now traverse the world stage.[11]

We can complain all we want about the burden of taking care of other people and other countries, but the reality is that we are entirely our brothers' keeper.

We can complain all we want about the burden of taking care of other people and other countries, but the reality is that we are entirely our brothers' keeper. The current world economic crisis brings this home to all in a powerful way. The financial crisis is finally causing us to reexamine our worldview and face what in the past we had the option to ignore. We can no longer afford that luxury. We must all adapt and accept our responsibility and become accountable. Angela Merkel, Germany's Chancellor and, in many ways, spokesperson for the Euro Zone that is on the chopping block right now, said: "A community that says regardless of what happens in the rest of the world that it can never again change its ground rules, that community can't survive."[12]

It is hard to see the forceful Angel Merkel, Germany's Chancellor, going to her people (which is how she governs) with this idea that Germany must assume the burden of other failed economies in the Euro Zone. Germany has been so self-disciplined while the other countries in the Euro Zone have not, and now Ms. Merkel will be asking her people to change and to bear the burden of the currency crisis in other nations, which has precipitated a crisis for Germany.[13]

Evolution and higher-order thinking have not come to all people; many remain at different rungs of the ladder, as in *Dante's Inferno* (Alighieri, 12th Century), and can move only at the speed of the lessons that come to them. In addition, we cannot force evolution, a process that will follow its course and pace no matter how much we wish or try to intervene. The bitter battle today around nationalism—and it is about nationalism, not money—in the European Union (EU) is the perfect example of the need for evolution in thought. Nevertheless, we cannot end our quest for freedom for all just because others are not there. Our purpose in the world is greater, and all evolved countries are called. Tony Blair, in his book *My Political Life, a Journey*, says: "America's burden is that it wants to be loved and knows it cannot be."[14] World leadership must release itself from the quest to be loved, and instead embrace with conviction the new paradigm that says: The world is my neighbor, and we will act like leaders and simply, with all the knowledge we have, do the right thing! We will not retreat from our vision of freedom for all people, everywhere. We will not seek the approval or permission from dictators or despots who are destroying their people.

The World Stage

If it sounds as though I am putting hope before experience, I am not. A strong military is a national imperative for the United States and the world, and the idea that we can spread that responsibility around and divert our attention to other matters is a myth. Robert Kagan, in his recent book *The World American Made*, lays out a convincing historical basis for why America must remain a strong and influential force in the world.[15] He contends that if America leaves the world stage, the current world order, as we know it, will shift in ways that will cause a decline in the number of world democracies and curtail freedom for many. As compelling as Fareed Zakaria's numbers seem to be, his case for an inevitable and desirable post-American world is, according to Kagan, perhaps not so strong.

Remembering that China and Russia are forever about the State and the preservation of its wealth and power, they will likely not take on the mantel of caring for the world. Remember that Nikita Khrushchev said he would bury the United States, and Soviet propagandist Georgi Arbatov said: "We are going to do the worst thing we can do to you. We are going to take your enemy away from you."[16]

We are going to do the worst thing we can do to you. We are going to take your enemy away from you.

George Arbatov

China also has no love for the US, and they continually manipulate trade matters in a free market that they would not support. The Chinese government keeps the Yuan artificially low, so Chinese goods undercut all competition. They keep as low a profile as a superpower can keep. Their army of peasant workers stays oppressed, and power rests in the state always. Somehow, we think business and international trade will change the designation of Red Russia and Red China as communist countries; it will not. Their form of capitalism will not allow free markets that benefit the larger world. Nor are they prepared, as Kagan points out, to wreck their economies to create a military capable of keeping the seas open and the skies free. A multipolarity of shared power or an attempt at equal footing for superpowers on the world stage would create competition, but not open seas, and free markets.

Such is clear with the refusal of China and Russia (⊙ February 4, 2012) to sign the United Nations (UN) Resolution condemning the atrocities of Syrian President Bashar al-Assad.[17] They do not stand ready to care about humanitarian efforts to protect the civilians who are being slaughtered *en masse*; rather, they support their vested political and business interests. This is not to say that the US does not support its vested political and business interests; it does, but the worldview is different.

China is a major user of world resources, but it gathers its oil from many sources.

The stakes are high at this point, with Russia being the strongest ally of Syria and with Putin saying months ago that he was not very interested in this part of the world, but obviously, he has keen interest.[18] The message is clear that at this moment, the only consideration is a consolidation of Putin's power and his desire for Russian dominance on the world stage and, with the fall of Gadhafi in Egypt, he needs to not lose another ally in the mid-east.[19] He needs Syria, although he does not care about the people. It is merely a strategic interest. China also has little or no interest in the people of Syria, and China is thinking only of its own economic interest. China is interested today in controlling the South China Sea, and sees it as an inevitable right to control this sea, which connects to the energy-rich Middle-East. At this moment, ☉ September 22, 2012, China is posturing to go to war with Japan over the South China Sea.[20] China is a major user of world resources, and it gathers its oil from many sources. The problem may occur for China or Russia when the Arab League, from which China and Russia do need resources, unites with the West to eliminate the Assad regime—certainly a possible scenario.[21]

Some of the other rising democracies, such as India and Brazil, have little interest in, and probably lack the financial capacity for, taking on leadership or dominance in the world order. As to politics, the West would like to see Putin lose power with a move to a more moderate leadership and to have China move further into the 21st century in terms of human rights and freer markets in general. This will probably not happen, no matter what the new Chinese leader-to-be, President Hu Jintao, says about improved relations when he comes to Washington (☉ February 2012). In addition, it will be a miracle if he is not booed in public for his country's position on Syria at the UN Security Council. For sure, he will drink his favorite champagne with Vice President Joe Biden. Leaders in the United States like to celebrate, always.[22]

So, again, as Kagan puts it, the myth is that a multipolar system of power distribution would bring harmony to the world and more progress to more people. Fareed Zakaria, to support his position on the decline of the United States, points out that China's gross domestic product (GDP) is the largest in the world (twice that of the United States) and growing—a direct path to a post-American world.[23] Kagan counters by explaining that while China's economy may be the largest in the world, it is not the richest.[24] The size of its economy is the result of the size of the population; in reality, unlike the US, China, in comparison, is a very poor country. When you look at the per capita GDP, the picture gets clearer: the US per capita GDP is more than $40,000, while that of China is only $4,000. Japan and Germany are also ahead of China in GDP per capita.[25]

For this reason, China will not likely be in a position to give up protectionist measures anytime soon and foster open or free markets, even if they wanted to. Forget their ideology; they are simply not rich enough to implement the military force to be a major player for world peace. Nor are they ideologically of the mindset that would give them the will to desire this as an outcome. It is not as though they do not understand the power of capitalism and the success of free markets; they do but are not prepared economically to embrace the realities of free markets in capitalism. They are still too poor. If in the United States, we have built some bridges to nowhere; the Chinese have built hundreds, maybe thousands of this sort of meaningless job creation work. They will not be ready to take over world leadership from the United States for another 20 years at the soonest, if indeed they continue to so desire.[26]

China will not likely be in a position to give up protectionist measures anytime soon and foster open or free markets, even if they wanted to.

Kagan's point is that the role of the leading character on the world stage must be well defined in the script, and not left as a matter of some artificial evolutionary process. Powers fall either because of a stronger outside force, against which they are unprepared to defend in might or will, or because of entropy from within. The United States is not unique in this history. Kagan makes a clear case for a strong and stronger part for the United States to play on the world stage, and, according to Kagan, the United States must secure the role with power. Free markets and trade exist only if the seas are navigable; this sounds too simple, but it is a reality that must be addressed. Therefore, it is for the government, through a strong military, "to keep the seas open and the sky free" and for the world, corporate structure to provide the technology and innovation that moves civilization forward.[27]

One of the latest books being discussed in diplomatic circles ⊙ September 2012 is Robert Kaplan's book *The Revenge of Geography*, which lays out several strategic messages for world leaders.[28] One point, so poignantly clear, in Kaplan's book is that the power of geography, the mountains, the rivers, the ports will not be overcome by technology, which has made the world flat in many respects; however, the technology, which has made globalization possible, will not, for example, eliminate the Himalayan mountains that separate India from the rest of Asia. On each side of the mountains, you have two vastly different civilizations. A second relevant point in Kaplan's writing is that it is easy to determine where wars will occur in the world when you look at a map. It is also important to note that while Kaplan's point of geography is a powerful one, without technology and innovation, which advances mobility and communication, geography would have to keep everything as status.

All nations seek power through control of territories with natural resources, particularly energy.

All nations seek power through control of territories with natural resources, particularly energy. Many countries seek this control as a survival measure, as with China who must import energy now and more in the future to support a vast population, which continues to grow despite the one-child policy. As I write, ☉ September 2012, China paid $570 million for 33% of the coal and shale, which will be found, going forward, in Colorado, Nebraska, Wyoming, and Kansas. Unlike the current US administration, which has spurned coal as a viable energy source, not even considering clean coal energy, the Chinese are embracing coal energy as a source, and buying everywhere, they can.[29] If the news that the Chinese are buying out the West is on the front page, we can only guess how much more buying is occurring that is not yet news.

Kaplan somewhat counters Kagan's point on multipolarity and the need for the United States to remain leader of the pack. Kaplan says that the burden that the United States now carries for the world is not sustainable in terms of cost and that it is strategic to begin to think how, as a nation, to become more self-contained and independent of resources from the rest of the world. He says the United States must find other like-minded counties to be willing to share the cost of freedom. He contends that he wants to see the US influence reach far into the future, but believes that it cannot happen without a reduction in our commitment to the world. I get his brilliant point; but I just do not see this happening. I do not know the answer completely, but I am sure that there is not another country that today is willing to even consider giving so much. It is my thesis that it is the worldwide corporations that must rise to fill the power vacuum or place, if there is to be one, and the multinational corporations, whose interest in world peace and economic stability, is market driven, must assume the responsibility of leadership sustainability. Governments must regulate and govern and corporations must lead.

CHAPTER 1

We Have Lost Our Way | We Are Warned Like the Man in the Dream

Beyond the Tipping Point

As witness to the unfolding of Fareed Zakaria's *The Post-American World*[1] and the "rise of the rest," the United States must begin the painful process of self-examination in regard to business and all international relationships and recognize the decided and fundamental loss of trust. Mary Shapiro, outgoing chairperson of the Securities and Exchange Commission (SEC), speaks of "dark pools of liquidity"; everyone and every corporation are storing money and not spending. The only way markets work and, therefore, the only way anything moves forward, is when money circulates, and this simply is not happening.[2] The estimates are that, as of this date (☉ December 2011), there is somewhere about $2.2 trillion in banks not tied to loans, and corporations have nearly $2 trillion that they are not spending.[3]

The manufacturing process will be reduced to one man and a dog, and the dog will be there to see that the man touches nothing.

David Altig

World over, there is no trust in government and faith in the future is weak. What has always made the United States strong—the ability to innovate—seems to have been sucked away by the slings and arrows of the outrageous fortunes of deceit and greed. The lesser thinkers want to point fingers to, for example, jobs that have gone offshore and the decline in US manufacturing. David Altig, senior researcher and vice president of the Federal Reserve in Atlanta, speaking about the decline in the US manufacturing sector, said that the output of US manufacturing has remained rather steady since the 1950s, but that the number of US jobs in manufacturing has declined for obvious reasons including technology and automation. Altig shared an inside joke from the Fed about manufacturing in the future, as he spoke to a group of business leaders at University of Florida, Gainesville, in November 2011. He said: "The manufacturing process will be reduced to one man and a dog, and the dog will be there to see that the man touches nothing" (Personal Communication, 2011).

However, the United States is not alone, if they are worried in China about how they are losing their jobs to Cambodia and Vietnam,[4] then the United States needs to stop looking back. The metaphor, from the Bible, for what happens, when we look back comes to mind: looking back turned Lot's wife into a pillar of salt—a salt lick, as in for cows. Now that is an exciting metaphor.[5] Neither China nor the United States wants these jobs to come back; the jobs that went off-shore were the low-end jobs, and the countries that inherited them have evolved a workforce to fill the demand and have even made innovations in the jobs and have grown an industry around these low-end jobs. It has been a win–win situation for the corporations and the countries. These jobs have made populations in other countries richer and more educated, thus creating more markets for everyone. What we as a society must do is not ask for the jobs to come back, but instead educate our population for the new jobs of the 21st century and consider education the major player for creating a modern workforce. It is such a populist and uneducated view to want the jobs that have gone abroad to come back. We want to help the population rise to the needs of new industries and corporations that require more skill and education. This is the natural and most progressive process for the entire world. More than 3.7 million jobs, ☉ October 2012, are unfilled in the United States alone according to the Bureau of Labor Statistics.[6]

We have evolved from an Agrarian Society, to an Industrial Age, to a Service Economy, to an Information Age, to a Knowledge-based Economy; and I would say we have moved again, even without an exact name, into a Communications Economy.

We have evolved from an Agrarian Society, to an Industrial Age, to a Service Economy, to an Information Age, to a Knowledge-based Economy; and I would say we have moved again, even without an exact name, into a Communications Economy. Look at the shift in power as significant as the Arab Spring, which rolled out beginning in December 2010 through the Arab world of Tunisia, Egypt, Libya, Bahrain, Syria, Jordan, Morocco, Oman, Kuwait, Lebanon, and Saudi Arabia.[7]

There is no prediction on how fast, how far, or in what direction this will go as evidenced by today's news on Libya,[8] but go it will! (☉ October 2012) I was a smart kid in high school, and thought I would major in history in college. I can remember clearly that my fellow students, who did not share my passion for history, would ask me the answers to the history essay questions in Mr. Murphy's class. I told them you could never go wrong, even if you do not know anything about the question, just use the words from the test question, and pair them with the statement: "The peasants always revolt." It is always the story, and while the Arab Spring seems no different than other such revolts in history, it has a striking and powerful significance in that it is so widespread and has moved so quickly; hence the new Age in which we live: the Age of Communication and expanded consciousness, dominated by instant information, 24/7, around the world. It is an exciting time to be alive, and like no other age before, we have the potential to make life better for the world. Instead, we are hoarding our money, stopping markets from working, walking with slumped shoulders, and having no faith in the future.

W. B. Yeats comes to mind:

Turning and turning in the widening gyre
The falcon cannot hear the falconer;
Things fall apart; the centre cannot hold;
Mere anarchy is loosed upon the world,
The blood-dimmed tide is loosed, and everywhere
The ceremony of innocence is drowned;
The best lack all conviction, while the worst
Are full of passionate intensity.
    —W.B. Yeats (The Collected Poems of W.B. Yeats) (Yeats)

Our Fiscal Future

It is easy to be critical of the current economic collapse in the Euro, but the US current economic system is not working all that well, and there is incredible loss of confidence in the Fed; however flawed, the United States does have both a monetary and a fiscal policy. The one thing that some of my colleagues, who are esteemed economists, forget to talk about is that economics is a theory based on a model, albeit a sophisticated model, with vast amounts of historical data. Fred Schultz (☉ who passed in 2009), vice chairman of the Fed under Carter, when he spoke at the Economic Roundtable of Jacksonville (Florida) reminded the group, that the economy is like a bean bag, we punch it here, and we have no idea where it will come out.[9] It is just a theory.

What must come forth now is a worldview that is held by the majority of evolved countries.

The lack of fiscal policy and strong nationalism makes the EU a hard body to organize. Moreover, in contrast to the United States, they have a more direct view of war because of their cultural heritage. Their wars, unlike ours, were fought in their front yards, which makes a major difference in how they see the world. The European worldview is less united than the US worldview (although you would not know this by listening to the constant political debates in the United States), but both are being challenged, as we speak, by other international bodies growing in strength. What must come forth now is a worldview that is held by the majority of evolved countries. Hopefully, it is through the younger and more clear-sighted generation world over, who are more adept at change and less prejudiced, and who seek international educations, that our hope for a strongly shared and more united worldview will be recognized. We do not need to be as extreme as Lyndon Johnson in the infamous *Daisy Ad* he ran in 1964 presidential campaign against Barry Goldwater, when he said: "These are the stakes: to make a world in which all God's children can live, or go into the darkness. We must all love one another, or we must die."[10] However, we must recognize that we are all connected by our financial markets and by our need for resources to run our world and provide enough energy for all people to live a better life.

Why Corporations Will Save Us

Only the global corporation has the power to save us! Ironic as it seems, this is where the power rests; certainly, it is not in government. The government guides us and the military keeps us free and safe, but corporations shape us, pay us, and provide for the movement and structure that is so necessary for life. The government does not initiate it only reacts, and often in a rather tardy fashion; world corporations can innovate and make a harmonious and sustainable life possible. It is this force that is alive, strong, and creative. The corporation provides our voice and allows our spirit to soar. Where else do the majority of people find work except in the collective, and this is a good thing. The corporation allows our endeavors to matter, to make a difference. The corporation is the vehicle by which the majority of people live, move, and have their being.

We have lost our moral compass, no doubt about it, and we will not survive this one unless we first acknowledge that we are lost, and then commit to the journey back to the center.

The problem is that the corporation has become dominated by greedy and myopic leadership in many cases, and not managed well by Boards, who should be watchful and accountable, and is deserted by real authentic leadership; it has thus failed to keep sight of its purpose to create and give us courage and hope. Corporations must examine their purpose and rename it clearly, and we must go to the rescue of the corporation and prop it up until it can right itself. Corporations must wake up and come to life, admit and examine where they are, and identify how they got here and how to proceed. We are in trouble, deep trouble, and we cannot just go to a new land and settle and start over. We must look to where the structure exists and see how that structure can best serve us now.

We have lost our moral compass, no doubt about it, and we will not survive this one unless we first acknowledge that we are lost, and then commit to the journey back to the center. There is no cure for something unless we name it and admit that we have the disease. This cannot be a recently discovered truth for anyone who has a modicum of sense. I do think our state of affairs is serious, more serious than any other time when major paradigm shifts occurred on the planet.

I equate this time to somewhere in elementary education, when as children, we had the science lesson on how the tectonic plates shifted under the surface of the earth. As the shift occurred, the landmasses divided and new continents were formed.[11] The plates are again shifting under the surface of the earth, and will be forming new worlds, connections, and cultures. The world needs to see this one coming and be a part of the process and lead the changes.

This formation will be accomplished through an affinity of values; however, more will be of shared values than ever before. We are living business history, which is really the history of civilization, now at a major turn in the human process of civilizing.

The Center Cannot Hold

We have history to teach us these things. We had World War I from 1914 to 1918, called, in oxymoron fashion, the "Great" War or the War to End all War, in which maybe as many as 15 million people died. This war centered mostly in Europe, and there are places today where you can still see evidence of this war in the countryside, places where people just did not rebuild because of such world ennui. We have the 20 years between World War I and World War II, a time of no or slow growth and great depressions. World War II in 1939–1945 was truly a global conflict that killed 70 million people and altered the political and social structures of the world.[12] Sometimes referred to as the "good war," yet, just yesterday (☉ October 2011), 30 of America's elite soldiers were shot down over Afghanistan.[13] Nothing seemingly good about that! But then again, as Papa Hemingway was known to say, "War is man's favorite game."[14] Only it does not look like a game anymore; the pictures are too graphic for me. W.B. Yeats said: "Things fall apart; the centre cannot hold" (Yeats).

Things fall apart, the centre cannot hold.
—Yeats

The center cannot hold because it has no traction, and it is hollow. We are almost numb to it since bad news bombards us every second with push news feeds on our phones that speak of destruction, man-made and natural, in places I cannot even pronounce. Still, I feel the instant connection and wonder at how things got so out of control. I have always said that in the history of civilizations, there are only two powers that have the force to change anything: one is love and the other, education. I still believe this, but my hopes were somewhat dimmed when individuals, who had lived free in the United States and enjoyed the benefits of freedom and education, flew a plane into the World Trade Center. It will take more than education; I see that now.

The Mandate for a More Evolved Education System

The weakness in the world educational system must be examined realistically, and the conversation has to shift, as with the historically strong political will of the Chinese one-child policy.[15] Tom Friedman, in his latest book with Michael Mandelbaum, *That Used to be US*,[16] sets up an interesting scenario when he puts forth post-advice he would have given to Hillary Clinton before she accepted the position of Secretary of State, if she had asked him for it (he notes, she did not). When President-elect Obama asked her to take on the job, she should have declined, saying that the position was tied to international diplomacy and set to frame the public and international policy of the United States, and she would be limited to interacting with only the heads of state for the countries of the world. Hillary should have asked to be Secretary of Education instead, explaining that she wanted to be in a strategic position for the nation's security and defense.

We can no longer talk about education as a social challenge, which has historically framed the discourse.

Got it!

We can no longer talk about education in the United States or in any developed country as a social challenge, which has historically framed the discourse. Education is an economic conversation and one involving national security. The fact that, in the United States, we have failed to reach a third or more of our students with developed skills even in the three R's as late as in the first part of the 21st century is amazing.[17] Moreover, in the United States, we remediate these subjects in junior colleges or even four-year universities. Really! The educational systems around the world are the core issue for economic growth and political stability for all countries.

Equally astonishing in the United States and beyond is the approach to ethics in higher education. Until the recent crisis in corporate leadership descended on the world, there was little interest in teaching ethics or leadership and the curriculum always yielded to quantitative courses. Ethics, in reality, should form the core of undergraduate and graduate programs in all business schools worldwide. Leadership and ethics would probably be taught best by an in-depth immersion in the liberal studies, not business case studies. After all, our leaders come from these business schools, where they are taught to lead and make decisions that impact and shape our lives. We so often fail to see the connectivity in our collective lives, and if it happens to General Motors or Toyota, it happens to all of us. The smog over China will come to the United States and be our smog because we all live on a sphere that rotates. Think about it. The nuclear disasters in Japan are the nuclear disasters of the world! The fish laden with mercury from the atomic reactors that failed when the tsunami hit Japan are now on the coast of California.[18]

The Age of Greed

When the US stock market crashed in December 2006 and in 2008, we did not fully grasp the meaning, but the flood of insight and information that rolled back the lid on the level of corruption and greed were shocking. The world over, we, however, must never "send to know for whom the bell tolls, it tolls for thee."[19] We are all part of what happened; people wanted and expected a 20% return on every investment, and they wanted it now. What the market demands, the market gets, and we got it. The price has been high: financial products that had no real definable value or source, such as derivatives, which Warren Buffet now calls weapons of mass destruction,[20] and hedge funds were created.

The total deregulation of the financial world[21] caused a collapse and bred distrust for a large segment of society. As Bernanke has pointed out on many occasions, we trusted free markets too much.[22] We trusted and now we do not.

In a world where a Bernie Madoff could happen[23] and continue unchecked for such an extended period, and involve such exaggerated amounts of money, we should be afraid. That he swindled so many people is not as surprising. His swindle played to the very worst of human nature, which is the velvet rope syndrome. We dream to make something for nothing, and long for some scheme, if we could just find it, that will make us rich instantly. The longer we are kept away from the action, as when customers are kept waiting behind the velvet rope for a premier performance or the best table in the house, the more we think the experience is great and that we are special for having been allowed across the velvet rope. Harry Markopolos, in his book *No One Would Listen,*[24] has written the Madoff story in what reads like a fictional Wall Street financial thriller. The problem is it is not fiction.

We trusted and now we do not.

Everyone was greedy and greed is not good! The US Federal Government, the states, and the cities and countries are now in financial chaos. Jefferson County, Alabama, filed for municipal bankruptcy (November 2011), with $3 billion in debt, the largest municipal bankruptcy in the US history.[25] At the same time, the state of Michigan is taking over the city of Flint, with broad new powers in place to break the union.[26] Unions are certainly part of the social order that has changed forever. Industries and corporations will function in a more healthy way when the last vestige of this dinosaur is gone from this cycle, and replaced with leadership that is corporately socially responsible to all stakeholders, including the planet. It is not a fairy tale, but a reality that is now thrust on us as a matter of survival. The world corporate structure will come to this place of moral participation as a matter of force, if not choice.

People tend to separate themselves from government in general; we are here and government is out there. The truth is we are government, and it is here. I listen to people say that governments are covering up, that there is money in Washington, the states, and the cities, and countries. This is what people believe; certainly many countries in the EU believe this about their governments. In fact, however, when the stock market crashed, Washington, the states, and the cities and many European countries were as heavily invested as the individual, and it is the collective that has lost. People who think they were not invested in Wall Street have only to look at their pensions and retirement packages. Wall Street is just fancy gambling, and as we like to think, gambling on a good thing—the corporation. It certainly works when we put money into things we believe in, but we do not believe in it anymore. That is the problem. The lines have become so blurred that investment decisions are not obvious, and even the best we do not trust. The impact of the recession and the fall of Wall Street are not limited to the United States; it is felt worldwide. The fall of Wall Street triggered an enormous reaction from a fragilely held world economy; the effects are reverberating worldwide, and the scandals continue with the latest, the Libor Scandal. This one may be the one that brings down the house.[27] We are one!

What Really Went Wrong

So, what really happened? It is not so simple, and it is tied-up in some ways that cannot seem to give clear answers. It was not a mass conspiracy, and it did not happen all at once. There was just so much money to be made, and people were emboldened by the ability to rationalize every decision as being for the greater good. Most of the people at the Enron table, for example, were able to rationalize that the creation of the subsidiaries designed to absorb and hide the bad assets was a good thing because they would be saving such an important company and so many jobs. They were, of course, making great personal wealth for themselves.[28] And, of course, it was legal at the time, and predated Sarbanes Oxley,[29] which now makes what was unethical but not illegal, illegal. The capacity to rationalize our conduct and our corrupt decisions over the moral core that tells us what is good or evil is what threatens to destroy us. However, let us be clear that a mere churning out of more rules like the Dodd-Frank Wall Street Reform and Consumer Protection Act[30] will not create ethical leaderships. For sure it may provide one of the 11 federal agencies more authority, but the bad guys are inventing ways around the "rules" the minute the rules are enacted.

The capacity to rationalize our conduct and our corrupt decisions over the moral core that tells us what is good or evil is what threatens to destroy us.

The things that we used to guide us in the past, we have thrown out in the name of obsolescence, their lack of modern application, and our desire to liberate ourselves from the past. This is unfortunate, as it is in the remembering of history and the embracing of stories that inform and guide us that we make progress. We are like children who pay no heed to their parents because they are old and "obviously" un-knowing people. We can stand no taller than the shoulders on which we stand, yet we are prideful and unwilling to pay the tribute that is owed. So much of the "me-generation" style and "look what my hands have wrought"[31] attitude still prevails. Yes, do look! We have failed to see what is obvious, and our perception is skewed by the fact that we stay in a reactionary posture and flee from introspection. We simply are moving too fast, and we rather like being numb. It is as though we can avoid it, if we are not conscious of it. Then, too, the state of the world and our lives seem so overwhelming that it is as if we are running in place.

We are like the man who is warned by a spirit in a dream that he will meet Death at the West gate, so he takes his wives, camels, gold, and food and goes out the East gate. There, at the East gate, he, of course, meets Death and he boldly says, "I was told I would meet death at the West gate." Death replies, "You were told you would meet Death. In addition, you did not ask any of the soul questions: Can I have some time to get ready to meet death? Is there something I should do before I meet death? Can I do anything to avoid meeting death?" The man realizes his foolishness. Death responds, "You took your life into your hands and used your mind only to plan an escape." We are more than mind, but we have forgotten that; and there is no escape, only the journey until we unite the mind with the body, and spirit.[32]

Buying Into Our Myths

We are morally bereft because we have not asked the right questions: Is there a highest and greatest good in this for everyone? Will the means be held to be of high value, no matter the end? Would my mother be proud of me if she knew everything about me? We rely on our minds to solve our problems; we trust only the mind. We are like the huddled masses, but unlike them, we are not longing to be free; we are longing to be right. We are empowered by our minds and we have come to believe in our own myths about money and power. Money is a wonderful thing, and I love all the things that money can buy and do. Some are really remarkable things that make life better in many ways for many people. However, we have come to worship these things as well as strive for them. Our decision making and our conduct belie any responsibility to the concepts articulated by the mantra, which we are now beginning to understand as our triple bottom line: people, planet, and profit.[33]

We rely on our minds to solve our problems; we trust only the mind.

Maybe it is when corporations break or lose their sense of fiduciary relationship with the real people who make up their business that the moral compass begins to slip. I do not know about you, but no amount of "Welcome to Moe's" at the front door of the bank convinces me that they really care. I have been with the same bank since I had my first real job at age 20, teaching school; the bank has changed names at least six times, but I have not changed. I had occasion to be in "my" bank on the day of the last official change in name and ownership, and there were balloons everywhere and a waiting line of greeters at the door. They had a camera set up to interview people, and the music that was playing was loud—the sounds of "Jeremiah Was a Bullfrog"[34] were ringing clearly. Somehow, it gave me pause, and I am sure they paid some advertising firm to dream all that up. It certainly did not make me feel secure or suggest the serious bond that should exist between a bank and its clients. Maybe that's it: the bond between the customer and the corporation has been so eroded that there is no longer a bond at all! Remember what the CEO of British Petroleum (BP), Tony Hayward, said during the oil spill crisis in the Gulf of Mexico, USA? He said he was speaking for the corporation, which was really concerned about all the little people. Most of what we hear, we recognize as just a slick PR campaign managed by a crisis communication specialist. It means nothing. However, the blatant arrogance of Corporate Leaders such as Tony Hayward, who took off for a sailing vacation instead of responding to the oil spill that wrecked and changed so many lives, underscores a truth of which we are all too suspecting, that no one really cares, and for all of us, who believed in the Wizard, the mask is off.[35]

We no longer seem to have the moral or political will to hold anyone accountable.

Altered State of Reality

We are so confused, and we have no real touchstones to follow. We have become desensitized to the moral turpitude at the highest levels. We think nothing of a congressional representative who takes nude pictures of himself and uploads them into cyberspace for all to see.[36] We have experienced it at such a visceral level that it almost does not register. It barely makes us break a yawn. We no longer seem to have the moral or political will to hold anyone accountable. The individuals, who should be the most accountable as leaders in world corporations, simply are out of touch and just surviving, rather than understanding the necessity to be morally responsible. It is more relevant to meet the needs of the shareholders with profit (and nothing else matters) than to consider all the stakeholders, including the planet. We have it in reverse, and we are making that end justify the means at any cost. We have failed the power that has been given to us; we certainly did not earn it, at any level. The only problem is that the end is not turning out so well, and the means seem to be catching up with us already.

We have lost our way; like a nation of sheep, we cannot find the Shepherd, and we have turned everyone to his/her own way![37] This is a separation that will destroy us and the only hope is to redefine, rebuild, and rethink the role of the corporation. The Corporate Leaders can be the Shepherd and can save us, but only if they have the courage to acknowledge the spiritual core.

The Spiritual Solution

Sometimes the mantel we drape over our actions is lifted, and we see a truer picture. The ideal is that we are always moving to higher-order thinking and to critical self-examination. It is only when a principled spiritual core becomes our touchstone that it makes a difference. Spirituality is not a religious matter, and true spirituality has to separate itself from religious dogma.

Therefore, successful corporations may not be Christian in the traditional sense of the word or they may be, but we need to have something that guides us. Mission statements are just words on the wall, and they often do not exist anywhere else. Certainly, mission statements can be relevant, but only as an expression for the image that the corporation has of itself; I cannot see living into a mission statement as being an overwhelmingly powerful motivator. An overhaul of the real meaning behind the mission statement is long overdue. A mission statement must be more than just an amalgamation of words; it must be a culmination of the voices of all stakeholders, and it must mirror that which is spiritual in man and in life.

The spiritual experience is relevant, but not as important as how we interpret it as we reach a higher consciousness.

I like the way Caroline Myss, author and speaker, talks about religion as a costume party, and how powerful it is that we all have a place to go to practice our rituals and learn more about our stories.[38] A brilliant friend of mine reminded me the other day of the importance of not being so judgmental about religions and their stories, such as the myths in Islam that promises that 72 virgins will minister to the male, who dies a sacred death.[39] My friend reminded me of how the Christian metaphor begins—with two nudes in a garden with an apple tree and a snake![40] The point is that in seeking the spiritual core, your specific theology matters not if you are a Christian, Buddhist, Jew, Taoist, or Hindu. We all come from some place and that place in its purest form is more than likely spiritual. It is important, I think, to see that where you are born and what your parents believe has been the most powerful force in determining what you believe theologically, and if or how you worship. This often narrow view is changing now for many, as we have access to spiritual teachings and information from all the world's religious traditions, and we can synthesize them into a spiritual pattern that works for us and in our own time. The spiritual experience is relevant, but not as important as how we interpret it as we reach a higher consciousness.

For the educated population, it is clear that all religions contain the same story patterns and archetypes, and it is the practice and interpretation of the stories that make people come together in one place and in one accord, and dwell in the collective conscious. It is evident that throughout history, there have been prophets, saints, shamans, and spiritualists who were enlightened and did show us the soul and its power to make us whole. Nevertheless, in these spiritual principles and archetypes, found in all evolved religions, is where corporations will find their way to open up the spiritual part that is now so completely missing.

The Spiritual Workforce

Dr. Kent Rhodes of Pepperdine set forth six components of workplace spirituality.[41] He admits that while the conversation has expanded, there is not yet consensus, and that complications in clarifying the meaning of spirituality at work have arisen more recently with the blurring of religious beliefs and political leanings in the United States. In his paper, he mentions Robert Bellah's statement, "The way 'spirituality' is often used suggests that we exist solely as a collection of individuals, not as members of a religious community".[42]

Workplace spirituality: emphasizes sustainability.

According to Rhodes, workplace spirituality emphasizes sustainability noting that such a program also has the potential to actually increase market value and attract investors; also values contributions made by employees who are empowered to view themselves as servants of employers, customers, and the community; recognizes that being creative is not necessarily reserved for a special few, but all employees; values individuals' life experiences and the lessons learned from them; supports the formulation of ethical principles that promote personal growth, long-term character development, and personal connections of faith and work development; and promotes vocation.[43]

It should be quickly noted, and with hope, that there are corporations that are moving toward, recognizing, and embracing a more spiritual part of the process. Companies such as Apple Computer, Raytheon Company, Cisco, Google, Yahoo, Medtronic, IBM, and others are taking steps to see that the spiritual nature of man is an acknowledged component in the process of man and his work.[44] Many of these companies have centers where employees can go during the workday and meditate or just be quiet. In addition, many have in-house chaplains who are employed just to listen and comfort. This practice of using chaplains as a substitute for or in addition to Employee Assistance Programs is seen in places where one might not expect to find them. Ford Motor Company, Coco Cola, and Tyson Food all have chaplaincy programs in place.[45] It may be just a sign of corporations experimenting with work place environments or an idea whose time has come. As the spiritual evolution takes place, an understanding, of the universe and its relationship to man, moves in stages—from egocentric, ethnocentric, and world-centric to cosmocentric. Therefore, the role of the corporation and its imperative to firmly create a mind, body, and spirit foundation come into focus.

International Insight | The Greeks Up-Close and Personal

I think I am so lucky to be an official baby boomer and have a beautiful 21-year-old daughter who, on top of what I read and research, keeps me real and very informed about this 21st century through her worldview. Catherine is studying in Greece (☉ Fall 2012) at an extension of the Hellenic International Studies in the Arts[46] on the Island of Paros, and when she wakes up every morning, she can gaze at the Aegean Sea from her dorm room. I have pictures of her jumping off the rocks into the Aegean Sea. What an experience!

She recently returned to the island after a week in Istanbul. This past Sunday morning (☉ November 2011), I rolled out of bed, grabbed my iPhone, and saw the push news that eastern Turkey experienced a major earthquake.[47] My heart went up to my throat, and I wished I had paid more attention to my geography classes. I frantically called a friend who had just come back from Turkey only to get voice mail (my mind does not always move in linear fashion). I then googled Istanbul, that only provided narrative, which was not what I needed. As I came to more sense, I googled a map and, with great relief, saw that Istanbul was on the far west of Turkey. However, I read this morning that Istanbul is hosting an armed opposition group waging an insurgency against the government of President Bashar al-Assad of Syria. Istanbul is providing shelter for the commander and dozens of members of the group, the Free Syrian Army, and allowing them to orchestrate attacks from inside a camp guarded by the Turkish military.[48] The seemingly endless turmoil and ruthless bloodshed in this part of the world amazes the Western audience.

My daughter, of course, has remained oblivious to the mayhem and madness. Her Facebook page is full of beautiful pictures of Istanbul with fellow students, all of them playing and having fun. The museums, she said, were more impressive and had larger collections than the museums in New York, Chicago, London, or Paris. (I could not help but pause, and think, when I was her age the longest distance I had gone from my Florida home was South Georgia.) She was impressed by the volume and depth of the collections. She also noted that mosques were on every corner—not an exaggeration, she said, really every corner.

I can add that Catherine is very Western in appearance and southern in manner, blond and beautiful. She said the women, who all wore burkas, and the men, who in volumes so openly made outrageous sexual callouts to her and other female students, confused her. She said, "I am thinking about this seeming incongruity, and plan to write about how it made me feel: insulted and vulnerable, and angry with the women for being so submissive." The women, she said, seemed sad and afraid.

From Istanbul, the group flew back to Athens, just in time for the temporary two-day peace, saw signs of the riots, and visited the Parliament buildings, where the riots were mostly staged. As we Skyped later, we compared the Western media coverage to what she saw and the Western media sagas seemed exaggerated to her. Catherine found the city dirtier than when she first arrived there in September, but she always felt safe. Back on the island of Paros, a warm shower and her bed were welcome.

She thinks she has more insight than many who are enrolled in the Hellenic school, as she made good friends with Elias, a young man on the island, and through him she met and spent time with his Greek friends and with Elias' parents, and has learned a few Greek words. She visited his home and found that his family and friends had much in common with her and, yet, many differences in lifestyle. The parents are retired but they make a trip to India once a year to buy jewels and bring them back to Paros to sell. By island standards, they are rich; they have a car and an iPhone. Catherine says that Elias's English is better than most, as his mother is German and his father, Greek, and the only language they have in common is English. Elias speaks all three languages. When I asked her if the islanders talked much about the current political debate, she said, "Yes, but I do not. They think that westerners are outrageous."

According to my daughter, the Greeks on Paros believe that if they returned to the drachma, all would be well. They do not like the rules of the EU and see no reason to be in the organization. They will never give up the siesta because it is so healthy. They all drink and smoke heavily and yet are conscious of their health, and drink all types of special teas. They do not work out, but all seem to have great bodies, and there are no overweight people. In addition, they want all Albanians to leave the island since they see Albanians as the root of all the Greek problems. This seems like the obvious answer to them, and is it?

She is somewhat enamored of Elias's lifestyle, as she says it is so unlike her world. For Elias and his friends, there appears to be no pressure. Most young people drop out of school and just go to work, knowing they can make enough money to have a house and a family. Elias works in a bar on the island during the tourist season, and he helped Catherine get a part-time job in the local bar. I cannot picture how this worked, since she would know nothing about the euro and does not speak Greek. She said Elias took care of her and told her he would protect her from the Albanians. The young man, who holds a German passport, leaves in November (☉ 2011) to enroll in a school in Düsseldorf. Catherine says many young men from the island go to Athens to enroll as well, but they do not attend school. To them and Elias, as he explained, it is just paper work; though this paper work apparently keeps them out of the Greek army draft. Families with enough money protect their sons, as they see it. Elias makes this journey with some other young men from the island every year. He leaves Germany after a visit and goes with his friends to Thailand to hang out. Elias will remain in Thailand until March or April, when the weather is better in Paros, and return to work in the bar (which is closed in the off-season months of November to March). His goal is to open a restaurant in Thailand and become a great chef! What an adventure and what a worldview she is developing.

The world is one big connected place, and we cannot go back from the connections, no matter how much the Greeks and any other player on the world stage may want to disengage. We are all actors in that theater. The more and the faster we learn about each other, the more progress we can make in the integration that is necessary for survival. The old idea that we are to become one big melting pot is passé; the new and more appropriate metaphor is that we want to be a mosaic. We must all come to the place where we understand that we are all part of one picture, while continuing to keep our distinct colors in the mosaic.

What is interesting to me about Catherine's experiences is how much they will shape her going forward and how strongly she sees and rejects the pattern of blaming someone else for the problems. The Greeks want the Albanians to go home, the Israelis want the Palestinians to go home, the English want the Muslims to leave, the Turks and the Armenians continue to fight, France now declares it a crime to deny the

1915 Armenian killings were genocide,[49] and the Germans are paying the Africans to go home in line with Angela Merkel's pronouncements that multiculturalism is dead. I do not think it is dead, but I fully see her view of the EU. I understand the frustration in the euro-zone countries in that they have a monetary policy, but not a fiscal policy as we have with our Fed (central bank), which determines universal rates across states.

Discussion Questions

- How does spirituality differ from religion?
- How does a corporation turn its mission statement into a course of action?
- How can a corporation inject or require ethical values in all relationships: employees, vendors, suppliers, clients, and the public message?

Exercise | Mission Statements | Mission Accomplished?

Every corporation today has a mission statement, and corporations are under pressure to have all the words and phrases such as transparency, sustainability, and diligence for all stakeholders in the mission statement. These statements are often crafted, not from inside the corporation itself, but by outside consultants, and other firms that now have a lucrative business, writing sustainability profiles and plans for corporations. Some mission statements rise to the level of religious fervor, and the superficial nature and the disconnect between the mission statement and reality is always observable first by the corporate family, and second by the public at large. Corporate executives found guilty of fraud and hauled off with hefty jail sentences often hail from corporations with lofty mission statements. BP's mission statement (quoted directly from the website section: Respect) is a case in point: "We respect the world in which we operate. It begins with compliance with laws and regulations. We hold ourselves to the highest ethical standards and behave in ways that earn the trust of others. We depend on the relationships we have and respect each other and those we work with. We value diversity of people and thought. We care about the consequences of our decisions, large and small, on those around us."

BP was found guilty of 14 charges of criminal counts including manslaughter and paid $4 billion in fines. That makes their disconnect reach major proportions. The following is part of Google's mission statement, taken directly from its website, which speaks more to an in-house mission statement and reflects more of how they see themselves as a company:[50] Once a company puts out a bold statement such as Google's, they will be watched more to see if and/or when they will sin. For this exercise, please go to the website and read the complete Google statement, and then complete the exercise.

Google—Ten Things We Know to Be True

We (Google) first wrote these "10 things" when Google was just a few years old. From time to time we revisit this list to see if it still holds true. We hope it does—and you can hold us to that.

1. Focus on the user and all else will follow. To consider how they might have been designed differently.
2. It's best to do one thing really, really well
3. Fast is better than slow.
4. Democracy on the web works
5. You don't need to be at your desk to need an answer.
6. You can make money without doing evil.
7. There's always more information out there.
8. The need for information crosses all borders.
9. You can be serious without a suit
10. Great just isn't good enough.[51]

Rate Google's adherence to these values based on research of the currently available information on Google considering the following:

Media	
Litigation	
Stock Price	
Consumer Feedback	
Personal Reflections	

A Case for Sustainability Manifestation | Patagonia: A Model for a 21st-Century Corporation

Our decision making and our conduct belie any responsibility to the concepts articulated by the mantra, which we are now beginning to understand our triple bottom line: people, planet, and profit.[52]

Patagonia, located in Ventura, CA, makes and markets high-end gear for outdoor active sports and lifestyles. Founded in 1972 by Yvon Chouinard, Patagonia has had a varied climb to success and currently maintains a committed client base that pays for the brand and the environmental image the company has created. The uniqueness of the company is mirrored in the founder, Chouinard, whose rare vision for life and the pleasure it can bring with a view to absolute sustainability, has created a company with a culture that abounds in creativity. The products that the company produces are not as relevant to the buyers as being a part of something in the 21st century that says we are different and care more for the world in which we live than the profit we make.[53]

The company has 50 retail stores throughout the United States, Europe, and Asia and survived the recession and the decline in retail 2009 by cost cutting, which included a hiring and salary freeze, and ending the 401K match. The backlash from the cuts cost the company in PR and the freeze and the benefits were restored in 2010.[54]

It should be quickly noted, and with hope, that there are corporations that are moving toward recognizing and embracing a more spiritual part of the process.

Comparing Patagonia to its chief rival and publically traded company, Columbia, it becomes clear that the highly profitable company capitalizes on its environmental image, which is more valuable than its retail line of clothing and gear. Columbia's annual sales in 2011 were $1.67 billion with over 4,000 employees and with a net profit margin of 5.7%.[55]

Patagonia is a model for a 21st-century corporation in that the focus on the environment is their brand. The concept that a company becomes known more for its vision of how it sees itself and how it interprets its role as a player on the world stage and finally for its product is a model that needs to be replicated. The philosophy of a company that says we are more about why we do what we do than the how or the "what" is an evolved view of a company that would be successful no matter what it produced.

This formation will be accomplished through an affinity of values; however, more will be of shared values than ever before.

Companies such as Patagonia have made a journey inward, and use their product as a vehicle to move forward their mission. They are the embodiment of the integration of the mind, body, spirit. From their webpage under the tab *Environmentalism: What We Do*, they say: "The wild world we love is fast disappearing. At Patagonia, we think that business can inspire solutions to the environmental crisis. This means that what we make and how we make it must cause the least harm to the environment. We evaluate raw materials, invest in innovative technologies, and rigorously police our waste."[56]

As a corporate goal, they seek feedback from environmentalists around the world, and demand transparency from all their suppliers and deliver transparency to their customers. Most recently in 2012, they owned a criticism from the animal welfare organization, *Four Paws of Germany*, for their use of feathers and down taken from live geese, who are raised for the production of foie gras, which force feeds the goose so that its liver grows bigger, considered a gourmet delicacy. Patagonia is actively seeking another source for its feathers and down.[57]

The *Common Thread Initiative* has a simple mantra: reduce, repair, reuse, and recycle. The company explains that we need to be less conspicuous in our consumption, see the value in repairing what we use, to reuse and share what we buy, and to recycle as a last resort. They encourage customers to return items for recycling to their store and Patagonia reuses the materials in making new gear products. This website explains: "We have just one planet to call home....reimagine a world in which we take nothing from nature that we can't replace."[58]

The *Our Common Waters Initiative* provides not only a tracking of the water consumption of the company in the manufacture of its products, but also involves research into reducing water consumption, and educating and raising awareness to the current world crisis in water shortages. This project is dedicated to the restoration of natural water systems through, for example, finding dams that once broken can restore rivers and other waterways.[59]

The *1% for the Planet Initiative* has, since 1985, pledged 1% of its sales (or 10% of its profit whatever is greater) to environmental work, which focuses on the preservation of and restoring of the natural world. The total award to date of cash and in-kind donations to both grassroots and directly to local communities is $46 million. Probably the most powerful part of this initiative is that the company selects and partners with vendors and suppliers who are of the same philosophy, who also are vigilant and transparent about their impact on the environment.[60]

Patagonia manufactures their products in 16 countries throughout the world. The footprints of each item the company makes can be tracked on the company website.[61]

By its own admission, Patagonia did not come to such a high level of corporate responsibility simply on its own inquiry. For example, the Kathy Lee Gifford scandal with the manufacture of her personally branded clothing traced to sweat shops in China, which revealed inhumane working conditions, led Patagonia to begin self-examination.[62]

The Corporate Leaders can be the Shepard and can save us, but only if they have the courage to acknowledge the spiritual core.

On their webpage blog, *The Cleanest Line*, Patagonia outlined the details of their supply chain and provided their rationale for corporate policies. The blog post outlines the mistakes as well as the success of the company. For a privately held company, the company provides a wealth of information not only about their mission to heal the environment, but also about their internal operations, which reveals much about how Patagonia perceives itself.[63]

Therefore, successful corporations will not be Christian in any sense of the word, but we need to have something that guides us. Mission statements are just words on the wall, and they often do not exist anywhere else.

Yvon Chouinard, Patagonia's Owner and Founder, along with Jib Ellison, and Rick Ridgeway authored an article for the **Harvard Business Review**, October 2011, entitled *The Sustainable Economy*[64] where the theme sounds like the line from *Murder in the Cathedral* by T.S. Eliot where he boldly states "To do the right deed for the wrong reason."[65] The team of authors sounds out the message clearly: "Even those concerned about only business and not the fate of the planet recognize that the viability of business itself depends on the resources of healthy ecosystems—fresh water, clean air, robust biodiversity, productive land—and on the stability of just societies. Happily, most of us also care about these things directly" (p. 52).

Chouinard has a life history of passion with the environment; he first bought a forging factory to make better steel-pitons for rock climbing, a sport that has been his life. Chouinard began to realize while the piton was stronger and better, it was doing damage to the mountain. So, he continued his quest to make better products from his own interest and knowledge of extreme sports, but with an eye to the impact on the environment. Financial success for this extreme sport person offered him the opportunity to create his company around his belief that employees were equal stakeholders in the business operation. The company was recognized by *Working Mothers Magazine* as one of the top places to work, and he created an employee-centric corporate environment.[66]

With the platform of a company that evolved into the current Patagonia, his sensitivity to and respect for the environment was provided a vehicle to create.

The spiritual experience is relevant, but not as important as how we interpret it as we reach a higher consciousness.

It may well be that Patagonia's success as a model company for sustainability and transparency happened more because of timing in that saving the planet is an idea whose time has come than from a totally altruistic place. However, the net result is overwhelming in its specific and positive impact on raising awareness to the sacredness of the planet and the urgent need to craft a plan that is reasonable and economically feasible at the same time. It is people, planet, and profit for Patagonia, which is a model for the corporation of the 21st century. Chouinard is also a model of forward-thinking leadership as he honors the environment. In addition, he is a leader who understands at a visceral level his product. Degrees from prestigious business schools are relevant for leadership; to know your product intimately can be a strength, but to have the spiritual connection to your world as Chouinard does is an imperative.[67]

Supplemental Reading

The following are scholarly and peer-reviewed journal articles, conference proceedings, and dissertations on the concepts discussed in this chapter.

- The Connecting Impact of Dark Trading and Visible Fragmentation on Market Quality, Hans Degryse, Frank de Jong, and Vincent van Kervel, November 2011 TILEC Discussion Paper No. 2011-026.
- The Failure of American Schools, Joel Klein, *The Atlantic*, June, 2011
- Collaborating to Further the Intellectual, Civic, and Moral Purposes of Higher Education, Gwendolyn Dungy, *Journal of College and Character* 13(3), 2012
- The Present State of Workplace Spirituality: A literature review considering context, theory, and measurement/assessment. David Miller & Tim Ewes, Princeton Faith and Work Initiative, January, 2011.
- Six Components of a Model for Workplace Spirituality, Kent Rhodes (2006) *Graziadio Business Review*, 9(2).

CHAPTER 2

How It Happened | Age of Reason | Everything Is a Cycle

The Evolution of Civilization

Simply put, we have played this game out; this game may have started with the Age of Enlightenment, and was surely marked by the French and American revolutions. The English 18th century was referred to as the Age of Enlightenment and, sometimes, the Age of Reason. In fact, up to the Age of Reason, much thought revolved around mysticism mixed with a strong measure of superstition. Nevertheless, the English 18th century— the age of science and literature—was framed by new thought and a significant paradigm shift from the world of the 17th century that seemed so chaotic. As every age is a reaction to the one before it, so did this Age of Reason shift its focus to the mind as the governing principle for all of life's questions. It was a time of open secularism, and the religion most practiced in the English colonies, for example, was Deism.[1]

The Deists were not practicing Christians, and they did not believe that the Bible was the literal or divine word of God, but was instead a great metaphor containing all truths about the human condition. They relied on reason and the power of the mind—not faith—as the test by which everything had to be measured. If, indeed, they had believed the Bible literally, they could not have been part of the rebellion against England. These young Americans saw power differently from the rulers of England; power would come up from the people and not down from the "divinely" appointed monarchs.

The men who founded the fledgling nation were clear about the separation of church and state.

It was a time of freethinking, and the Americans considered them-selves men of Enlightenment and expended much tolerance in the crea-tion of the nation. They were wealthy and successful businessmen who saw opportunity for themselves and their fledgling endeavors to become great; they were men of vision and tenacity. Leadership grew naturally out of the people, and these leaders, such as Jefferson, Franklin, Madison, Adams, and Washington, established a culture of government of the people. And it was of the people and by the people, with strong governance and much breadth for personal tolerance. These men of intellect understood what had been missing in the world of England from which they came; it was, of course, economic freedom and free-dom of thought, which would allow the consciousness of man to flour-ish and grow. These men believed in reason, natural law, universal order, and embraced a scientific and rational thought for all questions related to religious, social, or economic life. The men who founded the fledgling nation were clear about the separation of church and state, the opposite of the status quo in England, the colonizer from whom they wanted to break, and held that there would be no laws that would limit or define religion. Having come from the oppression of the mix of church and state in England, they were clear that religion was not to be a matter of law.[2]

Jefferson, the principal author of the Declaration of Independence, specifically represents the rejection of a formalized religion and yet in an almost eerie manner, he demonstrated the longing for answers from what seemed a spiritual source. Jefferson produced the 84-page volume in 1820 entitling it, *The Life and Morals of Jesus of Nazareth*. He had pored over six copies of the New Testament, in Greek, Latin, French, and King James English. He cut out passages with some sort of very sharp blade and, using blank paper, glued down lines from each of the Gospels in four columns, Greek and Latin on one side of the pages, and French and English on the other.[3] In essence, he created a Jefferson ver-sion of the Bible. He categorically eliminated any mention of the divin-ity of Jesus and any reference to the miracles in the New Testament of the Bible. Jefferson goes so far as to completely alter the text and remove the supernatural, but sees the teachings of the Bible and their value for the shaping of ethical behavior. Jefferson was able to accept what was rational and see the intrinsic worth without the supernatural. It is a small but amazing story that underscores the intent of the Founding Generation that man should be governed by laws of reason and not religion.[4] The Smithsonian has restored this 1820 Jefferson Bible, *The Life and Morals of Jesus of Nazareth.*[5]

> *More than any other figure in history, Newton embodies the Enlightenment.*

It would also be relevant, as we look at the impact of the Revolution and the Age of Reason on contemporary thought, to examine the impact of the achievements and writings of men such as Sir Isaac Newton, the English scientist, whose work spanned the late 17th and early 18th centuries. He brought the world to an understanding of the governing power of the natural forces, such as gravity—a fixed principle through which the universe and man would be understood. Newton did not, of course, create gravity; his discovery, documentation, and naming of this fixed principle was radical and absurd to many, particularly the Catholic Church. More than any other figure in history, Newton embodies the Enlightenment, and the fact that he was fascinated by the Bible and spent as much or more time studying the Bible than other scientific writings speaks loudly of man's quest and need to understand the interior life beyond the pale of scientific thinking and methods. In all fairness to this interpretation, Newton, like many scholars who studied the Bible, sought to decipher the secrets of the universe that he believed were encoded in the sacred text. For Newton, the Bible was a multifaceted work. In his work *Mathematical Principles of Natural Philosophy* 1687, Newton wrote: "This most beautiful system of the sun, planets, and comets could only proceed from the counsel and dominion of an intelligent and powerful Being. This Being governs all things, not as the soul of the world, but as Lord over all, and on account of His dominion He is wont to be called Lord God, Universal Ruler."[6] It is only relevant to know that the man, who so epitomized the Age of Reason, was drawn to wonder over the power in the universe.

Still on the subject of the mind and reason to establish unity, balance, and order: In his famous essay, *What Is Enlightenment?* (1784),

Emmanuel Kant,[7] the 18th-century German philosopher, defined the movement as follows:

> *Man's leaving his self-caused immaturity. Immaturity is the incapacity to use one's intelligence without the guidance of another. Such immaturity is self-caused if it is not caused by lack of intelligence, but by lack of determination and courage to use one's intelligence without being guided by another. Sapere Aude! [Dare to know!] Have the courage to use your own intelligence is therefore the motto of the enlightenment.*

The Founders of the United States dared to rely on their own intelligence, leave off from the unintelligent thinking that kept people so oppressed through limited thought, and embraced free thought. If allowed to erupt, free thought could extricate people from the darkness of unenlightened thinking, for them to be molded by reason and rationality. If there were natural laws that governed the universe with precision, then there were the same natural rights to govern society and the community of man.

> *The Founders of the US dared to rely on their own intelligence, leave off from the unintelligent thinking that kept people so oppressed through limited thought, and embraced free thought.*

We are true children of the Enlightenment and have embraced rational thinking and the natural laws of the universe as the source of our power and the touchstone by which all things are measured. And why not? It is what we see and understand, and that is what is so validating to the explanation for our existence. The laws of the universe are so precise and pronounced that in the 21st century we can send a man to the moon in a spaceship and calculate its landing time to the second. Yeah, Sir Isaac Newton! We have arrived at the apex of the manifestation of scientific thinking, the application of the scientific method, and the scientific way of life. It has brought us many powerful things and things of wonder. We have mechanized and ordered our world for great comfort and success. We are the products of the Enlightenment, and we have put off nonintellectual thinking (at least for the most part, but that is another book).

All the great thinkers and scientists who brought us the Enlightenment and the doers who followed their precepts are to be praised, for we are the beneficiaries who were delivered from the Dark Ages by brave and bright people. The US Founding Generation handed it to the fledgling country and these English settlers ran with it. The United States and its businesses are productive and powerful beyond their imaginations. As a country, the United States enjoys a land that is far more habitable than most and of great size. The United States dominates the air, sea, and land, yet the United States and the world is in a mess now!

The current state of affairs can be charged to a reliance solely on the patterns of the Age of Reason to sort all our thought processes. We so embraced the power and rightness of the mind to direct us and keep us free that we ignored probably the most important part of man, **the spirit**. The power and rightness of the mind to direct and retain freedom was so much the focus that as a world we ignored probably the most important part of man, the spirit.

We have dominated the air, sea, and land, yet we are in a mess now!

Evolving from Mind and Body to Mind, Body, and Spirit

Man and all that we create have become dominated and controlled by the idea of mind and body. Reason and the body leave out the spirit. Man is all three—mind, body, and spirit—and what we have come to is the avoidance of any focus on the power of the spirit, or the need to protect and cultivate it or allow this part of man to flourish. In fact, in our current state of affairs, and using a foolish interpretation of multiculturalism, we have dwarfed the soul to silence. Like large cities that host great world events such as Super Bowls and Olympics, which shuffle their homeless and undesirable population out of sight, we have hidden away the homeless soul. The things that do not reside in the mind and body are the core competencies that are missing from our current culture and, to a great extent, the explanation for why we are in such a state of panic. Residing in the spirit of man are hope, faith, optimism, innovation, will, calm, and peace.

I was sitting at a lovely outdoor graduation at a small liberal arts school in the south, patiently waiting for yet another boring graduation address. The Dean of Students came forward to provide the "invocation" and his avoidance of any reference to God, Spirit, Soul, Universe, and Force for Good or Power reached absurd proportions and drew an enormous amount of attention. At least it was not dull. Then it was the turn of the commencement speaker, Carla Harris, a Wall Street financial analyst and managing director of the Strategic Client Group and the head of Emerging Managers Platform for Morgan Stanley.[8] In a most gracious but loud and penetrating voice, Ms. Harris said: "God is good . . ." A few in the audience, including myself, joined her, "all the time, God is good!"

It was simply amazing, and she went on to deliver one of the most articulate and memorable graduation addresses in my memory. Google her and see what she is about and what she represents as a new type of leader. Ms. Harris represents a new breed of intellectuals not tied to any specific religious practice, but fully conscious of the spiritual part of life, work, and the corporate world.

We can no longer sustain ourselves, much less our world, because we are soulless, and the spirit where the soul resides has been stunted by the lack of use.

Sustainability

We can no longer sustain ourselves, much less our world, because we are soulless, and the spirit where the soul resides has been stunted by the lack of use. The prowess of mind and body has carried us a long way from the Dark Ages, but it can carry us no further. It is a new journey we must make, and make both individually and collectively, back to our whole self: mind, body, and spirit.

Some responsibility for the demise of the spirit or the neglect of the soul belongs to organized religion, which at times has failed to be more than institutionalized power for its own sake. It has, in many ways, kept us weak in that it points to a savior who, from outside of us, will save us. It is an immature view of the human condition; we have the God potential in us, and we can find that soul that resides in us and embrace the spirit that connects us to the rest of humanity. We can and are certainly free to embrace a religious practice which maybe a good thing, but it is not a requirement in being spiritual.

We can no longer sustain ourselves, much less our world, because we are soulless, and the spirit where the soul resides has been stunted by the lack of use.

We have experienced war, recessions, depressions, natural disasters, and corporate corruption. Fareed Zakaria, in his book *The Post-American World*,[9] talks about the 1980s in America. He speaks from his view as an 18-year-old student from India coming to America: "American was in rough shape. That December, unemployment hit 10.8 percent, higher than at any point since World War II. Interest rates hovered around 15 percent. Vietnam, Watergate, the energy crisis, and the Iranian hostage crisis had all battered American confidence. Images of the helicopter on the roof of the American Embassy in Saigon, of Nixon resigning, of long lines at gas stations and of the hostages blindfolded were all fresh in people's minds. The Soviet Union was on a roll, expanding its influence far beyond its borders from Afghanistan to Angola to Central American. That June, Israel invaded Lebanon, making a volatile situation in the Middle East even more tense."

What he goes on to say presents the real challenge—that America was open and Ronald Reagan, even with low approval rating, was the rallying point for optimism, as he presented real leadership qualities. Fareed adds that everywhere he went he sensed the optimism and the openness of an America that welcomed him.

The difference today is we have a shift in the economy that will take us down as a result of not only bad business decisions, but also the loss of the moral consciousness on a scale so large there are not enough mystics in place to absorb the fallout. Yeats said: "The pieces fall apart, the center cannot hold."

The peace we should find eludes us, and we have drugged ourselves with food and mindless pleasures.

I am not sure Fareed would find that same welcome today as he did in the 1980s. A fear has gripped the world that makes us unwelcoming of all. We are only in competition with them for natural resources and trade. Countries world over are completely market-driven: the research, innovation, and alliances revolve around what impact they have on market share. The market has no spirit, only body and mind!

Spirit-Based Leadership

We have no gravitational leadership to pull us together; rather, government leaders seem to polarize us more, to separate rather than unite us. Corporate leadership has so demoralized itself that we are totally disenchanted with what we see. There is a lack of conviction, and we try to just reason our way forward. Conviction is a product of that spirit that we have so long denied; if we are absent in spirit, we have no convictions.

We have lost total confidence with the people in power, and there is no optimism about the future; every day when hope is supposed to arise anew or spring eternal, we have a report that thwarts our faith. We are gradually losing our will to try and hopelessness is pervasive. The peace we should find eludes us, and we have drugged ourselves with food and mindless pleasures. Nor can we be creative in the face of such dire warnings of disaster, natural and man-made; and that innovation that we so crave is sucked up simply by a desire to connect with people. If somehow we can find body warmth then maybe the cold will not seem so dark.

International Insight | Immigrating to Ellis Island

This story is just one of many that demonstrate the evolving culture. A fellow author shared the story of her family's tale of immigrating to Ellis Island and four generations of upward mobility, only for her children, despite these advantages, to face an uncertain future. Just as so many families, her ancestors emigrated from Europe at the turn of the century. Each found their way to neighborhoods in New York City. Her father's family actually changed their last name during the immigration process to hide the fact they were Catholic, thinking that it would give them a better chance at success in the land of opportunity. Interestingly, this worked, but it also set the stage for an erosion of cultural and religious values in the name of financial success.

In the beginning, each lived in neighborhoods with neighbors of similar origin, fostering a sense of community. Her mother's family lived in a two-family home with their extended family and other family members lived within blocks. Her mother's upbringing included a close-knit family and a family pickle business. My friend's parents were of different ethnic origins. Their marriage set the stage for abandoning some of the traditions and customs of their ancestors' respective native lands. This was followed by a move out of the close-knit community to the suburbs. Although her parents remained connected to their families through frequent visits, they were no longer part of a homogeneous community. Her childhood home was in what was part of an emerging type of neighborhood composed of families of similar economic stature but varying faiths and ethnic backgrounds. Upward mobility became the name of the game.

As certain neighbors recognized increased financial successes, they moved to new bigger homes in more exclusive neighborhoods or transferred across the country due to a promotion or new job opportunity. There was a national obsession with status, which resulted in cultural differences between family members. While certainly these successes were to be commended, they also set the stage for a disconnect between generations. No longer were younger family members able to experience the sense of being connected to their heritage. More and more people's self-worth was derived from their possessions. The late 1960s and early 1970s ushered in the age of easy credit, no longer did people save for major purchases; store lay-a-way became a thing of the past and then the age of easy to obtain mortgages, which of course is largely to blame for the current economic landscape. Paying off a mortgage seemed foolish, rather, it became common to upgrade or refinance and use the equity to further enhance one's lifestyle. Keeping up with the Jones was the name of the game.

Therefore, what first became a separation from one's cultural roots evolved into an erosion of the extended family. At the same time, culturally diverse communities ended school prayer. Churches and religion fell out of favor often in the highly published light of financial and sexual misdeeds of church leadership. Churches became focused on the perceived sins of others, as opposed to centers of spiritual growth. To some the Bible became a weapon of mass destruction.

She cited another interesting perspective with respect to her story when she said that she noticed within her family that outward appearances became more important than what went on inside the home and that it was clear that her parents were struggling emotionally in order to sustain the lifestyle they had worked hard to create. It was clear that for her family and many of their neighbors, the financial successes of her parents and their peers was far greater than their emotional intelligence. Fear of failure made it easier and easier to engage in moral and ethical lapses in the name of success. Cheating on taxes, padding expense accounts, and similar types of seemingly innocent practices were viewed as acceptable because everyone else was doing it.

Along the way, each generation became more educated and worldlier. A college education, which for many of the greatest generation as Tom Brokaw described in his book, was not an option.[10] Post-college education became standard practice. Then along came the advent of the student loan. While her parents' savings paid for this woman's education, her children's education was financed by easy-to-obtain student loans. This seemed to make sense because the investment in education would yield a high-paying job that would more than cover the loan repayments. Sadly, by the time her children graduated, a good education no longer guaranteed a good job.

Moving ahead down this timeline, no longer was there a corporate culture of the benevolent employer and the loyal employee. Corporate mergers led to lay-offs; jobs were shipped off-shore; cities whose primary employer was a single large corporation could be wiped off the map by a strategic move to an area of the country with lower labor costs and bonuses and raises were no longer expected. There was no type of assurance that future generations could anticipate greater wealth than the generations before, rather it was quite likely to be exactly the opposite. My friend told me her father worked for one company his entire career; she changed jobs several times, sometimes in order to obtain a better position, other times because of lay-off or downsizing.

My friend was resigned to the fact that it was quite likely that three generations of upward mobility was no assurance of a continued trend for her children and grandchildren. There no longer was a large and prosperous "upper-middle class," rather, by the beginning of the 21st century, catch-phrases such as class warfare became the staple of the evening news on some channels. More importantly, all Americans were not getting the same news. The less fortunate were viewed as living off the hard work of others and corporations largely control the political process through massive donations.

From today's vantage point, rich and poor both seem to lack a moral compass, with both sides engaging in behavior that appears ethically challenged. As the rich seek tax shelters and profits regardless of who is hurt in the process, those with fewer resources feel compelled to do things such as work under the table, cheat on their taxes, and scheme to become eligible for entitlements once intended as a safety net.

At the end of her story, she mentioned that her accumulation of possessions, lavish vacations, and private educations all seemed propitious. Living in a home that had lost its value and with little retirement savings, she does not envision retiring and feels it is quite likely that she will be forced to rely on her children for financial support in her old age. Her story is not at all uncommon. More and more families began living under a single roof again for economic survival. In her words, the latter half of the 20th century for her and her family was an interesting but largely pointless experiment. Her standard of living became unsustainable, and as a result she was forced to abandon many lofty dreams and return to a style of living that was more focused on a close-knit family as the center of support.

Discussion Questions

- What is the corporation's role in enabling the evolution from the pinnacle of enlightened thought to spiritual values in the new age of communication and information?
- How can corporations restore optimism in their corporate message?
- How do corporate leaders end the disconnect with employees, the public, and find a consistency that changes the current course?

Exercise I Thomas Jefferson I World Religion

Thomas Jefferson constructed a book that he entitled *The Life and Morals of Jesus of Nazareth*. Assembling excerpts from the four gospels of the New Testament, he rearranged them to tell a chronological and edited story of Jesus's life, parables, and moral teaching. Jefferson cut from printed texts in four languages—English, French, Latin, and Greek—seeking to clarify and distill Jesus's teachings, which he believed to be "the most sublime and benevolent code of morals which has ever been offered to man."[11]

With a mindset similar to Jefferson's, rework the following religious passages into similar statements. Can you understand what Jefferson was trying to accomplish? Considering the following excerpts from sacred texts, rewrite each as an ethical principle for a corporation. What do you think about using the "sacred text" of the world's great religions to serve as an ethical model?

Judaism The Torah Exod. 23:10 | For six years you shall sow your land and gather in its yield; but the seventh year you shall let it rest and lie fallow, so that the poor of your people may eat; and what they leave the wild animals may eat. You shall do the same with your vineyard, and with your olive orchard.[12]

Christianity Proverbs 14:23 | In all labor there is profit: but the talk of the lips leads only to poverty.[13]

Muslim Quran   9:34 | O ye who believe! there are indeed many among the priests and anchorites, who in Falsehood devour the substance of men and hinder (them) from the way of Allah. And there are those who bury gold and silver and spend it not in the way of Allah: announce unto them a most grievous penalty.[14]

Buddhist Teachings | Think not lightly of evil, saying, "It will not come to me." Drop by drop is the water pot filled. Likewise, the fool, gathering it little by little, fills himself with evil.[15]

Hinduism. Bhagavad Gita 16.21 | There are three gates to self-destructive hell: lust, anger, and greed.[16]

Taoism. Tao Te Ching 46 | There is no crime greater than having too many desires; There is no disaster greater than not being content; There is no misfortune greater than being covetous.[17]

A Case for Being of the People and for the People: Ford Motor Company

*Henry Ford |
Founder Ford
Motor Company*

Henry Ford in 1903 founded Ford Motor Company in Detroit, MI.[18] Not only did Ford revolutionize the development of the automobile as a product, but he is also the visionary behind the innovation of mass production. Ford's ability to make automobiles affordable for the masses is cited as a driving force behind both the automobile industry and the creation of a middle class in America. He built his company on ethical and moral principles. Henry Ford once said, "there is a most intimate connection between decency and good business".[19] In 1925, Ford took out a full-page ad in the *Saturday Evening Post* titled: *Opening the Highways to All Mankind.* He stated that the goal of Ford Motor Company: "was to make safe and efficient transportation accessible to everyone—not just a wealthy few".[20] His legacy emphasized both the importance of the individual employee and the natural environment. In 1914, Ford employees were being paid $5 a day, which was, at the time, far above the average wages of the day.[21] Current chairman, William "Bill" Clay Ford, Jr., continues to affirm that employees represent the only sustainable advantage of a company. The younger Ford has maintained his grandfather's legacy by taking a leadership role in improving vehicle fuel efficiency while reducing emissions and has been quoted as saying, "I believe the distinction between a good company and a great company is this: a good company delivers excellent product and services; a great one delivers excellent products and services and strives to make the world a better place".[22] Bill also stood before a news conference in January 2006, and signaled a shift in the consciousness of the company; he asserted a new direction for the company when he said: "True customer-focus means that our business decisions originate from our knowledge of what the customer wants, both today and tomorrow. 'If you build it, they will buy it'—that's business as usual, and that's wrong. 'If they will buy it, we will build it' is right—and we're going back to it".[23] Ford's reputation in the marketplace proves that the company is committed to these standards as they are reflected in the manner in which they do business. The company's code of ethics covers conflict of interests for directors, improper personal benefits from stocks for any member of an employee's family, and any dealings with third parties that can affect Ford. Directors may not receive gifts nor use company assets for personal use.[24]

> *We got here because we relied solely on the patterns of the Age of Reason to sort all our thought processes. We so embraced the power and rightness of the mind to direct us and keep us free that we ignored probably the most important part of man,* **the spirit.**

Ford's current business strategy is embodied in what is referred to as the "ONE Ford" plan that includes a four-point business plan for achieving success globally. The four-points include:

1. Aggressively restructure to operate profitably at the current demand and changing model mix.

2. Accelerate development of new products that customers want and value.
3. Finance the plan and improve the balance sheet.
4. Work together effectively as one team.[25]

Through strict adherence to this plan over the years, Ford has weathered several economic downturns, including in 2008 when they were the only major US automaker not to take advantage of government loans to avoid bankruptcy.[26]

But 2008 was not the first time that Ford experienced economic pressures; in the autumn of 1920, Henry Ford was in trouble. He owed money to bankers, sales were plummeting, and the company was losing $20 on each car produced. This crisis inspired a key element of "lean manufacturing." By the spring of 1921 Ford had paid all his debts and the company had a cash surplus of $20 million. Productivity had increased with a reduction in labor cost.[27]

We have experienced war, recessions, depressions, natural disasters, and corporate corruption.

Today, Ford Motor Company is a global leader in sustainability. Ford's Code of Basic Working Conditions, Human Rights and Corporate Responsibility (Policy Letter 24)[28] applies both to company operations and to the company's over 2,000 suppliers making 130,000 different parts at 7,500 sites in 60 countries. Each year, the company reports its progress in its Sustainability Report Summary[29] it has been publishing for the past 12 years. In addition, through their commitment to the U.N. Global Compact, they continue to integrate sustainability into all organizational structures and business processes, including complete transparency in sustainability reporting. Ford has been at the forefront of incorporating the environmental, social, and governance principles of the United Nations Global Compact and is one of the 50 institutional investors who pledged to follow these principles.[30] With stakeholders that include shareholders, suppliers, dealers, customers, employees, and communities in 200 countries, Ford has recognized its role as a thought leader and center of influence with multinational oversight. With sales and operations in 200 countries, Ford recognizes that it is in its interest to promote stability and peace throughout the world.[31]

We can no longer sustain ourselves, much less our world, because we are soulless, and the spirit where the soul resides has been stunted by the lack of use.

Ford responded to environmental advocates' criticisms by developing hybrid and flex fuel vehicles. By July 2006, they had invested $1.6 billion bill to develop technology with a goal to improve the Ford Focus to the point it has 70 mpg fuel efficiency. In response to the European Union's requirement that, by 2015, 95% of the materials used to build a vehicle be recyclable, Ford is developing "Model U" concept car using biomaterials.[32] They have also committed to reduce waste generated in Ford plants as well as rely on landfill gases as a source of energy for plants and converting paint and solvent waste for other uses.[33]

We have lost total confidence with the people in power, and there is no optimism about the future; every day when hope is supposed to arise anew or spring eternal, we have a report that thwarts our faith.

World affairs directly impact Ford. As a global automotive company, Ford continues to strive to be recognized as a credible, leading source of information with respect to the formation of such policies across a range of issues including manufacturing, climate change, energy security, health care reform, human rights, trade, education, and vehicle safety, among others. Ford strives to shape policies that are economically, environmentally, and socially sustainable for Ford and for the world. Informed policy makes for better policy, whether at the international, national, regional, state, or local level.[34]

The difference today is we have a shift in the economy that will take us down not only as a result of bad business decisions, but also the loss of the moral consciousness on a scale so large there are not enough mystics in place to absorb the fallout.

That is not to say that Ford Motor Company does not make mistakes; in the early 1970s, it was discovered that there was a design flaw in its Pinto model that could cause the car to burst into flames even in minor rear-end collisions. Ford did a cost–benefit analysis and decided that the cost of fixing all Pintos on the road (about $11 each) would result in higher overall costs than paying damages to people injured or killed in car fires, which it estimated to be about $270,000 each. When juries learned of Ford's cold-blooded comparisons of spare parts and human lives, they gave victims multimillion-dollar damage settlements. Ford voluntarily recalled the and repaired the Pintos. The company lost millions of dollars, and its image suffered for years among the car-buying public. This came at a time when the demand for sub-compacts was rising on the market. The car was designed by Lee Iacocca who had specifications for the design that were uncompromising. "The Pinto was not to weigh an ounce over 2,000 pounds and not cost a cent over $2,000." To correct it would have required changing and strengthening the design.[35]

As a country, we are completely market-driven: our research, innovation, and alliances revolve around what impact they have on market share. The market has no spirit, only body and mind!

Bill Ford | Executive Chairman | Ford Motor Company

Ford is an example of a corporation that continues to remake itself, and continues the focus of its founder, to make a product that is safe and accessible to everyone. In an industry that is impacted by world energy resources and the political winds that prevail, Ford is forced to rethink its strategy and its values. Ford is a leading corporation, at the moment, that is proving that it can and will continue to refine its process and remain committed to the public trust through transparency and accountability.

Supplemental Reading

The following are scholarly and peer-reviewed journal articles, conference proceedings, and dissertations on the concepts discussed in this chapter.

- Spirituality at Work: An Exploratory Sociological Investigation of the Ford Motor Company[36]
- Workplace Spirituality and Organizational Performance[37]
- Individual Differences and Workplace Spirituality: The Homogenization of the Corporate Culture, T. Winters Moore, *Journal of Management and Marketing Research*, Volume 1, December 2008[38]

CHAPTER 3

Why Does It Matter? |
Only Business Can
Save Us

A New Vision for Corporations

Large global corporations now control the whole planet, employ most of the people, and make the profit. Literally, the corporation is the life-blood of the world as we know it. If we are to continue to survive and thrive, it is going to be the corporation that recognizes that the Age of Reason has reached its limit of applicability, and the real enlightenment is that we are not just a force of two—body and mind—but a trinity that includes the spirit.

Reviewing the composition of the charitable giving and its impact on real-time sources of monies that keep the majority of R & D endeavors, and other causes world over, funded shows that if corporate giving were ended, so much of the progress we are making in curing disease and building infrastructure in underdeveloped countries would go away.[1] Two percent of the US GDP is charitable giving. Of the 3 billion given in 2011, 73% was individual and 5% was corporate. Foundations account for 14% of all giving. Bequests account for 8%. Family Foundations, such as the Bill & Melinda Gates Foundation or the Rockefeller Foundation, are formed out of corporate profit contributed to philanthropy. Notably Warren Buffet and Bill Gates, in what started as a challenge to 11 of their wealthy friends to give away half of their wealth to philanthropic causes, has grown to a list that is over 100 and gaining recognition.[2]

Corporations are vilified and scorned; the "little people," led by politicians, and often the media, call for more taxes on the "evil" corporations.

Corporations are vilified and scorned; the "little people," led by politicians, and often the media, call for more taxes on the "evil" corporations. Who do you think makes up the corporation? The "little people," whom else? So often, the protesters are short on facts and have only the micro view of the way the world works and are not armed with much more than their own anger with their own lives and desire to have someone else to accuse of tyranny. The corporation is the easy target. But the protest is misplaced as with the Occupy Wall Street people. It is all people, as well as the planet, that will suffer or be destroyed if corporate leaders do not assume the responsibility that goes with the rights to make money. Certainly, corporations can and must make the profit and continually invest and innovate in ways to make more profit. The "however" is that if corporate greed continues to be epitomized by graduates from prestigious business schools then we have no chance for upward movement in corporate responsibility. It is just a farce. In 2011, the Wharton Business School at the University of Pennsylvania approved a new vision for MBA education, "grounded in flexibility for our diverse student body, academic rigor, continuous innovation of course content and a commitment to lifelong learning, with an integrated focus on ethical and legal responsibility in business."[3] This curriculum change came in the wake of the financial crisis; however, it did not go unnoticed that, in recent years, two Wharton MBAs pleaded guilty to securities fraud, and Wharton graduate and Galleon Hedge Fund Manager Raj Rajaratnam was convicted of fraud and conspiracy.[4] In the words of one student interviewed at the school's 2011 graduation: "You spend four semesters learning to push to the edge, to identify any possible advantage," he said. "And just one half of one credit on ethics. That's just six class sessions. It's amazing that there aren't more of these cases."[5]

According to Dean Thomas S. Robertson: "At Wharton it (ethics) is central to our mission, business can and must be a force for good."[6] In a recent *Huffington Post* Blog, Robertson discussed the power of the corporation in even greater detail when he said the following:

"I believe that business, arguably the most powerful resource on the planet, must take a leading role in addressing the challenges the world faces, and not just in the economic sphere. Environmental degradation, global climate change, poverty, disease, and human exploitation are all concerns that business should help address. All the better if this responsible reaction to the world's problems can promote profits at the same time that it improves quality of life. When businesses work to solve social problems, they endorse connectivity and collaboration. The goal is to increase the velocity of commerce that drives progress and creates newly-empowered generations of consumers eager and prepared to embrace the security and rewards of middle class life."[7]

"I believe that business, arguably the most powerful resource on the planet, must take a leading role in addressing the challenges the world faces, and not just in the economic sphere." Dean Thomas S. Robertson, Dean of Wharton School of Business.

Sadly, this rhetoric around saving the planet remains just that, rhetoric. A review of the largest global companies, including country of origin, by industry, in terms of annual revenue, and number of employees proves that the corporations are the organized unit within our world today that can bring sustainability to our current unsustainable trajectory. In looking at just the top ten, it is also remarkable that the nine out of ten in revenue are involved in the oil industry. Listing the top ten in profit has some differing players in terms of industry representation.

Top 10 companies in profit and number of employees[8]

Rank	Company	Country	Industry	2011 revenue in USD	Total employees
1	Royal Dutch Shell	The Netherlands	Petroleum	$484.4 billion	90,000
2	Exxon Mobil	United States	Petroleum	$452.9 billion	99,100
3	Wal-Mart Stores	United States	Retail	$446.9 billion	2,100,000
4	BP	United Kingdom	Petroleum	$386.4 billion	79,700
5	Sinopec	China	Petroleum	$375.2 billion	640,535
6	China National Petroleum	China	Petroleum	$352.3 billion	1,668,072
7	State Grid	China	Power	$259.1 billion	1,564,000
8	Chevron	United States	Petroleum	$245.6 billion	62,196
9	Conoco Phillips	United States	Petroleum	$237.2 billion	29,700
10	Toyota Motor	Japan	Automobiles	$235.3 billion	317,716

These numbers speak volumes about where people earn their livelihood and what a powerful force these corporations with a global presence are in the life of our world.

The Role of the United Nations

It is not as though we do not know what we need to do; it is a willingness to go beyond the power paradigm and to find the political will to implement in a manner that says that leadership in the world is about doing the right thing and following the purpose of the UN, which is to protect human rights around the world and to see to it that nations can self-actualize and self-govern. The League of Nations,[9] which was formed after World War I, was a good idea, but the League's failure was the result of goals that were too unrealistic and possibly naïve for the world stage, and consequently major world powers, such as the United States, Britain, France, Germany, did not support the League's mission.

The League failed politically more than socially while many of its programs have affected social policy around the world in regard to human rights, the treatment of women, and the eradication of disease in underdeveloped countries. The League of Nations set the stage for the dialogue around internationally agreed upon goals.

The United Nations,[10] which was formed after World War ll, has not, in the eyes of some, yet achieved the world peace or balance of power according to its vision. The UN is funded chiefly by the United States, which means US financial support is integral to the ongoing efforts of the UN to provide the forum for an international voice. The UN budget was $5.41 billion per year (2010–2011), and it spent $7.2 billion per year (2010–2011) on peace-keeping activities around the world. The United States pays dues of 22% of the UN budget.[11] This year (2012), for the first time, the UN cut its budget by 5% for the second time in 50 years.[12]

The connection for the UN in terms of ethics is that the eyes of the world watch for the increased acceptance of the rule of law. Unfortunately, standards in underdeveloped countries rise slowly. Some of the political places where the UN has sought to intervene highlight a conflicted struggle for some members in the body, and for the UN who must operate in a world of greed, corruption, and deceit. A case in point, the Syrian massacres are so horrific that Kofi Annan, former Secretary General to the UN, a man who has devoted his life to peace, was appointed as the joint UN Arab-League special envoy to Syria in an attempt to end the increasingly violent uprising that began in March 2011. He left Syria and came back to the United States without any encouraging words. He conceded that it was a lost cause! Annan also stepped down as Secretary General.[13]

The call is for leadership that can make the hard choice and speak the truth without political bias.

Nevertheless, the UN remains an essential international body, under Secretary General Ban Ki-moon, where world voices can come to the stage and be heard. However, these days (⊙ July 2012), the body is again polarized, with Russia and China refusing for the third time to sign the agreement, supported by most people in the world community, calling for an end to the brutal reign of Bashar al-Assad, the Syrian leader who has devastated his country and is killing his people *en masse*.[14] It is more a jockeying for power and further indication that the world is more, and perhaps best now, controlled by corporations than by governments. The call is for leadership that can make the hard choice and speak the truth without political bias. Sounds like a fairy tale perhaps, but without an intervention and insertion of truth in leadership, we are perishing as a world. The connection can be made that the perceived weaknesses in an international body such as the UN are a microcosm of the macrocosm and that what is missing is the spiritual understanding that the world is one and that the urgency is for this international dialogue.

The UN often cannot compete with corporate power, even in the face of such challenging world needs; the refusal of Russia's Putin to intervene in Syria has little to do with anything other than the amassing of his own power, and the need to be in opposition to the West as he secures his power (☉ March 2012) by winning another 6 years in office. Putin is interested in the most self-serving way with Syria, not the people, just the strategic location of the country in the Mideast. Having lost Gaddafi as an ally, Putin can ill-afford to lose another. Putin will be stopped only when the economic interest and power of Russia's corporate business grows stronger and demands it. Even in a state-controlled country such as Russia, the democratic power of business is at work.[15]

China's refusal to side with other countries in the UN, and notably with the United States, in condemning Assad, is explained in part by the fact that China draws much of its imported oil from Iran and has deep concerns about Western military intervention. China is flexing its muscle as a world power; add to this how they observed the war in Afghanistan and its cost first to Russia and now the United States. China would not want the economic impact of a war in Syria in which they might be engaged. They care little or nothing about the violation of human rights; it is not in their DNA. Further, China fears Muslim extremist interference, and they are seeking new allies.[16]

The UN Global Compact deserves major attention and is an example of a seminal and spiritual idea, and a testament to the vision of the UN that business and the corporations along with this international body have the power to make the biggest difference in the world. Few have signed on to it, but it points to the reality of the direction in which we must move.

The 10 principles enjoy universal consensus.

The Global Compact of 2001, which was inspired by the speech of then UN Secretary General Kofi Annan's to the assembly, is an important marker for the awakening of the giant.[17] The 10 principles of this compact are intended to draw together business from all over the globe and create a density or critical mass that moves the planet in the direction of healing through a common bond.[18]

The 10 principles enjoy universal consensus and are derived from:

- The Universal Declaration of Human Rights
- The International Labor Organization's Declaration on Fundamental Principles and Rights at Work
- The Rio Declaration on Environment and Development
- The United Nations Convention Against Corruption
- The UN Global Compact asks companies to embrace, support, and enact within their sphere of influence, a set of core values in the areas of human rights, labor standards, the environment, and anticorruption.[19]

The Ten Principles

Human Rights

Principle 1: Businesses should support and respect the protection of internationally proclaimed human rights; and

Principle 2: Make sure that they are not complicit in human rights abuses.

Labor

Principle 3: Businesses should uphold the freedom of association and the effective recognition of the right to collective bargaining;

Principle 4: The elimination of all forms of forced and compulsory labor;

Principle 5: The effective abolition of child labor; and

Principle 6: The elimination of discrimination in respect of employment and occupation.

Environment

Principle 7: Businesses should support a precautionary approach to environmental challenges;

Principle 8: Undertake initiatives to promote greater environmental responsibility; and

Principle 9: Encourage the development and diffusion of environmentally friendly technologies.

Anticorruption

Principle 10: Businesses should work against corruption in all its forms, including extortion and bribery.

Adherence to the Principles

The UN Compact has disinvited 2,500 members in 2011 for noncompliance.[20] I urge you to go to the website (UN Global Compact) and read all about the compact, and if your corporation or your school or business is not yet part of this critical mass, join today. This very simply represents an enlightened and global view of the role for all people and for all corporate entities, public and private.

The UN Compact disinvited 2,500 members in 2011 for noncompliance.

The goal of the UN Compact is to double its current membership to 20,000 by the year 2020. These numbers are small (under 10,000 now) considering the over 70,000 multinationals that exist, plus the millions and millions of corporations worldwide that should easily be a part of this agreement. That the UN Compact has delisted 2,500 members this year (© 2011) for noncompliance is two steps forward and one back![21] For the UN, and the UN Global Compact specifically, to be a strong voice and effective on the world stage for sustainability, or for peace that protects citizens around the world, more support and commitment is needed from the corporate community.

The power to create a regulatory board, **A Watch Force** as it were, for sustainability will come from the list of the top 100 corporations in terms of profit and numbers of employees that must intervene and do what the UN has yet to do, create an international body funded by all the top world corporations and whose agenda will be to have 100% participation in a Global Social Sustainability Model for people, planet, and profit. A corporation should not be allowed to exist if its only goal is profit.

People or Profit

Mark Schwartz, associate professor of Law, Governance, and Ethics at York University, Canada, in his new book *Corporate Social Responsibility, An Ethical Approach* (2012), echoes this idea. The book serves as a counter to Jeffery Skilling's view of the corporate role of leaders, in that Schwartz's position is that a corporation that exists to make profit only should not exist and should be caused to close.

Schwartz in this text has consolidated the five dominant terminologies surrounding corporate social responsibility, business ethics, stakeholder management, sustainability, and corporate citizenship into a Venn diagram of ethics, legal, and economics to show the equal relationship to the Value a corporation needs, the Balance required for managing stakeholder interest, and Accountability, in terms of total corporate social responsibility. Schwartz's research represents a definitive movement to what and how we will train leaders going forward and what will be required of corporations. The tide has changed in what we teach and how we teach leadership most specifically as it relates to corporate social responsibility.[22]

> For too long Wall Street and the other stock exchanges of the world have held sway over corporate decision making, and this must change, and corporate life must end the cycle of owing its soul to the middle men who manipulate what a corporation can and cannot do.

If the reason corporations refrain from joining the UN Compact is political, rather than the absence of real transparent principles and sustainability as the major thrust of doing business, or both, then we must have a group rise up, that as Jeff Immlet, the CEO of GE, refers to as "domain experts,"[23] who will bring the power and leadership, who will come with a well-defined code of ethics and along with the industry-specific knowledge to form **a Corporate Social Responsibility Watch Force**, a name I am coining. The power for this international body would come from its influence with all the world investment exchanges, including Wall Street, in that investors will not invest in a company that fails to meet the test of true, transparent, and real social responsibility, no matter how profitable or how much their revenue value. In addition, this body will end the dominance that exchanges have over corporate life. Corporations will be freed from the overweening and capriciousness of demands made by exchanges that are counter-culture to the life of the corporations. Moving forward with the creation of this body, **the Corporate Social Responsibility Watch Force** creates a palpable sense that forms an energy that always accompanies an idea whose time has come.

For too long Wall Street and the other stock exchanges of the world have held sway over corporate decision making, and this must change, and corporate life must end the cycle of owing its soul to the middle men who manipulate what a corporation can and cannot do. The Financial Exchanges of the world from China to Japan to London do not care for the people, or the planet. We need a straighter line between the corporation and the stakeholders. We see how much fraud and how innately corruptible the exchanges have become with the latest installment being the high-speed trading that only a small number of traders even begin to understand, much less can any of the government agencies control or regulate. The regulators do not understand the high-speed process enough to regulate it and are always responding after the events have devastated large sectors of the economy and destroyed peoples' lives.[24]

Currently, World Exchanges have no soul and therefore, they are without a moral fiber, individually or collectively to lead.

The need for citizens to become vested in companies as shareholders is paramount to a company's ability to be successful and to have the capital to continue innovation and growth. The vast power that we see executed by the World Exchanges to dictate leadership change in a corporation or to determine product focus for a company has to end. These exchanges should not be allowed to be the interloper and dictate what a company can do; they can evaluate but their power to dominate must be curtailed.[25] Currently, World Exchanges have no soul and, therefore, they are without a moral fiber, individually or collectively, to lead. The UN is a most logical international body to execute on the plan for there to be a significant force that brings corporate power together. However, if the UN proves, in short order, that it cannot accomplish this along with its other responsibilities, then, we must call onto the world stage a **Corporate Social Responsibility Watch Force** to execute the vision and provide the collective and collaborative leadership necessary for a world order to survive. These men and women must tackle the challenges to the globe and its people: water and energy resources, poverty, and disease in Third World countries, a broken education system, and the financial crisis. A **Corporate Social Responsibility Watch Force** would establish standards and weighs to evaluate CSR across the board and across the world. I see people such as Bill Gates, Warren Buffet, Michael Bloomberg, Tim Cook, Jeff Immlet, Meg Whitman, Larry Ellison, Indra Nooyi, Edgar Bronfman, Jon Huntsman, T. Boone Pickens, Richard Branson, and there are others, who own enough of the world stage and who have achieved success and lived with authenticity to have a loud voice and to make a difference.

International Insight | Reviewing the UN | You Decide

International Insight | Reviewing the UN & Syria | You Decide

John F. Kennedy in his "ask not" speech said: "Americans do not start war." He believed that and most citizens in the United States share that belief. Why would we need to start a war, we have everything we need, which is the attitude that also sucks the United States into conflicts. The premise is that we go to war to help the oppressed who seek basic human rights and freedom, and whom we believe should have the rule of law which will ensure those human rights. A leader like Afghanistan president, Hamid Karzai, who has an extreme hatred for the United States and all the Western allies, believes that Americans start wars just by being who we are and showing up. Karzai often talks about how impossible it is for his government to govern when any Westerner is present. And so we leave Afghanistan now, and we will all see the outcome. We engender such vitriolic responses from leaders like Karzai because of the wealth we cannot hide. Going back to the comment that Tony Blair made in his book, *A Journey: My Political Life*, when he said: "America's burden is that it wants to be loved and knows it cannot be." (Blair, p.xi) Robert Kagan in his book, *Of Paradise and Power*, takes the position that not only do we want to be loved, the United States puts money and will into that process, and one place where this is evident is the United Nations with all its reach into places where the light needs to shine in the world where human rights continue to be abused.[26]

So Syria is on the world stage and anyone viewing the spread of sectarian violence has to see the Bashar al-Assad regime as a classic Greek Tragedy which always has five acts, and this is act five for sure (March 2013).

While the UN Global Compact website stated that there are 44 participants in Syria, it is difficult to find solid information with respect to the program's successes in this region. Currently, any assessment of what is going on inside the Syrian world, which is also spilling over into bordering Turkey, where hundreds of thousands of Syrians are displaced, presents a clear picture of oppression and civil war. The country has a brain and labor drain that will not easily or quickly be repaired, with possibly more than a million refugees who have fled the country, many of whom are now receiving humanitarian aid through the UN. The abuse of human rights and the absence of the rule of law allow the tyranny to continue. The UN today has not been successful in negotiating peace. Kofi Annan's six point peace plan launched almost a year ago had no lasting effect on the Assad's reign of terror, and this compounded with Annan resigning as special envoy for the UN in Syria (⊘ August 2012), citing disarray in the international community, chinches the deal. Syria will not come to peace talks anytime soon.

Below is a series of opinions intended to give the reader an overall sense as to the administration of the program in areas where human rights abuses are common. Please note that when the author attempted to access the Global Compact Website for Syria (⊘ March 3, 2013), it said the account was suspended.[27]

On the other hand, as of ⊘ December 2012, the following overall description remained on the UN Global Compact Website, touting successes in the region: (quoting directly)

Initiating the Incremental Impact by Shared Values United Nations Development Programme (NUDP) *UNDP Pushes into High Gear with Syria's Private Sector.*

Summary from website:

"The past ten years has provided a unique opportunity for the private sector to engage in high-level dialogue with governments from around the world and identify promising trends and opportunities for business community contributions to the Millennium Development Goals (MDGs). Secretary-General Ban Ki-moon put it best by saying: 'The common thread runs through almost all companies' experiences in bringing the Compact's ten principles to life: expanding markets and advancing the economic and social well-being of people and societies can be two sides of the same coin"…

(Ali Ahmad, UNDP Syria).

Private sector leaders have launched corporate practices, exemplary collective action and innovative business models for contributing to development in the areas of poverty and hunger, maternal and child health and HIV/AIDS, access to education through innovative Informations Communications Technology, innovations for financial inclusion, empowering women and achieving equality and greening the economy.

(Ahmad).

Today, Syria stands as the UN Global Compact's fastest growing network in the Middle East, with 43 members and USD 4 million in the United Nations Development Programme (UNDP) lead private sector partnerships. This fact speaks volumes about what the initiative can do in a country, no matter what the economies of scale. At the same time, it provides an indication of how mature the private sector can be when engaging in global development.

(Ahmad).

These statements articulate a position that we would like to be so, and it follows a pattern that has been successful for the UN and the promotion of its partnerships with business to bring stability, domestic and international, to developing economies and peoples around the world. The problem in Syria is that the tyranny of the Bashar Assad regime threatens so much of an already fragile existence in the Middle East. Going into its third year civil war has not moved to resolve, with the continued support for Bashar Assad by China, Russia, and Iran and even with extreme economic sanctions and humanitarian support from Britain, the US, and the arch-enemy, Israel for the rebels. These players make a strange dual, and no one can imagine a war among these players (Gayathri, March 23, 2012 6:01 AM). However, Fouad Ajami, an expert on the Middle East in the *Wall Street Journal*, February 28, 2013 writes: "Syria is the place where the will of Iran can be broken." If this is the case and if the voices for support of the Syrian rebels grow from the UK's David Cameron, and with former Secretary of State, Hillary Clinton, the secretary of Defense, Leon Panetta, and chairman of the Joint Chiefs of Staff, Dempsey, and the director of the Central Intelligence

Agency, Morell, all of whom support arming the rebels and joined today @ March 4, 2013 with the articulate voice of the senator, and soon to be face of the Republican party, Marcio Rubio calling for this armed support, it is any one's guess on how this will roll out. It will not be simple unless it is a decisive and clear position taken by world powers. It will require that the world community supports this no matter who takes the lead; the stakes are too high and the players too powerful. The UN is the logical place from which these powers can agree, at least on the obvious that the Assad regime must be displaced. And as we have learned again and again, as with Egypt and Libya now, it is not enough to unseat the despot, if there is not a strong and immediate government that goes in place immediately that has the will of the people, what fills the vacuum that is created can be worse. Not an easy play to stage! But at this moment, it seems inevitable that the US, and hopefully through the UN which has the best shot at bringing the world voices together, will need to lead on this one and this time for all the right reasons.

Consider that when a Tunisian fruit vendor set himself on fire and set in motion what we have called the Arab Spring (Paulson, 2011); the whole world is challenged to focus on the two things that causes this type of revolutionary response: property and human rights and the rule of law (Paulson). As flawed as these systems are, even in developed countries, they represent the core practices that lift a people to a civilized state. There is no other way.

The Secretary General made this statement (quoted directly from the UN website on 2 March 2013)—The international community must act with unity to achieve a political solution and end the suffering in Syria, Secretary-General Ban Ki-moon and the Joint Special Representative of the world organization and the League of Arab States, Lakhdar Brahimi, stressed today during a meeting in Mt. Pelerin, Switzerland.

Both expressed deep frustration at the failure of the international community to act with unity to bring an end to the conflict, and regretted that the Government and the armed opposition forces have become "increasingly reckless with human life," according to information from Mr. Ban's spokesperson.

They also emphasized the importance of ensuring accountability for war crimes and crimes against humanity.

Up to 70,000 people, mostly civilians, have been killed since the uprising against President Bashar al-Assad began in March 2011 and more than 900,000 people have fled to neighboring countries. In addition, 2 million have been internally displaced and over 4 million people are in need of humanitarian assistance.

During their meeting, Mr. Ban and Mr. Brahimi reaffirmed their conviction that the international community should remain focused on pursuing a political solution to arrive at a peaceful, democratic Syria that protects the right of all of its communities.

The two men also discussed recent statements by the Government and the opposition indicating their willingness to engage in dialogue and said that the UN would welcome and be prepared to facilitate a dialogue between a strong and representative delegation from the opposition and a credible and empowered delegation from the Syrian Government.

When evaluating the UN, we must remember how and why the UN was formed, and how its successes and its failures demonstrate the state of the world at any time, and what it says about us as a people on this planet. It is up to you to decide how effective this international body remains. Since the UN grew out of World War II in 1945, the mission has been straightforward in that it seeks peace and freedom from war for all people and an end to world hunger and the protection of human rights. Often small countries overshadow larger countries and the mission is mired by politics. The Global Compact remains a big deal and as you read the principles again, you understand that the power it has comes from the people and yet, it cannot be all-powerful in that this omnipotence would defeat its core purpose. Negotiating power and bringing the atrocities still committed somewhere in the world to the attention of the world has to be its real power, but its voice to end violence now in Syria is loud, pronounced, and direct.

You Decide!

Discussion Questions

- Why should a corporation doing business primarily in the US need to concern itself with what seems like global issues?
- Why is government so ineffective in regulating corporations?

- How can corporate diversity translate into a corporate value as opposed to a subject for litigation?

Exercise | Principles by Which to Measure | UN Global Compact

- This exercise is designed to provide a real-world illustration of how the UN Global Compact's principles could be used to unify corporate power globally creating high moral ground, transparency, and a sustainable future for all peoples. The UN Global Compact has created a self-assessment tool for corporations to evaluate their business operations with respect to adherence to the 10 principles of the Compact. The process yields a comprehensive overview and sets forth best practices for consideration.

Step One	Select a corporation that is not currently a member of the UN Global Compact (www.unglobalcompact.org/participants/search)
Step Two	Create a login and use it to log into the Self-Assessment Tool (www.globalcompactselfassessment.org)
Step Three	Read the Section entitled Getting Started, then answer one or more of the questions in each of the four areas (Human Rights, Labor, Environment, and Anti-Corruption).
Step Four	Click on Export to Excel tab to generate a follow-up report.
Step Five	Based on the results, draft a letter to the Chief Ethics Officer of the Corporation, listing some suggested courses of action

- Supplemental exercises and projects | consider the following:
  One–Create a Communication on Progress (COP) using the provided template. http://www.unglobalcompact.org/docs/communication _on_progress/Basic_COP_Step_by_Step_Guide.pdf
  Two–Using the Global Reporting Initiative create a report for the Corporation. https://www.globalreporting.org/resourcelibrary/ English-Lets-Report- Template.pdf
  Three–Review the Environment, Social, Governance Investor Briefing and create a report of the Corporation. http://www .unglobalcompact.org/docs/issues_doc/Financial_markets /ESGInvestorBriefingFramework.pdf

- For an additional exercise, review the websites for the World Justice Project (http://worldjusticeproject.org/) and Ethisphere (http://ethisphere.com/) and note how it differs from the UN Global Compact. In a short paper (1200–1500 words), prepared for oral presentation including PowerPoint, compare and contrast the three organizations, include mission/vision, history of organization, membership, funding, current status, and conclude with research that takes a position on the power of each organization to effect sustainability going forward.

Case Study | A Case Study for Collaboration | Accenture and the UN Global Compact

When a circumstance is forced, sometimes it creates strange bedfellows. For a successful global consulting firm such as Accenture to team up with the UN seems like such a match. Why would a company, which generated net revenues of US$27.9 billion for the fiscal year ended August 31, 2012, be willing to partner-up with or accept an invitation from a world entity such as the UN?[28] Because we have come to a tipping point in the progression of civilization as we know it. All the thought leaders today know that the world's resources must be managed not for one country or for one corporation, but for the world. The 2010 collaboration between the UN and its Global Compact and Accenture is given wings by the selection of Accenture as the author of the *CEO Study 2010*, and the UN Global Compact gives Accenture the credibility of authenticity as a business that it merits.[29] It may be that the UN knows what to do and Accenture knows how to have it "Delivered."

> *It is not as though we do not know what we need to do; it is a willingness to go beyond the power paradigm and to find the political will to implement in a manner that says that Leadership in the world is about doing the right thing and following the purpose of the UN which is to protect human rights around the world and to see to it that nations can self-actualize and self-govern.*

The UN functions from the inside out, and they know **why** they are in business, and that is to provide a global forum where what is happening anywhere in the world, can receive notice by a world community that is now rediscovering why it must care. The UN also knows **what** they do: provide arbitration for world challenges with intervention in strife-torn places in the world with resources such as the International Monetary Fund and a system of 30 organizations, which rescues countries and champions causes around the world. Accenture seems to be providing the **how,** or more of the vehicle, for the UN to "Deliver" the why and the what.

The United Nation's headquarter in New York is the site where 193 countries now come to talk and bring to the attention of an international body grievances and needs. Ban Ki-moon, Korean born with an impressive history of public service, is the Secretary General, elected to serve through 2016.[30] The focus of the organization is only generally understood and the achievements are often not as noted as the defeats. Just the mere fact that there is an international stage where the causes of humanity have a forum is nothing short of a miracle. Among the causes that challenge the advancement of civilization and are championed by the UN are human rights, gender equality, diseases such as AIDS, poverty, child labor, safe air travel, secure telecommunications, drug trafficking, refugees, and food and water shortages.[31]

The UN Global Compact (Contract) deserves some attention and is an example of a seminal and spiritual idea, and a testament to the vision of the UN (even in view of the body's current anemic impact on world negotiations) that business and the corporations along with this international body have the power to make the biggest difference in the world.

The report represents the largest research ever conducted on sustainability, including the survey of 799 CEOs and interviews with 50 of the top CEOs worldwide. The research indicated that even the world economic crisis has not changed the course of commitment to sustainability. In fact, it has heightened it, according to the findings, in that sustainability is now viewed as a positive impact on the bottom line and understood as a way to create strong ROI. Instead of sustainability being an add-on, it is seen as a driver for economic growth in entering emerging markets. The report acknowledges the progress that has been made: "The survey results indicate that businesses are taking sustainability more seriously. In a similar survey conducted in 2007, 50 percent of the CEO respondents said that sustainability issues had become part of their company's strategy and operations. In the 2010 survey, that number jumped to 81 per cent. While recognizing the scale and complexity of global challenges, many CEOs say there has been progress over the past three years in making the transition from developing a sustainability strategy to execution."[32]

Peter Lacey, the managing director of Sustainability Services for Accenture, said that the report shows a major move forward:

If sustainability does become fully integrated into global businesses within the next decade, the regulatory, technology, investment and consumer changes required will be staggering, creating significant winners and losers across businesses and industries. Still, it's great to see that some progress is being made, and that the movement toward a more sustainable economy and business context is clearly gaining momentum.[33]

The call is for leadership that can make the hard choice and speak the truth without political bias. Sounds like a fairy tale perhaps, but without an intervention of truth in leadership, we are perishing.

At a recent (November 2012) World Affairs Council Global Affairs Luncheon in Jacksonville (FL), a presentation on the future prospects for

US trade with Cuba provided insight and enlightenment. Dr. Joseph Scarpaci, executive director, Center of the Study of Cuban Culture and the Economy and author spoke to the Council. Dr. Scarpaci is Cuban, and his biography is impressive; he talked eloquently and with an in-depth view of the state of life in Cuba and referenced a shift that would occur when what he called the "biological endings" came, referring to the time when Fidel and his brother will die. The talk was full of information on the power of the entrepreneurs and the courageous spirit of the Cuban people. A question from the audience, however, provided the strongest point of the day. A lawyer from the audience introduced himself and explained the back log of legal challenges that surround Cuba's land use, finances, and the illegal incarcerations in which he was personally involved. The current reality is that without the rule of law in Cuba, you can have nothing, no relationship, no trade, no economic growth, or promise of a consistent future. The point was made with me; at the end of the day, nothing else matters or can make a difference without the rule of law in place.[34]

The connection here is that for the UN to be effective in places where it is intervening, it will first take a cultural reality drawn for an anthropologist understanding of the country, and of the people, and how close the people and the country can be moved to a rule of law. Next, and this is the force of power, in order for the country to have economic growth or to access the sources of energy to keep their country going, the country must have political stability. Where *Accenture's CEO 2010 Report* becomes relevant is when the humanitarian intervention is not delivered with the belief that it will bring democracy, but with the knowing that the aid will provide for a self-actualization of a people or a country to begin its own journey to freedom and liberty.[35]

Supplemental Reading

The following are scholarly and peer-reviewed journal articles, conference proceedings, and dissertations on the concepts discussed in this chapter.

- An Annual Review of the United Nation Affairs, The Global Compact: An Organizational Innovation to Realize UN

Principles[36] Institutionalizing sustainability: an empirical study of corporate registration and commitment to the United Nations Global Compact Guidelines. This needs a footnote number to Waddell.

- United Nations global compact guidelines[37]
- Company Delistings from the UN Global Compact: Limited Business Demand or Domestic Governance Failure?[38]

CHAPTER 4

Leadership and Leaders I What Should They Look Like?

Leadership Failure

Leadership has failed us, and we all have feet of clay. We have demanded great leadership but have been patient and complacent with the mediocre. In his research on leadership, Warren Bennis, the great scholar and academician, reveals three things that have the power to destroy civilization, as we know it: a pandemic, nuclear war, and the loss of leadership.[1]

Certainly, this is the case today. "Where have all the leaders gone?" could be the question, and the rather sarcastic answer is "to jail." Leaders today have more ambition for themselves than for the people they lead, and the executive compensation packages seem obscene. It is the corporate ego compared with the "spitting contest" in places like the NFL, where the badge of courage goes to the team that has the highest-paid quarterback. We pay our CEO more than you pay your CEO, so ours is better! The bigger the ego, the less the man or woman, and, thus, the less the corporation.

Government has very little power over business because business has the money that government needs.

Government has very little power over business because business has the money that government needs. Moreover, brainpower and expertise resides in the corporate world. We do have exceptionally bright and talented people in public service, but they are outranked by the depth and breadth of the brainpower in business. The Security and Exchange

Commission (SEC) is just one small example. As one of 11 federal agencies, the SEC is tasked with overseeing and protecting investors.[2] The mortgage debacle could and should have been averted via more oversight by the SEC, who, under Chris Cox, were anything but vigilant. In an environment of fully deregulated markets, beginning with the Clinton administration, financial products were created from a ball of nothingness, sold to investors, and put into portfolios. Loans were made by banks that accepted the money at a ridiculously low borrowing rate and agreed to lend money to everyone who wanted their dream home! The dream became a nightmare because, in the process, banks and mortgage companies agreed to the deal to have lower prime but discharged their fiduciary responsibility by not holding the loan for more than 45 days.[3]

Where Government Failed

The practice became impersonal and, by now, also devoid of accountability or transparency. These loan packages go off to places such as Fannie Mae and Freddie Mac, where they are put together, lumping the good with the bad, and cut up into things called derivatives and sold as "solid" investments to individuals, pension funds, and state and local governments for investment. When the loans are defaulted on, it is hard to even find the source because the loans are buried deep in the package. However, former Security and Exchange Commission (SEC) chair Chris Cox and the SEC staff were undermanned and so without the resources to even begin to manage anything of this scale.

> *The essence of innovation is you don't know what you're going to build, what it's going to be called, or how much it's going to cost.*
>
> Michael Bloomberg

I am sure much could be said about the bias in government agencies as well as the result of how individuals are appointed to the agencies that are tasked with regulating. They are all political appointees who come from places such as Lehman Brothers and Goldman Sachs, and, in fact, not always domain experts. Do a bit of research and sketch how people who are in current leadership roles got there. It often is not connected to their expertise in a particular area. Government is not the answer; it cannot control business or the corporation. For instance, the late Steve Jobs reportedly told President Obama he needed to create more business-friendly policies.[4] I did not sense any malice aimed at the president in that comment, just an insightful statement about the actual power of the corporate arena.

The reason that government cannot be the force to save us was summed up in part by Michael Bloomberg, successful businessman and Mayor of New York City, in his comments at the recent (© May 2011) C40 Summit of Mayors in Brazil. In an interview with freelance writer Sridhar Pappu, Bloomberg explained the mystique of innovation; he said: "The essence of innovation is you don't know what you're going to build, what it's going to be called, or how much it's going to cost."[5]

Obviously, these are the first questions that government must answer. Only business can innovate, and in the place we find ourselves, innovating and reinventing ourselves is the point of initializing. As only the seemingly arrogant Bloomberg can, he unloaded profound pronouncements in the discussion on the challenges faced by cities recovering from natural disasters (such as storms and tornadoes in the Midwest) and zeroed in on Hurricane Katrina. Bloomberg said that the hurricane actually gave New Orleans an opportunity to start over and try something new and fresh in its school system.[6]

This is the kind of view that business, not government, has: seeing the possibilities presented even by a disaster. The kind of thinking exhibited by Bloomberg and Jobs is an example of power thinking, and when we add to this the soul that must be part of the process for a corporation, we could have the winning formula. As individuals, leaders such as Bloomberg and Bill Gates have foundations and philanthropies that represent the best of the merger of the corporation with the mind, body, and soul. These are men who understand the triptych that is necessary to succeed.[7] If corporations run their businesses with the sole aim of gaining more market share or earning more profits, they may well lead the world into economic, environmental, and social ruin.

If corporations run their businesses with the sole aim of gaining more market share or earning more profits, they may well lead the world into economic, environmental, and social ruin.

Kyosei

What we are talking about here are ideas that many leaders have seen before. In a *Harvard Business Review* article, Canon Copiers CEO Ryuzaburo Kaku said: "Because multibillion-dollar corporations control vast resources around the globe, employ millions of people, and create and own incredible wealth, they hold the future of the planet in their hands. However, if they work together, in a spirit of kyosei, they can bring food to the poor, peace to war-torn areas, and renewal to the natural world. It is our obligation as business leaders to join together to build a foundation for world peace and prosperity."[8]

Kaku's words were true 15 years ago (© 1997), but at that time, we were not there. Here, at the beginning of © 2012, we have reached critical mass in terms of reinventing ourselves and the very face of capitalism. The corporate philosophy of Canon is kyosei. A concise definition of this word would be "living and working together for the common good," but ours is broader: "all people, regardless of race, religion, or culture, harmoniously living and working together into the future." Truly global companies must foster good relations, not only with their customers and the communities in which they operate, but also with nations and the environment.[9]

Unfortunately, the imbalances in our world in areas such as trade, income levels, and the environment hinder the achievement of kyosei. Through corporate activities based on kyosei, Canon strives to resolve imbalances in the world. They must also bear the responsibility for the impact of their activities on society. For this reason, Canon's goal is to contribute to global prosperity and the well-being of mankind, which will lead to continuing growth and bring the world closer to achieving kyosei.[10]

Author, filmmaker, and social critic Michael Moore would have us dismantle capitalism and throw out our leadership, but it is not clear exactly what he would put in its place. It is well known that Moore is in the top 2% income level in this country and, smilingly noted, that he made his money in a capitalistic system. According to many accounts, he is, in fact, obsessed with money. He would substitute capitalism for what, communism or socialism?[11]

To the extent that any world leader or anyone who really understands the principles governing economic life and wants human beings to live and grow prosperous, he/she can and must be an advocate of a form of capitalism, at least on paper. The system has flaws, as does any human system, but you cannot abandon the most successful economic system in history in terms of the greatest good for the greatest number of people. This would be like the cliché of throwing the baby out with the bath water. In the pure form of capitalism (with many variations on the theme), there is a self-interest, which, however benevolent, operates along with the profit motive that demands economic freedom. The environment is the government's responsibility; however (and this has been historically validated), government interference in the economy produces inflation, depression, economic stagnation, poverty, international conflicts, and war. It is becoming relatively clear that as we have moved from a service economy, to an information economy, to a knowledge economy and beyond that the next step for prosperity and survival may be through hard work and productivity. As Jeff Immlet says, we may need to actually make something to return to efficient capital allocation, to the time of savings, and technological innovation.[12] What caused many of our economic problems was the government's failure to act and enforce the laws on the books (specific blame falls on oversight agencies such as the SEC), coupled with its blind decision to keep corporations from falling under the weight of their own bad choices.[13]

Operating with only the mind and body is what brought us to this situation.

The government turned a deaf ear to the growing concerns that financial institutions were expanding beyond control. Simply put, if government did what it was designed to do, regulate, and did not do what it was not designed to do, intervene, we would be in an entirely different place today. Again, operating with only the mind and body is what brought us to this situation.

Ayn Rand's novel *Atlas Shrugged*,[14] which had the audacity to suggest that values are objective and not prey to a subjective interpretation, supports the notion that capitalism is a higher-order thinking. The image of Atlas is like that of the United States, with more load added to the already heavy weight of the world we carry on our shoulders. Rand makes the suggestion that if we blackmail the world by taking away the thought leaders and the creators of industry, then the world would be forced to stop and government would be forced to act in a more responsible manner. With wealth and resources, we may be tempted to just shrug like Atlas. However, in reality, we cannot just abandon capitalism, or just clean it up and leave it weak and anemic, or just shake up corporate leadership to suit the purpose of this economic system. We must look realistically at the system and at its strengths and respect the place it has brought us to date. Why would we abandon capitalism when all the other economic systems have been moving more toward a form of the capitalist's model, embracing that wonderful creature we call the entrepreneur, and rescuing and sustaining the middle class, who reside between the 2% of the Michael Moores of the world and the poorest?

The Soul of a Corporation

So, what should the corporate soul look like and how do we find it? Initially, we must seek and demand a new kind of spiritual purpose in leadership. We can look for patterns of leadership in history; there are so many extraordinary individuals to whom we can point. The problem with reviewing the past as the principal pattern to discovering what kind of leadership we need now is that it has minimal value at best; at worst, it keeps us from facing our own world. There has never been a time exactly like this one, or people exactly like us. We must consciously have absorbed the stories of leaders in the past: the good, the bad, and the ugly, and from that we must create new ones. Today, leaders must spring from a different crucible than the one that produced the outstanding corporate heads of the late 1950s and 1960s.

Corporations must reinvent themselves NOW! We must have leaders who can see it coming, chart a new course, and move quickly.

We live in such a reactionary posture, and we move and have our being without a thought. It is easier that way. We are thinking all the time, but it is not a real thought; it is merely about what we need to do next, never asking what this needs to look like or be like in the long term. What is long term, by the way? Current leaders are even more in this paradigm than the workers are in terms of the need to take the long view. The challenges inherent in instant information can change the market on a mere picture (e.g., Steve Jobs looking not so well) on the Internet or the front page of a significant paper. They are so over-whelming that they almost defy setting or following a strategy for more than a day or even less. This has never been the case in the past. We have corporations that are large brick-and-mortar structures that cannot sustain themselves and cannot change course. They are pretty much like the stately Queen Mary going through the ocean at full speed ahead and such that she cannot change course quickly. When what we need are smaller PT boats that can turn on a dime. Who could not have seen the Red Box coming, yet Blockbuster is bankrupt because it suffered from the forest-trees syndrome.[15] Corporations must reinvent them-selves NOW! We must have leaders who can see it coming, chart a new course, and move quickly.

They were the war heroes, majors, and generals who were capable of executing on that command-and-control model, and inspiring the troops to follow. The days of command and control succeeding to lead a contemporary corporate entity are over—have been for some time already. I have been teaching team building since 1985, as the chief means of moving work along, and now it is the collaboration of teams that forms corporate governance and demands a culture of cooperation. It is not possible to micromanage and achieve success. Leaders can and will get work done only through their people, and as the workforce becomes more democratized, teams will assume the leadership role as opposed to an established hierarchy. Leaders must display the entire gamut of emotional intelligence: self-awareness, self-discipline, empathy, motivation, and social skills.[16] Leaders will get work done through their people only if they care about the people, the planet, and the profits. Theodore Roosevelt said: "People do not care how much you know until they know how much you care."[17]

Leaders cannot care without the soul!

The Soul of a Leader

Leaders cannot care without the soul! Moreover, we are like dogs and kids: you will not be able to fool us anymore! The new breed of leaders will be, for example, the antithesis of the world of Pfizer, the largest international pharmaceutical company, and its deposed CEO, Jeff Kindler, whose castigation of employees and misuse of power threatened to destroy the giant corporation. The story of Kindler plays out like a true Garden of Eden being corrupted by the snake. Its moral is the same one I told my fellow students to use on their history essays: the peasants do revolt. No matter how successful and smart Kindler the trialawyer was, people refused to be treated in such a brutal manner. True, the Pfizer Board should have acted sooner, but the bottom line is that they did act and Kindler is gone because he did not possess the spirituality necessary for real leadership! Game over. Time to rethink and rebuild.[18]

Many American and world corporations such as Pfizer are in a state of disgrace and crisis, suffering from a loss of identity, failed leadership, and no sense of ownership by the people who work inside their hallowed halls.[19] To go forward, a real reshaping is necessary, starting with a new breed of leadership. This is central to understanding how powerful a corporate culture is and how it is created. Culture comes from the top down, and when you have leaders who have stayed with the company for a long time and have come up in the culture, that is one animal. If a company has a leader who comes in from outside, you have another kind of animal. Make no mistake: either way, the culture is a top-down process.

In his book *Good to Great*,[20] Jim Collins explains that truly great leaders, when they appear, will have more passion for their company/their people than they have for themselves. What a different animal this will be. It is all a numbers game, and the isolation inherent in leadership and positions of power keeps many from even seeking these positions. In Collins's latest book, *Great by Choice*,[21] he crafts his thesis of leadership around the concept of a leader who is patient and caretaking, and like Odysseus (my metaphor), ties himself/herself to the ship's mast to avoid the lure of the sirens' song. This is no small feat today, when we are just beginning to see that the one who destroys the company, culture, and people by moving too quickly does not win the race. Note, for example, the current crisis in the IPO of Groupon.[22] When we move too quickly, we make mistakes that cost us in credibility. It is the balance that matters: move within your industry, and change and correct course quickly; however, be cautious with growth that should remain steady and consistent.

When we move too quickly, we make mistakes that cost us in credibility.

Great by Choice outlines what constitutes a great company with a study that Collins began 11 years ago in 2002 and notes that a company can know everything except what the future will bring. Collins also talks about the chaos of the 9-year period covered by the study, as the United States awoke to a new world: the bull market crashed, Clinton's surplus turned into the Bush deficit, the attacks of terror on September 11 (the single act that would change the face of the world for decades to follow), war, and technology that is almost beyond comprehension and changes the level of expectation beyond comprehension. It is obvious that great companies can survive through chaos, but what is it that allows some to not only survive, but also thrive? In his study of 20,400 companies, Collins selected seven (something interesting about the magic of this number) as examples of companies that have strategies that allow them to grow in good times and in bad. He dubs them the 10X companies because they increased their industry index by 10 times the average. The companies are: **Amgen**, a pioneer biotech firm (located in Thousand Oaks, California); **Biomet**, the world's leading medical instrument manufacturer (Warsaw, Indiana); **Intel**, a multinational and the world's largest semiconductor chipmaker (Santa Clara, California); **Microsoft**, which designs and manufactures home and office computing systems, and dominates this market (Redmond, Washington); **Progressive Insurance**, which provides personal automobile insurance, other specialty property and casualty insurance, and related services in the United States (Mayfield Village, Ohio); **Southwest Airlines**, the largest US-based airline in terms of domestic passengers, operating 3,400 flights a day with 552 airplanes (Dallas, Texas); and **Stryker**, a world leader in orthopedic technology (Mahwah, New Jersey). What has pulled these companies successfully through some of the toughest times in business and industrial history? One thing that jumps out of Collins's study reminded me of the counseling mantra: you cannot control the things that happen on the outside; you can only control how you react to these things. Since we can know everything but the future, we must prepare ourselves with a philosophy that will take us past those siren songs. These companies did just that, remembering also that these companies have resisted the call to expand too rapidly or speculatively. Their leadership has not been so hungry for profit that it clouded their decisions, which were made for the highest and greatest good for all, not just the call for profit. Profit is not always the answer and it has ruined so many good ideas!

When the culture of a corporation has flaws, be they in disclosure, ethics, quality, transparency, accountability, or customer service, the problem is at the top!

The 20-Mile March

Collins likens the cocoon philosophy that encases the butterfly of these companies to the 20-mile-march metaphor, wherein the individual (in this case, the company) adheres to a strict goal of conservative and consistent growth (hence only 20 miles a day in good times or bad). All the while, the company continues to innovate but vigorously eschews the temptation to grow too quickly for profit or to outdistance competition—that is, it resists the urge to speed up the 20-mile pace. Collins calls it discipline and points to the special breed of leadership, who cares more for the long view of the company than for the immediate growth and profit.[23] I would rather say it is the manifestation of the prototype of the corporations that have found their souls and accessed a spirituality that sets them apart. It is *the* model! The question is how to dial it back in areas such as executive compensation, which is tied to profit; especially when payment for failure continues to abound. When the culture of a corporation has flaws, be they in disclosure, ethics, quality, transparency, accountability, or customer service, the problem is at the top!

I like the metaphor for leadership of the conductor who must turn his/her back on the audience in order to conduct the orchestra.[24] The necessity to focus with such single-mindedness on the purpose of the music that is delivered is powerful. The audience is the recipient of the product, but, in the moment, has no say in its creation. When the conductor communicates in this way, it is precise and with purpose. Leaders, like the conductor, must have the courage to turn their back on the audience, no matter how powerfully it clamors, and focus on their charge, which is to care for their company/their people... If there is a flaw in operations, the leader is responsible. If he/she did not know it, he/she should have.[25]

Boards must find their soul as well and use it!

The Role of the Board of Directors

Board members are equally liable and in the same way. We must reform our thinking about Boards and make the individuals who sit on them more than just advisory. Although advisory boards are important because of the brainpower they bring, there must be more sitting Boards with authority, voice, and accountability in the corporate structure. Board membership has become more self-serving than is healthy for a corporation. Boards must find their soul as well and use it!

Sometimes it is hard to discern what is in leadership or what the core beliefs are in a leader. The media and the manipulations of a public relations team often mask it; corporate leaders are like political leaders in this measure.

It is essential to understand when the corporation indicates that it fulfills its obligations to all stakeholders; it is missing a piece if it is not clear that the largest stakeholder is our whole world, and we hold our breath as we wait to see if the transformation will come in time. It is a huge responsibility. When we say society, it means the whole—the sustainability of the environment and, literally, the life of all the citizens of the world. More than just corporate social responsibility, which we have talked to death with little more than green washing; it is the real manifestation of spirituality in leadership, right here, right now!

How do we really get to know who they are and what their substance contains? We try to read people to know what or who they are. Even if we are not students of behavior, it is behavior or the manifestation of behavior that we use to evaluate character, in which we are most interested. Pictures of powerful people in predicaments or awkward positions often create such a powerful message that nothing they say can change the perception created by the picture. The list is legend of political figures who committed such errors with their pose: Nixon and the five-o'clock shadow in the debate with Kennedy; Michael Dukakis in the military tank with the helmet; John Kerry, butt in the air, on a racing bike; Bush the first, on a golf course taking a swing as the Persian Gulf War was raging; and Bush the second, viewing the disaster of Katrina from an airplane. The picture that sticks in my mind may not be as well recorded, but I noted it at the moment, and knew it meant disaster at many levels. When John McCain was running for the presidential nomination in 2009, he left the campaign trail to fly to Washington and meet with Bush, the cabinet, and economic advisors about what was the beginning of the economic collapse of AIG and all the others that followed.[26] When he came back from Washington, he was photographed getting off the plane with his suit disheveled, his hair a mess, and his expression pained. His whole body spoke of world-weariness, as if he carried the weight of the world on his shoulders; he looked very tired and very old! I knew at that moment that he would not be elected president. Contest over! Now, after that time, it is easy to understand how a man like McCain would have been overwhelmed and disgusted with what was being sanctioned at the time by the government. Yet, he could not speak of it with the detail that he had in that point and he did not have an alternative answer!

It seems to be a matter of character, character that is missing in men and women who ascend to power.

In addition to looking at leaders and the image they project with the nonverbal, we must listen to them as well, or at least try to. However, the feeling that we get most often, is one of general distrust; we really expect to be lied to, and perhaps we are complicit in this as well and bear equal blame with leaders, who if the truth is told that we cannot have 20% profit from our investments—that we must have less services and higher taxes in this country—the leaders would not be elected.

It seems to be a matter of character, character that is missing in men and women who ascend to power. Michael Lewis, in his book *The Blind Side*,[27] set in the world of big-time athletics, says that when people in power positions fail, it is not a lack of skill, ability, or experience, but a defect in character. This is clear in terms of what we see on the field today. Lewis's experience is that of a big-time financial figure on Wall Street who became so disillusioned with the game that he dropped out to write about its corruption, which is to the core. The question is how challenging and deep must the crisis become before people who can lead step up and make the hard calls? Where are the men and women with character? The next question is if these men and women did appear, would we follow them? We have become so jaded because people in high places and positions of power and even honor disappoint us, leave us, and deceive us, so that the faith to follow is hard to come by these days.

The Karma Connection

The rest of this story is that we often just get what we ask for. If we had leaders with strong moral character who spoke the truth, then we would also have to strengthen our moral character. For example, we would not cheat on our taxes, look for loopholes in the law, and lie to our kids or ourselves. The Madoff scandal is so well chronicled and so amazing in the breadth and depth of its lie that it boggles the mind. Yet it speaks of character on both sides—Madoff's and the people who bought in. The greed that compels us to believe we can profit beyond a reasonable level is the greed factor that comes from that flawed character, and the stakes get so high; then the critics ask what is reasonable profit? If you are smart enough to get a 20% return on an inside investment, then why not? It is a reward for your smarts.[28]

Someone I talked with at a party confided in me that they had taken a position with a small company and a one-person office and were being paid under the table. They were so happy because they could still draw unemployment insurance. They added that learning the payroll system would be challenging since some of the people were paid on the table and some below. This monologue was laced with the perfect belief that this was more than acceptable, and a really damn good idea! It is never about how big or little the lie is but, rather, that the lie comes out of our character.

> *It is never about how big or little the lie is but, rather, that the lie comes out of our character.*

As a people, we are like the ancient Greeks in that we have fashioned our Gods and our leaders in our own image. They cannot truly be above reproach, and we long to know their character flaws so we can identify with them. We expect them to fall and are not surprised when they do. Secretly, we are probably relieved since the bar is not set so high now. Take Zeus on Mount Olympus: as the head Greek God, he had many affairs and, at the slightest annoyance, would banish mortals or other lesser Gods to ridiculous lives of pain and suffering. The Greeks could easily worship Zeus, serve at his temple, and bow down to him because he was like them: flawed.[29] Thus, the prayer was not so much "forgive my sins" as "you understand my sins, which makes me okay in your eyes," My God.

What is the full measure of leadership for the 21st century? Men and women who are made of the right stuff must appear now; it is time. Where will we find these queer animals, how will we know them when we see them, and how will we discern them when we hear them speak?

It is mandatory that corporations find and fill the vacuum of leadership that exists today by cultivating the talent required for such a time as this. Strong leadership development programs within a corporation will not forecast success, but a company without one has no chance of success. It has to be an integral corporate strategy and priority in the corporate structure. As more and more multinational companies take the world stage, it is imperative that methods to recruit and retain high potential players be refined and modernized. We must all understand that we are global now, not local or regional, in terms of power and influence. Corporations must be more creative than ever before to find and lure leaders who fit the mold for the 21st century and have true spirituality.

International Insight | Kyosei 2.0—Universal Design

"Canon is proud of its long and unwavering tradition of protecting and preserving our most precious of resources—the world we share. We work to harmonize environmental commitment and economic interests in all our business activities. We believe this balance is essential to sustain prosperity for future generations. This is not a new thinking at Canon. As a global organization, we at Canon understand our responsibility for the impact we make on society and the environment. That is why, from our founding, Canon's corporate philosophy has been Kyosei—which we define as "all people, regardless of race, religion, or culture, harmoniously living and working together into the future."

At all of our office locations, and throughout our manufacturing and sales operations, Canon maintains a deep commitment to social and environmental responsibility. This determination to live and work together for the common good permeates everything we do: from research and development, to product manufacturing, marketing, sales, and distribution.

At Canon, we believe every manufacturer has a responsibility to ensure its operations and practices are environmentally sound. We apply this standard for environmental respect to every stage of our operations. At every step, we make energy and resource conservation and the elimination of hazardous substances our most important goals. That is why Canon is recognized for producing some of the world's most energy-efficient products. Canon built a successful business model based on their dedication to *Kyosei*. According to their website, "Kyosei guides our tradition of commitment to protect and preserve our most precious of resources—the world we share, the communities we serve, and the lives we touch. We do this through environmental conservation, recycling, and sustainability initiatives.

We also practice *Kyosei* through **social** and **educational** programs on behalf of young people and those in need. This is our corporate philosophy, and it unites all Canon companies and employees together in contributing to the prosperity of humanity and the protection of the world we share." One of the by-products of Kyosei was Canon's "universal design," a concept developed to predict and understand all the real-world problems users may encounter when interacting with products and then to devise solutions to as many of these problems as possible. Canon says that this approach leads to products that anyone, at any time and in any situation, can access and use comfortably.

According to the company website, regardless of how good a product performs, if its operation causes stress, it fails to fulfill its purpose. We think of "universal design" as something that appears in the posture of the user when interacting with the product. Therefore, the slogan of our universal design initiatives is "designing user posture." Not only do we analyze how and where customers interact with a product, we also watch customers' typical behavior before and after using a product. This leads to discoveries about various issues that we would not find just by looking at the product. Markings are difficult to see in dark rooms or in direct sunlight. People also find it difficult to see after moving suddenly from a dark area to a bright area or vice versa. Products must be designed to be easy to see in many different environments. The Principles of Universal Design are as follows: After obtaining a thorough understanding of the customer's usage circumstances, Canon gives every consideration to the inherent usability of the design in keeping with the product's purpose and usage environment. They continually pursue innovative idea creation that goes beyond simple problem solving in order to create products and services that customers really want to use. They also apply Canon's leading technologies to products to improve customer convenience and to create richer, more comfortable lives.

Canon defines universal design as being able to flexibly address all kinds of issues by thinking from the customer's standpoint instead of following a set of fixed development rules. This guide organizes various issues that customers may encounter when using products and was created to encourage designers to put themselves in the customer's shoes. Interestingly, and similarly to Kyosei, which was liberally shared with the international business community, although the guide was intended to be used as internal guidelines, Canon released this guide to the public, so that this sustainable and logical approach to design can lead to similar developments in other industries. There are 29 specific guidelines ranging from issues related to physical abilities and movements, issues related to vision and hearing, issues related to awareness and thought, and issues related to emotions.

For example, with respect to physical issues, the guide points out that women generally have about 60% of the physical strength of men. Seniors and children often have even less physical strength. Products must be designed so that they can be operated easily with little physical exertion. With respect to visual considerations, the guide notes that markings are difficult to see in dark rooms or in direct sunlight. People also find it difficult to see after moving suddenly from a dark area to a bright area or vice versa. Products must be designed to be easy to see in many different environments.

We live in a fast-moving society. The guidelines address this by acknowledging that users cannot always focus on operating the product, as they attend to telephone calls and other sudden interruptions. Products must be designed to provide users with the ability to quickly recall and resume an operation where they left off for some reason. From an emotional standpoint, people tend to rush their tasks if others are waiting to use a machine. People also make mistakes with simple operations when being watched. Canon's take away from this observation is that "an important function is the ability to use a product without it weighing on your mind."

It is clear from Canon's universal design development guidelines, which drill so deep into addressing differences in color perception, that Kyosei is far more than a mission statement or even a corporate culture. It is the underlying principle in every business decision that is made. By sharing these guidelines freely on their website, it is clear that Canon feels that it would be in the best interest of the company, the business community, and society as a whole if similar guidelines were incorporated into other product lines.

Discussion Questions

- How can corporations sustain the "20-mile pace" concept and stay competitive? Is it a realistic goal?
- What is the role of the schools of business in training ethical leaders who care more for their people than their profit?
- Is the spirit of Kyosei viable for the corporate arena?

Exercise | Mission, Vision, and Reality

It is essential that a corporation is able to align productivity and output with the reality that a shift to spiritual principals will have on overall operational impact. To illustrate its impact on the bottom line, select two corporations. Select one with a past or current challenge (i.e., Monsanto, Enron, or Penn State) and the other that has been praised for its ethical operations (i.e., Accenture, American Express, Johnson Controls). On the basis of the event giving rise to the media attention, review the Mission Statement, Corporate Leadership, and similar information and evaluate whether what went wrong or right was based on the overall corporate culture. For example, answer the following questions:

- Were the expected standards of conduct articulate, clear, and specific?
- Were they clearly communicated to all stakeholders and, if not, what were the communications disconnects?
- Was there an ethics or policy breach?
- Was the media-worthy event directly related to a recent change in corporate policy?

- Was the stated principle realistic?
- Was the action industry specific or based on a management tactic that crosses all lines of business?
- What role did leadership have?
- Was this an aberration, an accident, unavoidable, or the intentional result of actionable objectives?
- Lastly, identify suggestions to either prevent future occurrences to the extent a breech has occurred and, with respect to the positive results, discuss the sustainability of the program as well as potential problems, and prepare a revised mission statement or other corporate communication reflecting your suggestions and observations.

Case Study | A Case Study for Leadership | Aung San Suu Kyi | Democracy for Myanmar: A Beginning

Résumé for Leadership

- Rafto éPrize and Sakharov Prize for Freedom of Thought 1990
- Nobel Peace Prize 1991
- Jawaharlal Nehru Award for International Understanding (from India) 1992
- International Simon Bolivar Prize (from Venezuela) 1992
- Honorary Citizen of Canada (one of four) 2007
- Wallenberg Medal 2011
- Congressional Gold Medal and Presidential Medal of Freedom 2012
- Elected to the Pyithu Hluttaw, Burmese Parliament, April 1, 2012

Certainly, that is the case today. "Where have all the leaders gone?" could be the question, and the rather sarcastic answer is "to jail."

She had the education, the genes, a loving marriage, the will of the people, and, following the elections of 1990, the party she helped formed, the National League for Democracy, came to power, and she was appointed general secretary of the party. Suu Kyi, even before the election, was under house arrest. From 1989 to 2011, she was under house arrest for 15 of the 20 plus years. Her father was a political force for democracy and is credited with forming the Burmese army, and for gaining freedom from Britain. He was killed by political enemies in 1947, when Suu Kyi was two. Her mother was an ambassador to India and Nepal and following her mother's stations of duty exposed her to a wide range of people and thinking.[30]

> *There has never been a time exactly like this one, or a people exactly like us. We must consciously have absorbed the stories of leaders in the past: the good, the bad and the ugly, and from that we must create new ones.*

As a follower of Mahatma Gandhi's vision for nonviolence and as a Buddhist, Suu Kyi found the strength and courage to lead in some significant ways, not from behind, which it might seem on the surface, but from within. As a leader, very connected to her people, she elected to remain in Burma, under house arrest, and forego her personal life and the option to be with her husband, rather than to abandon her call to be a tangible and spiritual leader for her people.[31]

> *In the pure form of capitalism (with many variations on the theme), there is a self-interest which however benevolent and which operates along with the profit motive which demands economic freedom.*

As Suu Kyi continues to lead her people toward democracy, she is focused not on herself, but on a long-term vision. Leadership so often in the current environment takes the short view of long-term needs. There is no quick, short, or easy path to victory. To have your voice heard, to receive justice as you seek social justice for the people you lead, the commitment must be deep and authentic. You cannot be "shoulder surfing" for yourself or your company. Shoulder surfing is what one observers at cocktail parties when someone is talking to you, but at the same time looking over your shoulder to determine who is the next more important person to whom they wish to talk. Leaders who "shoulder surf" for themselves and for their companies do not have the anchor needed to weather the storm. They could in no way wait out the storm or remain in house arrest with faith in the future and taking the long view.

Many who called themselves leaders today are mere strategists, and unlike Suu Kyi, can easily move from one industry to another plying their wares. There is superficiality about their aura, and you sense it is all about the money and the power for them. This fact is supported daily in the news when we see such a high level of corruption and failed leadership world over. The mighty have fallen and we are disgraced everywhere. Leadership can never be about the money or the power when it is, it becomes not leadership at all but a veil for ego, which is hollow and vacuous and can never find the spirit. Suu Kyi's life to date is a new look at seemingly the lost values of leadership: Courage, Conviction, Character, Caring, Commitment, Clarity, and Competence.

To the extent that any world leader or anyone who really understands the principles governing economic life and wants human beings to live and grow prosperous, he/she can and must be an advocate of a form of capitalism, at least on paper.

Tom Friedman in his NYT opinion piece for September 22, 2012 remarks about the democracy leader of Myanmar, Burma, Aung San Suu Kyi, who this week was awarded the US Congressional Medal of Honor for her courage. Former presidential candidate, former prisoner of war, and highly decorated US Veteran, John McCain presented the award on September 19, 2012 and said Aung had taught him about courage. "Aung, highly educated and with a long family heritage of political commitment to Burma in her fight for democracy for her people was in house arrest for over 20 years and remained in fear of her life for most of that time. She did this for what she believed was the right thing to do for her people. In April 2012, Aung and her party the National League for Democracy came into power."[32] At the ceremony, McCain quoted her mantra: "it is not power that corrupts but fear. Fear of losing power corrupts those who wield it, and fear of the scourge of power corrupts those who are subject to it."[33] Friedman well notes that this phrase sums up where we are today in terms of our national leadership. Friedman's article *Hard Lines, Red Lines and Green Lines* highlights the fact that it is this fear of losing power that has our leaders so frail in acting with conviction and keeps them from doing the right thing. Few people in leadership are willing to tell the hard truth for the fear of losing power.

Friedman ends the article with a powerful observation:

"My gut tells me that this deficit of global leadership can't last. For one thing, the world is getting so interdependent that weak leadership in one country now deeply impacts so many others. Think euro crisis, Israel-Iran or Chinese pollution. And, for another, I don't believe the two most powerful disciplining forces on the planet—the market and Mother Nature—will sit idle for another decade and let us keep building these huge financial deficits and carbon surpluses without one day delivering some punishing blows that will require herculean leadership to deal with. So let's honor The Lady from Myanmar, not just with a medal, but in a way that really matters—with emulation."[34]

Supplemental Reading

The following are scholarly and peer-reviewed journal articles, conference proceedings, and dissertations on the concepts discussed in this chapter.

- C. William Thomas, April 2002, The Rise and Fall of Enron—When a company looks too good to be true, it usually is.
- Jim Collins: Good to Great in 10 Steps, Kimberly Weisul, May 7, 2012, Inc.com
- Ryuzaburo Kaku, The Path of Kyosei, *Harvard Business Review*, July 1997.[35]

CHAPTER 5

For Profit Must Stay | Capitalism Going Forward

Capitalism

While there is no such thing as pure capitalism, we can analyze the evolution that forms our knowledge of and maneuvering within the system. However, the form of capitalism practiced in the United States, and emulated by many governments, is by far the most stable economic model, but without the soul, it has been so abused that it can scarcely function. We are so wrapped in short-term thinking, with over-the-top speculation spurred on by a constant contact frenzy, that what is flowing through our veins is not blood but a magnetized solution that draws us to invest in or buy things we know nothing about just because it might make us a profit. Look at the corporate buyouts that brought some of the big houses down. In the greedy quest for growth and expansion and the merger magic, they did not really know what they were buying; it turned out that they were buying bad assets and merging with entities they did not understand. We must reverse this tide; in fact, it may reverse on its own as part of the natural process of the cycle.

> *We are so wrapped in short-term thinking, with over-the-top specu-*
> *lation spurred on by a constant contact frenzy, that what is flowing*
> *through our veins is not blood but a magnetized solution that draws*
> *us to invest in or buy things we know nothing about just because it*
> *might make us a profit.*

In his new book *Exile on Wall Street*,[1] Mike Mayo, a 20-year veteran financial analyst with Credit Suisse, Prudential, Deutsche Bank, and now Credit Agricole Securities, tells us what we really do not want to know and what the banking industry really did not want to hear: that the majority of financial advisors are not to be trusted. Mayo does not say this directly, but it is a meaning that comes through clearly.

I have written about financial advice and advisors and have indicated that I equate financial advisors to nail techs. I got much pushback and open criticism for that one! Financial advisors are people who only have to pass a test every so often to keep their license to practice, and they can open up shop anywhere. These are rather harsh words, I understand, but here is the reality for me: talk to me about your research, what you know about the industry, and the stats on the company that is paying you; make suggestions for me to buy; and tell me what you think about my financial picture and what products are best suited for me, and you have told me nothing! Talk to me about who holds your mortgage, which is tied to what, where your money is invested, and how diverse your portfolio is; prove it, and I will listen.

Economics Versus the Economy

I remind all of my esteemed colleagues who are economists that economics is a theory. Economics is a theory based on a model, and even with all the historical perspective contained in the best research, you would be hard pressed to explain where we are now with a mere economic model. Models do not factor in my feelings or those of the larger collective body. You can tell me how we have acted, responded, and produced before, but the past, in terms of where we are today, has little relevance. There is no real model for this one!

Mayo's book details his research on the banking industry and his life as an analyst, talking about publically traded financial firms that control more of our economy than the average person understands. Mayo began to see the trend in banks as early as 1999, because there was little or no regulation after the interstate banking laws were passed in 1994. The major risk lay in more and weaker loans (because mergers were no longer the way to grow rapidly); the overblown executive compensation, wherein salaries are tied to the profit, thus encouraging the taking of greater risk (in all industries); and the totally ludicrous and out-of-proportion advice on the buy/sell information that was distributed in the banking sector and others. The more interesting statistics in the 1,000-page research report that he prepared for Congress were those in the late 1990s: Merrill Lynch had buy ratings on 940 stocks and sell ratings on seven; Salomon Smith Barney had 856 buy ratings with four sells; and Morgan Stanley Dean Witter had 670 buy ratings and zero sells. This would be a red flag to even a weekend player, as not all companies can be that solid.

Economics is a theory based on a model, and even with all the historical perspective contained in the best research, you would be hard-pressed to explain where we are now with a mere economic model.

The picture Mayo paints is that people somehow now intuit that there is no truth in the advice. I mean as a financial advisor, you work for someone, so there is vested interest; and the information you give me is always tied to your paycheck. How can you have my best interest in your heart? It will always come second to yours. As a financial advisor, Mayo reported his concerns within his industry, where he was ridiculed and threatened. If he issued sell on bank stocks, the banks would no longer be friends to his company and provide all the other sources of profit to the firm because of the relationship. He also testified before Congress, to which he admitted that so much of what happens in the market is the result of advice from financial advisors who are not always transparent with investors because of all the backhouse deals that are part of the industry's stock and trade. Mayo asserts in his book that financial analysts are the force that can bring the conscious or the accountability back to Wall Street; I am not convinced.

Mayo is a free market guy and contends that the reason regulation does not work (other than the one I suggest—that the brightest people are not in the regulatory positions and the government is corrupt and complex) is because the regulators are always reactionary, dissecting things that have already tanked, in which the damage is already done. Just look at the current status and complexity surrounding Jon Corzine and MF Global, which was a major global financial derivatives broker, or commodities brokerage firm, as a perfect example. The case is closed, they are out of business, and now that the damage is done, federal regulators are investigating what happened. Everyone has been printing money for a long time now, and we are at the end of that saga. Both the Commodity Futures Trading Commission (CFTC) and the Securities and Exchange Commission (SEC) were asleep on this one. Still no one has gone to jail![2]

Mayo argues that what we have now is the worst of capitalism, and I see his point. We have so many rules, yet so many rules are not enforced, and loopholes open up the minute a rule is in the way of achieving profit. Since they are operating with only the mind–body contingency, the proverbial handwriting is on the wall.

Everyone has been printing money for a long time now, and we are at the end of that saga.

Mayo would not throw out the rules completely in his quest to have free markets control everything. I found his description of what he would not propose entertaining. When he wrote this, I think he just tore a page out of the current banking playbook. I very much agree with him when he says: "We need a cultural, perhaps generational, change that compels companies to better apply accounting rules based on economic substance versus surface presentation" (Mayo, Why Wall Street Can't Handle the Truth, 2011).[3] In other words, we must not be so overwhelmed with the size of the profit, as to be unaware of how the companies got there. Too often, government is too eager to collect the corporate tax and look the other way. Hence, also, the way political campaigns are funded.

Spiritually Sound Economics

Spiritually sound economics, combining the brilliance of our mind, the wisdom of our body (which contains the DNA of the collective conscience), with the spirit from the soul, will only happen when the change is transformative at the spiritual level. It is clear to me that what unfolds in the next year or less (© January 2013) will reveal what can no longer be covered, and that is the extent of the exposure in the

United States to European Sovereign debt and the fragility of European banks and financial institutions to absorb the liquidity needs of the failed economies of entire countries. The fact that so many companies that have bloated the foreign debt are now insolvent is about to unravel the manner by which we have always done business.

The cultural change that Mayo sees is the reduction of the power of banks (and other public companies) and a forced transparency, so that people like him—the 5,000 sell-side Wall Street analysts—can scrutinize the banks and provide investment advice for their clients. This is meant to preserve his profession because without such access, financial advisors (who have the most superficial advice to offer in the first place) have nothing. He is basically just blowing the whistle on the industry and complaining that the access that was denied him and his colleagues made the difference here. The problem is that when he did start reporting on the problems he saw in banking, Congress did not want to hear it. For one thing, many are not smart enough to understand or have no time to do their homework; for another, many are personally and heavily invested in the banking industry and would not want to start losing money. Financial investment firms should not be involved in banking.

Financial Investment firms should not be involved in banking.

Banking is also a powerful lobby! Of course, the solution that no one wants to hear is to make banks function like banks—in the current model of credit unions. Separate the banks from their large financial investment arms and have the banks concentrate on the banking needs of their customers and make a profit from pure banking operations. In other words, break up the banks. The loans that banks extend should be carefully selected, based on their customers' capacity to pay. I understand that, recently, some financial houses were made into banks by federal charter to save them from insolvency, but that is over now. We have allowed two separate functions to merge to our detriment. Banks simply use their proprietary platform with masses of customer connections and strong branding for a built-in customer base. Banking and investing must be separate businesses, but no one wants to pull this trigger. We must break up the big banks as we did the telecommunications industry in the 1980s.[4]

I realize that it is not that simple, as the crisis is real and threatens to destroy financial markets around the world. It is also more complex than just the banking woes we have, although these woes are typical of the problems in other industry sectors of the economy. A new breed of corporations is necessary, one that builds on the for-profit model but in a transparent and accountable manner.

We cannot, as some might suggest, create a whole new world and eliminate capitalism (the mantra of "Occupy Wall Street"). One example presented by those who would change the capitalistic structure and create a whole new world concept is the for-benefits movement, which proposes a corporate structure that completely changes the DNA of capitalism, and the removal of the for-profit model. The defining characteristic of all Fourth Sector organizations, as they are called in the for-benefits movement, is that they attempt to integrate social and environmental aims with business approaches.[5] Not a bad concept. Some Fourth Sector organizations go further by embodying features such as inclusive governance, transparent reporting, fair compensation, environmental responsibility, community service, and contribution of profits to the common good. Good so far.

One of the most downloaded *New York Times* business article to date is *"Make Money, Save the World."*[6] This is yet another sign of one of the hottest trends in business today: corporations doing well while doing good. It is a concept that is "not only here to stay; it's now a full-fledged business model," says the article. As an example, the article cites Altrushare Securities, of which the majority owners are two charities. Therefore, the question is: "Is it a for-profit business or a nonprofit fund-raising machine?" The answer is both. To quote the expression coined by the article, "it's a for-benefit corporation."

There should really be no distinction between a not-for-profit and a for-profit company.

The term may be brand new, but the concept has been around for a while. Since its creation over half a century ago, the idea of a for-benefits corporation has been dedicated to the notion that a corporation can do good in emerging markets through investments in private enterprise by helping companies of all sizes access opportunities in domestic and emerging markets. The focus is more clearly seen in emerging markets. The article says it is just one of the earliest examples of the Wish it were so. I do see the value in the dialogue, but to draw an analogy, if you are building freshwater wells in Africa, and you are not making money or gaining public capital at some place along the line, the freshwater wells will remain untapped. The money can be the hard dollars that you make by assembling all the apparatus for the "good" venture or the soft money via the public relations and image building that you accomplish, and the relationships you forge for future for-profit ventures, but the profit, hard or soft, must be there.

For Profit Philanthropy

There should really be no distinction between a not-for-profit and a for-profit company. Both corporate types should be held to the same standards and scrutiny. If the not-for-profit firm were a corporation, operating with the same model as its for-profit counterpart, there would be more accountability, more visibility, and probably more money for the not-for-profit firm. Not-for-profit and for-profit firms differ only in how they spend their money. Often, not-for-profit firms attempt to or are unable to follow a solid business model with accountability and transparency, and want to hide behind the **"worthiness"** of their cause as a reason for their existence. This is no more worthy than the corporations that focus on profit only.

The for-benefits model is not going to happen, not in this go-round! If it did, it would defy the human condition. What I am proposing is a regrowing or rediscovery of something that the individual and the collective possess in sufficient quantities to make a real difference going forward: the soul! To bring forth spirituality does not mean giving up the for-profit model of capitalism; it means embracing the power found in acknowledging that the corporation is not a machine but an organic entity that must be viewed as human in every way. It is much more than having a strong values statement; it means living in a shared set of beliefs about the human condition that transforms the corporation into a caring entity that makes money because of its focus on value using a 360 approach.

> *To bring forth spirituality does not mean giving up the for-profit model of capitalism; it means embracing the power found in acknowledging that the corporation is not a machine but an organic entity that must be viewed as human in every way.*

Corporations create themselves for the market and put on the face that the market demands; there are steps that must be taken to change this approach. First, we make a paradigm shift and buy into the fact that we are lost. That is hard because we are still so insulated and have such a good standard of living in developed economies around the world. Social media have greatly empowered us with instant access to information. We have never lived in a more exciting time for business or individuals, wherein there is so much complete and instant access to what we want to know, when we want to know it. However, information cannot save us; if it could, we would have been saved already. Instead, the instant access to information has created a sense of anxiety around a level of expectation that we cannot reach. The mind has reached capacity.

Dr. Cliff of the University of Bristol in a white paper prepared for Her Majesty's Treasury (HMT) explores and attempts to make clear to HMT the ways (using his Foresight Model) to get to the challenges of stability and ways to control future global financial markets. The white paper sets up the converging of three technologies that will change, and he states, disrupt, our lives, as we know them now. He cites the World Wide Web, the expansion of slick and fast computing as with the ICloud, and the spread and advancement of Artificial Intelligence. Cliff adds to this the practices that are in place for mind enhancing psychopharmacology drugs, which will so expand the brain's cognitive capacity that the future that can be created move beyond natural selection. His thesis is that an understanding of these elements will provide a controlled way to determine how citizens interact with each other, how business is conducted, and how companies and people will communicate with institutions of government. Cliff says: "...this project is proposed because there are multiple simultaneous developments in science and technology, and in the maturation of business processes and regulatory environments and societal norms and expectations, that all look set to converge in ways that justify examination by Foresight's methods."[7]

For there to be economic stability in global markets, the individuals in the global markets must trust leaders, and leaders must have integrity and act with conviction, convincingly.

What I think he misses in his research, which is fascinating speculation, laced with strong historical data, is the real human factor, which no history or study can predict as a way to control global financial markets. For there to be economic stability in global markets, the individuals in the global markets must trust leaders, and leaders must have integrity and act with conviction, convincingly.

As a caveat to what may begin to sound like an "end-time" and nonintellectual discussion of the state of our world, let me be quick to underscore that all of life and other-life is a cycle, and it is vital to know where you are in the cycle. There have been sophisticated civilizations before ours, and there will be such after ours is destroyed. Cultural anthropologists tell us some of the things that have destroyed past civilizations, and history tells us what has destroyed empires before ours. We would not go back to the age of mysticism because, for one thing, we would just not go back, and the times in this far distance and those immediately remembered are filled with superstition and ignorance. I do not believe in end-time reverie, just the cycle; there is always the circle, and we are moving in it. Sometimes we make real progress as a civilization and sometimes we do not. Jim Collins, who writes about the patterns of behavior for successful leaders and companies, compares the status of the United States in the first part of the 21st century to the height of the empires of Egypt, the golden age of Greece, the Roman Empire, and England at its glory in the reign of Victoria. Sometimes we come to the real end of the cycle, and another world is born.[8]

International Insight | Bill Clinton's Global Initiative

While there are many domestic and international micro-lending programs, in general they raise more awareness than capital. On closer look at several of the programs, many of the mirco-financing websites are not quite as person-to-person as their marketing materials may appear.

On the other hand, **Bill Clinton's Global Initiative** is an international commitment to action at a local or multinational level. Founded in 2005, to date, members have made over 2,300 commitments impacting over 400 million people in more than 180 countries. Every commitment must meet three basic criteria: (quoting directly)

1. **New**: Many commitments involve new approaches, while others draw on promising solutions that can be scaled up or replicated. Members can also join existing commitments by providing in-kind support or technical expertise that will help expand current efforts. CGI asks only that a commitment is made in addition to their current work.

2. **Specific**: Commitments should articulate a desired outcome and approach to addressing a specific problem, have clear and feasible objectives within a defined period of time, and incorporate an effective approach to implementation.

3. **Measurable**: Each CGI commitment should have specific quantitative and/or qualitative goals that can be used to evaluate their

progress over time. CGI asks members to report on their progress, providing a database of information we can use to help other organizations engaged in similar work. All commitments are available in a database on the organization's website. Interested parties may support a commitment in cash or in-kind.

Clinton's Global Initiative commitments are dedicated to alleviating poverty by helping people start and grow entrepreneurial businesses. Because of the Clinton name, the CGI is able to partner corporate leaders with the Third World start-up companies in order to provide guidance, training, or funding for entrepreneurs in the developing world. OneRoof is just one of many stories. In this case, the partnership was a microfranchise. In 2005, OneRoof committed to launch a chain of franchise cyber cafes in the rural developing world. Each business provides a variety of Internet services, from e-mail to job skills training. OneRoof has also developed a web-based management information system to provide franchisees with tools that help them manage their finances and other aspects of the business. Though the system was built to optimize operations in OneRoof Centers, soon OneRoof began to hear from nonprofit telecenter networks, private cyber cafés, and from government officials showing strong interest in the management information system. By the end of 2008, it shifted its focus to meet a demand for this tool among the 1,000,000+ telecenters and cyber cafés that provide primary access to the Internet for 100,000,000+ people, largely in the developing world.

In 2009, OneRoof launched the first web-based MIS for public access computing that facilitates profitable, effective, and sustainable management of telecenters and cyber cafés. Built to optimize operations in OneRoof Centers, they had requests from nonprofit telecenter networks, private cyber cafés, and government officials with strong interest in OneRoof's MIS. As a result, OneRoof shifted their focus to meet a demand for this tool among the 1,000,000+ telecenters and cyber cafés that provide primary access to Internet for 100,000,000+ people, largely in the developing world.

With a 5-year goal of launching at least 2,000 businesses, World Corps commits to do the following over the next 12 months: launch at least 100 businesses in India and Mexico; identify other regions in India and Mexico and additional countries for expansion; and establish strategic partnership for provision of loan capital to franchises.

The organization will be structured as a private, "not-for-loss" international franchise with headquarters in San Francisco. The initiative grows out of the work of World Corps, a Seattle-based NGO that has launched rural Internet telecenters in India, Kenya, Mexico, and the Philippines. World Corps has done this work in partnership with institutions that include the Ford Foundation, Hewlett-Packard, UNDP, the state government of Andhra Pradesh, India, and numerous civil society organizations. World Corps has been recognized by Microsoft for our "superior approach to training," and World Corps Mexico was selected by the Mexican federal government as the only provider of advanced training for operators of the "e-Mexico" program, a network of 7,000 government-funded telecenters.

The new organization will aim to build an international network of franchised "social businesses" that use the market to deliver essential goods and services to the world's rural poor. These businesses will begin as Internet telecenters providing access to information and communications services and over time will expand access to other goods and services, including some or all of the following: solar electricity, appropriate technologies, clean water, microfinance, essential medicines and health care, sanitation, and access to markets. The following is an overview of some milestones within the organization.

April 2009—Since launching its first franchised businesses in 2008, OneRoof worked to build a web-based MIS as part of its proprietary business infrastructure. The MIS was designed to optimize processes and provide value-added data to franchisee entrepreneurs operating OneRoof Centers.

This MIS provides employee productivity tools, hourly computer utilization rates (for optimizing hours open and knowing when it is profitable to add computers), operating expenses for yielding monthly financial statements and profit and loss reports, customer demographics, blind benchmark center comparisons, and instant, retroactive retrieval of user data to comply with new antiterrorism laws in certain countries.

OneRoof designed the MIS to make understanding the essential business data for cyber café operations easy via intuitive graphical displays; localization in most languages; multistore enterprise reporting; anywhere/anytime browser access; and SMS data push.

Interest in OneRoof's MIS, now called **OneRoof Reports**, from other cyber café and telecenter businesses, nonprofits, and government programs has far surpassed anything anticipated, and the demand for this software as a service far exceeds the original, limited purpose for which it was designed. Early customers for MIS product, include telecenter networks with which OneRoof has collaborated since 2005 and other new partners.

In March 2009, **OneRoof Reports** were installed in telecenter networks in Chile, and more installations are planned in Brazil (May 2009), Mexico, and Colombia (early-mid-summer), and Spain (late summer).

OneRoof acquired the Canadian subsidiary **CyberCafePro**, Inc. from Global Gaming Factory, a Swedish company, in April 2009. This acquisition gives OneRoof complete proprietary source code control—from POS data collection to browser display.

OneRoof Center operations continue to grow in India managed by its Indian subsidiary OneRoof Services, and expanded their product and service offerings in 2009 under the new OneRoof brand, **Connect Here.**

August 2008—Launched and opened the first nine OneRoof stores in May and June. Trained 18 store operators (two per store) in April and May. Refined the business model to accommodate infrastructure and technology needs. Identified likely partners whose goods/services will be brokered in OneRoof stores. Received strong initial responses from businessmen in India interested in future franchising opportunities with OneRoof.

July 2008—OneRoof, Inc. launched its franchising in India in December 2007. Since that time several rounds of training have been conducted in Chennai and 15 franchises have been launched in the states of Tamil Nadu and Andhra Pradesh, India. OneRoof franchises are owned and operated by local entrepreneurs who receive training, technical support, and service partnerships from OneRoof.

OneRoof opened four new centers in Veracruz, Mexico during the summer of 2007 for a total of 12 communities in Mexico. Ten out of twelve OneRoof stores in Mexico were sold to their operators at favorable terms and continue to serve those communities in Yucatan and Veracruz as independent entities.

June 2007—Raised capital to fund Phase II (2007–2008), the next round of rapid regional expansion of OneRoof stores through franchising to local entrepreneurs; secured, to date, over 75% of $5 million in private investment needed to fund Phase II operations in 2007–2008. Shared business plans and profit/loss results and projections are a part of this with a range of interested private and institutional investors in the United States and abroad. Drafted the franchise agreement and documentation that will be the legal framework under which franchisees will be recruited and new, franchised stores will operate in the next Phase of operations. Continued to refine Phase I operations, training, and product offerings in 18 company-owned OneRoof stores/internet centers in rural Mexico and India. Selected sites for next round of OneRoof centers to be opened in Veracruz, Mexico. New operator candidates were selected and are currently in training. Of 18 OneRoof stores opened since Spring 2006, 16 continue successful operations and 4 more are set to open this quarter.

Plans to open four new communities in Veracruz, Mexico in Summer 2007. Plans to finalize franchise agreement and start recruitment, selection, and training processes for first OneRoof franchisees.

October–December 2006—The OneRoof store in rural Acanceh, Mexico—one of the first 18 company-owned stores opened in 2006 and broke even in October in its fifth month of operation and had strong showings in November and December as well. This indicates that the projections OneRoof made for their future Mexico franchises may be easily reached and even surpassed.

All 10 OneRoof stores in rural Tamil Nadu, India, added educational services to their offerings and most had great success with "livelihood" classes—teaching students just out of high school how to prepare themselves for the world of work. Over 200 young people paid roughly USD $3 for a 3-hour course and men signed up for further classes on English and computers.

Staff of OneRoof San Francisco reworked their business plan to plan growth of franchises and to do profit/loss projections through 2014.

OneRoof began meetings with individuals and institutional representatives as they seek to raise $5 million in capital for 2007–2008.

March 2006—The "Concorida" Community Information Center in Becal, Mexico, has been established as the first OneRoof franchise. Four young adult men who are the owners of the "Concordia" Community Information Center will, over the next 4 months, convert their cybercafe into a full-service OneRoof store. The cybercafe in Becal (town of 6,000 people in Campeche state) was 1 of the 30 set up around the world by graduates of World Corps—the NGO that has now become OneRoof. The Becal owners will make their store an early model/demonstration center for OneRoof, allowing us to test a range of new products, services, and educational materials in several areas: financial services, education, health, clean water, clean energy, employment creation, and more. Two of the four owners will also work at the offices of OneRoof Mexico lending technical support and assisting with our training program for new operators and franchisees.

February 2006—The first 10 rural communities were selected in India and Mexico as sites for the first company-owned OneRoof stores (9) and franchises (1). Staff of our subsidiaries in India and Mexico spent much time in various towns (population 3,000–20,000) to determine the best sites for our first company-owned OneRoof stores, now set to open in late April (Mexico) and early May (India). Two people from each community will receive 3 weeks of training so they can serve as operators of the stores.

December 2005—We have successfully transitioned from working as a Seattle-based NGO, World Corps, and have incorporated a new C Corporation, OneRoof, based in San Francisco to do our work as a for-profit social enterprise. We have also incorporated affiliates in India and Mexico and will launch the first 10 OneRoof stores in those countries in the first quarter of 2006.

Milestones Reached: Five OneRoof centers in Tamil Nadu continue to operate as company-owned stores. Plans for rapid expansion of the franchise are underway. OneRoof centers are currently operating or slated to open under franchise in six districts of Tamil Nadu.

OneRoof codified its internal policies and social mission to earn third-party designation as a B-Corporation, a growing international network of purpose-driven businesses dedicated to setting a new standard for social and environmental performance, and creating benefit for all stakeholders and not shareholders alone.

OneRoof, Inc. finalized partnerships with new IT-based service providers Alison and Smart Ticketing Agency (STA) to add top-quality computer literacy courses and cash-based bus, rail, and airplane ticketing to the services offered at our centers in southern India.

SEEKING: financial resources.

OFFERING: best practices information, media, and marketing assistance.[9]

Discussion Questions

- What changes would need to occur in the business model for a for-benefits movement to evolve into a viable business model?
- How can we stop the cheating rather than just using government monitoring and economic sanctions that have no impact on the life of the corporation?
- What should be the 21st-century model for lending and banking?

Exercise I Not-for-Profit Versus For Profit

- Select a for-profit and a not-for-profit publically held corporation of similar size as far as number of employees and revenue generated.
- Compare salaries, bonuses, and revenue.
- Create a business plan and revenue projections that could be recognized by the not-for-profit entity if they operated on a for-profit basis.
- Based on research, list some of the reforms that need to happen to make not-for-profits more accountable and transparent.
- Research the number of not-for-profit and investigate the impact and ethics of consolidating not-for-profits and research if increase services would occur.
- Investigate the need to consolidate some not-for-profits and increase services.

A Case for For-Profit Philanthropy |
DMT Mobile Toilets

Isaac Durojaiye, a.k.a Otunba Gadaffi, was born in Lagos, Nigeria (deceased March 2012). In 1991, while in charge of security for Kola Abiola's wedding, he discovered that there were only two toilets available for the expected 10,000 guests. When he brought this to the attention of the planning committee, they instructed him to find a mobile toilet company, of which, there was none in existence at that time. He then constructed toilets for the event, which gave rise to DMT, *a for-profit enterprise,* that has gone far beyond serving the need for portable toilets.[10] In Nigeria, water and sewerage problems are the norm. To make matters worse, most Nigerians cook, clean, and drink unfiltered water. As a result, infectious diseases such as dysentery and cholera are common and are the second-largest cause of childhood death in Nigeria.[11]

While there has been a great deal of humanitarian relief effort focused on the sanitation problems of this region, the DMT model, engaged the local population, and as a result not only addressed the sanitation issue, but also inspired at-risk youth, created jobs, and improved the educational, economic, and environmental conditions in Nigeria.

DMT initially focused on renting toilets for parties, religious activities, and other outdoor events. Funded in part from revenues generated from these sales, DMT now manufactures plastic, portable toilets and strategically places them at bus stops and in densely populated areas in major cities where they operate as public toilets. Each of these public toilets serves about 100 people a day.

We are so wrapped in short-term thinking, with over-the-top speculation spurred on by a constant contact frenzy, that what is flowing through our veins is not blood but a magnetized solution that draws us to invest in or buy things we know nothing about just because it might make us a profit.

A small fee (about 2 cents US) is charged for their use. Young at-risk men, known as the Area Boys, are engaged as the proprietors of the toilets. Instead of paying them an hourly wage, each earns a percentage of the revenue generated by the toilets they maintain. The young proprietors keep 60% of the revenues generated and remit 40% to DMT. These young men and women earn about US $15 a day, which is well above the average income in Nigeria. In addition, they are able to experience the self-worth that comes from meaningful work experience and adding value to their community.[12]

DMT's holistic and dynamic approach to a social problem reaches far beyond the problem of waste management. In addition to providing a much needed service, DMT has been able to improve overall sanitation, improve the quality of the water, control disease, and create hundreds of jobs. Durojaiye, who died in 2012, was selected as the Schwab Foundation's Social Entrepreneur of the Year in Nigeria in 2005 and has been widely profiled in the media including the BBC and the *New York Times*.[13]

Sense and Sustainability

Unlike many not-for-profit models that operate in a more paternalistic mode, DMT engages and empowers the community.

DMT covers 93% of their operating expenses from revenue generated from events and sales of goods and services. DMT also sells toilets globally. These revenues seed the placement of basic toilets. Using a sliding scale enables the organization to creatively finance their multipronged mission. The results have been overwhelmingly positive impacting the country socially, economically, and environmentally. DMT provides a much needed service, but the manner in which the services are provided contributed greatly to the company's success and improved the quality of life for all the citizens of Nigeria. The keys to the success of DMT are straightforward. In addition to their pricing model and taking advantage of a readily available local workforce, DMT established strategic partnerships that were critical to the sustainability of the endeavor and sells advertising space on the toilet units.

I remind all of my esteemed colleagues who are economists that economics is a theory. Economics is a theory based on a model, and even with all the historical perspective contained in the best research, you would be hard-pressed to explain where we are now with a mere economic model.

This additional source of revenue underwrites much of the company's manufacturing costs. The toilets are produced locally, the by-product of which both enriches the community and reduces transportation and other expenses. Unlike many not-for-profit humanitarian efforts that are largely dependent on outside resources, DMT has virtually eliminated the need for any outside resources. As a result, the local economy is the direct benefactor. Area residents are being taught valuable skills and earning wages that are much higher than the national average, and there is a sense of accomplishment and sustainability. In comparison, had these toilets been provided via a traditional humanitarian not-for-profit organization, it would be likely that off-shore, tax-deductible donations would be used to purchase the toilets, which would be in turn shipped to Nigeria. Depending on the range of vision and available funding, the toilets would either be maintained by the organization's volunteers or perhaps just be dropped off without a plan for sustaining the effort and maintaining the facilities. The DMT model provides for a fair exchange and all stakeholders share in the rewards. Had this project been facilitated by outsiders, it is not likely that the ripple effect would have been recognized. The project, while well intended, would have been managed by parties with little intuitive knowledge of the culture and existing infrastructure. As a result, it would be likely that the successes would not have been as far reaching or as lasting.

To provide a general overview of the successes of DMT, since 2003, DMT has manufactured over 3,000 toilets. It has provided and managed toilets at national events such as the All African Games. Recognizing the positive impact the company has had on Nigeria, the Nigerian government recently donated 2,000 free toilets to DMT. DMT is expanding its scope by increasing its efforts to recycle waste in order to generate bio-gas, electricity, and fertilizer for farmers. They are also using a portion of their profits to provide free toilets at local schools.[14]

There should really be no distinction between a not-for-profit and a for-profit company. Both corporate types should be held to the same standards and scrutiny.

Lessons Learned

DMT has contributed tremendously to a cleaner environment and improved sanitation in major cities in Nigeria as well as motivate Nigerian youth, encouraged business ownership, relied on local resources to reduce costs and create opportunities. By operating a commercial enterprise, DMT was able to underwrite some of the expenses of manufacturing the public toilets. The company improves the overall quality of life in Nigeria by addressing other social problems such as poverty, crime, and employment by factoring in area residents into production and operations. They engaged in strategic partnerships and continue to grow in a manner that considers the needs of area residents. In the words of DMT Mobile Toilets founder Isaac Durojaiye: "Sustainability through self-sufficiency is the only guarantee for future survival."[15]

We have never lived in a more exciting time for business or individuals, wherein there is so much complete and instant access to what we want to know, when we want to know it, information cannot save us; if it could, we would have been saved already However. instead, the instant access to information has created a sense of anxiety around a level of expectation that we cannot reach. The mind has reached capacity.

Supplemental Reading

The following are scholarly and peer-reviewed journal articles, conference proceedings, and dissertations or blogs on the concepts discussed in this chapter.

- Fairness, Spiritual Maturity And Socio-Economic Theory, Angela Schnaubelt, Illuminate Me
- For Profit Philanthropy, Dana Brakman Reiser, *Fordham Law Review* 77(5) Article 14, 2009.
- Illicit Financial Flows Explained, EJ Fagan, Task Force on Financial Integrity & Economic Development, Global Financial Integrity, September 7, 2012.

CHAPTER 6

What We Can Do About It? |
Collective Conscious |
What About Prayer? |
What Is It? | Does It Work?

What we can do about it? I think we can pray. We all come from some point of reference, and I cannot imagine any rational thinker believing that we can be one nation or world without allowing all people to think and believe as their conscious or traditions dictate. We have always been mindful of the separation of church and state, and that will be more articulated going forward!

As fascinated as I have always been with the writing and teaching of Carl Jung on the collective unconscious and the primordial images that are a part of his teaching, I am now much more intrigued by the power of the collective conscious.[1] Its evidence is everywhere—from the profoundness of the Arab Spring to the loudness of big college football stadiums. It works; you have large numbers of people in one place and of one accord, and for a time, all energy is concentrated on one event, goal, mission, or desired outcome. You can feel it, you may even see it. It is powerful and real. For the first time in history, we can all be present with this collective conscious wherever it is, and we can participate with our energy as well.

For the first time in history, we can all be present with this collective conscious wherever it is, and we can participate with our energy as well.

I was somewhat intrigued with Franklin Graham's interview with Christiane Amanpour of ABC (© April 24, 2011),[2] when he announced that he now understood how the Christian prophecy that every eye would see and every knee shall bow (to acknowledge Jesus Christ as Lord) in the second coming. He revealed that as he had wondered in the past about how this prophecy would be fulfilled, he now saw that the social media would be a vehicle that could fulfill this prophecy. He added that all people now have cameras in their cell phones, so that pictures would be taken of the second coming of Jesus Christ and shown around the world.

It is hard for me to get my mind around this one, and I am reluctant to criticize the Grahams, as they have had such a wide sphere of influence and have touched the lives of thousands of people for the good. However, this type of literal interpretation of sacred text, no matter the tradition, seems to reduce the power of the message to complete ludicrousness. The metaphor for the people who would acknowledge the stories and messages of unconditional love on a collective conscious level and thereby be transformed seems much more palatable. Many would call this the coming of the Christ-consciousness, which in the past 2,000 years has been embodied in the message of the prophet Jesus. The message of Jesus mirrors the evolved soul in principles that end man's inhumanity to man, man's fight with nature, man's interior struggle with himself, and man's ego race to be all powerful!

The prayer we need to pray at this moment should contain a petition that we receive our souls back or are able to regrow them. The manifestation of this would be that we recognize where we are in space and time, what we have done to deplete the natural resources of the earth that sustains us, and the unwholesome things we have done to our bodies that we should have revered as sacred temples. We have continued to take and not give back, and we are coming to this party so late. However, nothing changes until it is forced to change. An accident kills someone at the intersection and then we put up the traffic light. The nuclear explosion destroys a company, weakens an industry, kills people, and degrades the health of the environment, and then we decide we need to put in new safeguards to prevent this from happening again. We must capture, regrow, acknowledge, find, solicit, and claim our souls in a proactive manner instead of waiting in the cave for the dragon to come in.

So what should this praying look like exactly? Literally, to each his own. However, the prayer that we must engage in now should be in unison and should have the power of the collective conscious.

So what should this praying look like exactly? Literally, to each his own. However, the prayer that we must engage in now should be in unison and should have the power of the collective conscious: one people, in one mind, and in one accord seeking the reemergence of the spirit or soul. We must reconnect, capture, regrow, acknowledge, find, solicit, and claim our souls. We must do this individually before we can do it collectively as a corporation. Be not afraid, it is not that we will give up our reason; it has served us well, and we will continue to feed it and sustain it. We are evolved, and we will not go back! We do not desire to go back to the time before the Age of Reason, but we are ready to make the shift to a collective conscious that contains high ethical standards, the wisdom of the soul, the purity of thought, the clarity of vision, and the full embracing of the spiritual part of the trilogy with the mind and body—because we simply have no choice.

In his book *The Mormon Way of Doing Business*,[3] Jeff Benedict lifts up some major players who are leaders of American corporations, such as Marriott International, Dell, Deloitte, Price Waterhouse, and Coopers, including notables such as JetBlue founder David Neeleman, Credit Suisse CEO Eric Varvel, and Gary Crittenden, former CFO of Citigroup and American Express. Stephen Covey and a Republican candidate for president—Mitt Romney—is also Mormon. Another major political figure, Newt Gingrich, places faith at the top of his list for how he sees and acts in the world. These people have in common a personal practice that stems from their religious beliefs and, as Stephen Covey (passed ⊘ July 2012) argued, they do what is essential for leadership, putting the creation and development of their family first. They rarely work Sundays, come home for dinner, and do chores around the house. Yet they compete very successfully against workaholics who routinely put in 70- to 80-hour weeks.[4]

We must put away the things that divide us in the stories that serve us well.

Without question, religion and religious practices of faith serve some of the leaders of today's corporations well, no matter how mired in myth or superstition some of the traditions were in the past. Today, these practiced faiths act more like major anchors that provide a pattern for the integration of the mind, body, soul rather than the mind–body template that has brought us to the precarious place where we now stand. It is the principles of the faith's practices that focus on the soul of a person and his/her humanity that must serve us now. We must put away the things that divide us in the stories that serve us well. The place to which we have come is scary and calls for the whole of a person to bring in full force the power of spirituality in the workforce. We need the attention of all practiced faiths and the will of nonbelievers as well to be part of the process in restoring the soul of the national, international, and multinational corporation. It is rather Jungian, I admit!

Will it work? I am not sure, and we simply may be, as I say, at a place that cannot be sustained. Since archeologists tell us of civilizations that have existed before ours, historians chronicle regimes that have come and gone, and scientists show us evidence of galaxies other than ours, it is logical that we may be at the end of an age. I am very sure that many before us had stories that helped and served them well, and some superstitions that were encumbering.

What I am also sure of is that which divides us, destroys us. We need to see how much we have in common and talk about those things.

International Insight | What to Do About Prayer: Is Pray at Work Viable?

While labor laws do require employees be provided time off to worship in accordance with their faith, most HR professionals will state that balancing the various religious practices can be difficult. While it is clear that spirituality has a positive impact on performance, it can create significant challenges. The following is a prime example with respect to devoted Muslims.

Dr. Syed Malik is a devoted Muslim who tries, and mostly succeeds, to pray five times per day, as demanded by his Islamic faith. He is also an accomplished general surgeon in Orlando, FL, who does complex operations that can last hours. Malik, 66, would never leave an operating table to pray. Instead, when surgery and prayer times conflict, he performs prayers before surgery or makes them up after.

"I don't care if this goes against what some scholars say, I feel very comfortable with how I approach prayers," said Malik. In fact, Islamic scholars generally agree that while prayers command high priority, they can be missed or performed later in extenuating circumstances. While Muslims differ about what constitutes extenuating circumstances, many successfully integrate prayer into their workday, often with help from their employers.

Still, employers and Muslim workers sometimes clash over prayers.

Recently, Hertz fired 25 Somali Muslim drivers at the Seattle-Tacoma International Airport, who refused to sign an agreement pledging to clock out during prayer breaks. Hertz says they initially allowed Muslim workers to pray during two paid daily breaks of 10 minutes each, but many workers took more than 10 minutes. Nine Muslim workers signed the pledge. The workers' union is challenging Hertz. But some Islamic scholars say that the rental car company offered the workers a solution compatible with their Islamic beliefs.

"Employers have the right to protect themselves. Unfortunately, there are Muslims who abuse the system," said Imam Yahya Hendi, president of Clergy Without Borders, an interfaith organization in Washington, D.C. Hendi said that it was un-Islamic to accept pay for work one did not perform, and chastised the fired Hertz workers for making Islam seem "complicated" and "inadaptable to America."

"If Muslims can do it on their own time, this is the idea," said Zulfiqar Ali Shah, executive director of the North American Fiqh Council, a group of religious leaders who offer guidance on Islamic law. "If there's a conflict between prayer and work, the Muslims should accommodate to work," said Shah. To emphasize that point, Muslims point to a hadith, or story, about Prophet Muhammad in which he prayed the midday and afternoon prayers together. Most scholars recognize the exception, but caution that it should be used judiciously, and not just to avoid uncomfortable situations.

"Would you step out of a meeting to use the bathroom or take a call from your son? Then why not take a few minutes to be with God?" said Hossam Al Jabri, an imam in Boston and former executive director of the Muslim American Society, an advocacy group.

"Being a little inconvenienced for the sake of God is not such a bad thing."

Most Muslims can complete their prayers in 3 to 5 minutes, although pre-prayer ablutions, or ritual washing, can take almost as long.

For each of the five prayers—pre-dawn, noon, afternoon, sunset, and night—Muslims have a few hours to make them, although some say prayers are best when made early. These times change throughout the year as the length of the days varies. Many Muslims find that employers are happy to accommodate their prayer needs.

In his 20 years with the same company in Los Angeles, IT Manager Soheil Naimi has seen supervisors come and go, but none ever prevented him from praying. In fact, Naimi's prayer space has improved as he's been promoted. When he started, he had no office and used to pray in open conference rooms. He later received a cubicle that was big enough to pray in, but was often interrupted by co-workers, who he tuned out while praying.

"I don't think I offended anyone," said Naimi, who asked that his company not be named. He now has his own office, so praying is easy. The only time performing prayers can be hard is when he's out of the office, said Naimi, who has prayed in his car, in a bathroom, and has occasionally missed prayer altogether.

Kelly Kaufmann, a program manager at a Chicago health insurance company, keeps a prayer rug in a Macy's tote bag at her office, and reserves one of her company's many meeting rooms twice daily for 30 minutes. Kaufmann, who also asked that her company not be named, text messages Muslim co-workers to let them know when she has a room reserved. "I am lucky that I make my own schedule and control when my meetings are, and can simply come to work earlier or stay later if needed to ensure the time taken to pray does not interfere with the amount of work I wanted to accomplish during the day," Kaufmann said.[5]

Discussion Questions

- Does prayer in the corporate arena make sense? If not, what are the alternatives?
- Whose role is it to bring the cultural transformation and to sustain it?
- Evaluating the corporations that have culturally embraced spiritual principles, are there differences in profitability and is sustainability a corporate focus?

Exercise | Religious Freedom

With the United States being a country of religious freedom, it is hard to imagine a culture where religious beliefs cannot or will not play a large role in a corporation. Select a country that has a national or prevailing religion and discuss how religious practices are incorporated into the workday, the work product, and customer relations. Compare or contrast the activities and policies that are based on religion, listing the benefits and challenges of operating in such a manner. For those activities that are of value to the religious-based corporation, transform the principle into a spiritual or ethical policy that retains the general concept of the secular ideal but is redrafted to reflect moral or ethical guidelines or general spiritual principles.

A Case for the Ethical Corporation | Tyson Foods

While Tyson's does not put itself in alignment with overt religious principles such as Chick-fil-a or Hobby Lobby, it does employ chaplains in-house for employees to seek solace and to have the opportunity for prayer. It is a company with adherence to the spiritual life incorporated into best practices. It is the belief and practice of this company that most directly in times of crisis, the employees have immediate access to someone and some place to pray. John Tyson, the company chairman, states clearly that he is a born-again Christian who believes that faith should be practiced inside as well as outside the company. Tyson is well known for its philanthropy, which seems to grow out of its need to feed the poor, as a direct commandment. Chairman Tyson says: "My faith is just an ongoing evolution, trying to understand what faith in the marketplace looks like, giving people permission to live their faith seven days a week,...If people can talk about the football game on Monday, why can't they talk about their faith?"(Bold Faith in the Workplace | Gospel Light Minute #73)

This Is the Tyson Story

Tyson Foods, Inc. (NYSE:TSN), founded in 1935 with headquarters in Springdale, Arkansas, is one of the world's largest processors and marketers of chicken, beef, and pork, the second-largest food production company in the Fortune 500 and a member of the S&P 500. The company produces a wide variety of protein-based and prepared food products and is the recognized market leader in the retail and foodservice markets it serves. Tyson provides products and services to customers throughout the United States and more than 130 countries. The company has approximately 115,000 Team Members employed at more than 400 facilities and offices in the United States and around the world. Through its Core Values, Code of Conduct and Team Member Bill of Rights, Tyson strives to operate with integrity and trust and is committed to creating value for its shareholders, customers, and team members. The company also strives to be faith friendly, provide a safe work environment, and serve as stewards of the animals, land, and environment entrusted to it.[6]

Tyson is often cited as a company that strives to operate in an ethical manner and is frequently honored as an ethical corporation. Ethisphere rates Tyson's ethics program "above standard," which they describe as: "Strong programs that exceed all government standards. Institutional commitment to ethics apparent with most measurement criteria met yet selective short fall may still be present, but easily improved".[7] In 2012, Tyson Foods, Inc. was named one of the "100 Best Corporate Citizens" by *Corporate Responsibility Magazine*. Tyson ranked No. 90 of the 100 companies on the 13th annual list. The magazine based its list on publicly available data related to seven categories: climate change, employee relations, environment, financial, corporate governance, human rights, and philanthropy.[8]

What we can do about it? I think we can pray. We all come from some point of reference, and I cannot imagine any rational thinker believing that we can be one nation or world without allowing all people to think and believe as their conscious or traditions dictate. We have always been mindful of the separation of church and state, and that will be more articulated going forward!

Despite ongoing commitment to ethics and corporate responsibility, lapses still occur and, interestingly, their program, which is widely accepted as a model for other corporations, was not originally created by choice. Rather, when it was discovered that Tyson executives were entertaining Mike Espy, who at the time was the United States Secretary of Agriculture, the company plead guilty to federal charges. As a result, Tyson Foods was ordered to pay a multimillion-dollar fine, and the company received 4 years' probation. In addition, Tyson's media director was found guilty of bribery and sentenced to the minimum term allowable, a year and a day of prison time. A condition of the probation was that the company develops an ethics office and code of corporate conduct.[9]

Dr. John Copeland developed the ethics department and corporate code of conduct for Tyson Foods. He wrote an oft-cited, detailed paper about the process. According to Copeland, "during the probationary period, there were more than 70 surprise visits to Tyson offices by inspectors for the USDA and OIC. They checked records of ethics training sessions, saw to it that posters proclaiming the existence of a help-line for whistleblowers were displayed prominently, and randomly questioned employees about the company's code of conduct. Had the inspectors been dissatisfied with Tyson's ethics efforts, its probation could have been revoked and serious penalties inflicted on it." Copeland is also quick to point out that oversight of an ethics department is primarily a management, not a legal function and that its success is contingent on extensive auditing, monitoring, training, and discipline.[10]

> *Without question, religion and religious practices of faith serve well some of the leaders of today's corporations, no matter how mired in myth or superstition some of the traditions were in the past. Today, these practiced faiths act more like major anchors that provide a pattern for the integration of the mind, body, soul rather than the mind–body template that has brought us to the precarious place where we now stand.*

Despite Tyson's high marks with respect to their operating practices and commitment to a strict code of conduct, ethical lapses continue. It appears that these breeches are not because the company does not take its commitment to ethical business practices seriously, rather they appear to be caused, at least in part, by the sheer size of the organization and the fact that they have operations worldwide.

In late June 2004, a plant manager for one of Tyson Foods' poultry processing plants in Mexico sent a memo to company headquarters in Springdale, Arkansas: two women who "most definitely do not work for Tyson Foods in Mexico" each were paid 30,700 pesos, or about $2,700, a month and had been for years. The women happened to be the wives of two veterinarians stationed at the plants as part of Mexico's effort to meet high sanitary and processing standards. The veterinarians certified products as suitable for export, a step required by countries such as Japan and increasingly sought after by Mexican consumers as an assurance of quality and safety for locally produced processed meats. While payments of this nature may be part of the Mexican business culture, they were a clear violation of Tyson's Corporate Code of Conduct as well as, the Foreign Corrupt Practices Act. Accordingly, Tyson agreed to resolve the charges with a deferred prosecution and paid a $4 million criminal penalty as well as an additional $1.2 million to settle related S.E.C. charges that it maintained false books and records and lacked the controls to prevent payments to phantom employees and government officials.[11]

Even more recently, Tyson Food's was the subject of widespread and instant backlash when the Humane Society of the United States released undercover video footage revealing cruel treatment of animals and inhumane conditions at a Wyoming pig breeding facility owned by a supplier for Tyson Foods. In reporting the incident, David Vinjamuri stated: "They kicked piglets like soccer balls, whipped them around by their hind legs, smashed them into concrete floors, and threw them high into the air. A few even threw piglets' testicles at each other and fed them back to the mother pigs for fun.[12]

Vinjamuri is quick to point out the following: "It's easy to cast Tyson and other mass-market companies as heartless villains, but the reality is more complex. The historical willful ignorance of consumers to know how their food is produced combined with a very competitive commercial marketplace has propagated practices that the average consumer would find morally unacceptable. A changing media environment suggests that more of these practices will come to light, and that they will provoke a stronger consumer backlash when they do. This means that it is in the economic interest of large consumer companies to bring their practices in line with the ethical and moral standards of their own consumers."[13]

What I am also sure of is that which divides us, destroys us. We need to see how much we have in common and talk on those things.

Tyson works with more than 12,000 independent livestock and poultry farmers and has long been an industry leader in animal welfare, employing more than a dozen veterinarians and maintaining an Office of Animal Well-being since 2000. The fact that the footage was from only one of the thousands of farms Tyson Foods contracts with, its impact was immediate and viewed by the public as a direct reflection of their standards of operation. This one short video created enormous potential damage to the corporation, so much so, it caused executives to immediately rethink the corporation's ethical standards. In response, Tyson Foods launched the Tyson FarmCheck™ Program to personally audit the treatment of animals at the livestock and poultry farms that supply the company. "Our company is made up of ethical, responsible, and compassionate people, and we believe the family farmers who supply us share our values," said Donnie Smith, president and CEO of Tyson Foods. "We know more consumers want assurance their food is being produced responsibly, and we think two important ways to do that are by conducting on-farm audits while also continuing to research ways to improve how farm animals are raised." Such an incident gives evidence to the fact that the ethical and moral standards of a corporation's consumers play a significant role in that corporation's profitability and sustainability.[14]

Tyson has received widespread praise for their program, even from their most vocal critics. Janeen Salak-Johnson, associate professor of Stress Physiology and Animal Well-Being at the University of Illinois: "Tyson should be commended for taking the initiative to develop and implement an on-farm auditing program. It's a step in the right direction and will help verify farmers are fulfilling their obligation to provide proper care for the animals they raise."[15]

The lessons learned at Tyson Foods are important ones. Doing the right thing and contracting with suppliers that do the right thing is not a social policy, it is a fiscal reality. The United States leads the world in criminalizing business misconduct. Even so, no longer is it enough to catch and punish violators, violations must be prevented in order to sustain an organization.

Ethical standards and a corporate code of conduct must be dynamic and reflect the landscape in which an organization operates. In the case of Tyson Foods, this means that Tyson's standards must be applied not just to Tyson employees, but also to their vendors and suppliers.

Supplemental Reading

The following are scholarly and peer-reviewed journal articles, conference proceedings, and dissertations on the concepts discussed in this chapter.

- Technical Spirituality at Work: Jacques Ellul on Workplace Spirituality, Cathy Driscoll and Elden Wiebe, *Journal of Management Inquiry* 2007, 16: 333.
- *Religion and the Workplace: Pluralism, Spirituality, Leadership*, Douglas A. Hicks, Cambridge University Press, October 2003.
- Christ and Business Culture: Another Classification of Christians in Workplaces According to an Empirical Study in Hong Kong, *Journal of Markets & Morality 12*(1) (Spring 2009): 91–111.

CHAPTER 7

Why Is It Time Sensitive | We Must Name It

The Power of the Corporation

Corporations are the power and force that can really save us now. Communities are filled with people who work in corporations and countries are fueled and funded by corporations. All the streams of our lives run down to the Corporate Rivers and the Sea is not full. The corporation has the capacity because it has fully functioning systems in place for ingathering and distribution—to move money, save people, and protect the planet. The challenge is that currently, the corporate structure is like the headless horseman; it is without leadership and without a core constituency that believes in the mission. We must create a culture governed by integral values that are comprehensive and embracing. The corporations must unpack, go back down to their core, and reassess their mission. Reassess, in light of the loss in confidence and the failure of corporations to come to the table with integrity for all the stakeholders: people, planet, and profit. The corporation is the most powerful institution in the world today, and the idea of social responsibility is one whose time has come, in that we must address the corporations' external effects on society and internal effects on spirituality. The most dominant institution in a society must take on the role of being in charge, and many megacorporations are beginning this transformation and demonstrating that they have a vision of the connectivity to financial success achieved by doing the right thing.

The corporation has the capacity because it has fully functioning systems in place for ingathering and distribution—to move money, save people, and protect the planet.

I am certainly aware that there may not be any truly American corporation or purely single-nation corporation today. I am sure I have always known that, but I think when a Belgium company bought Budweiser (Anheuser Busch) and the beer and the bullfrog commercials at Super Bowls were funnier than ever, I got it! We are so interconnected and, as Shakespeare said: "what is done, cannot be undone."[1]

Emerging Patterns in Leadership

We must, however, examine corporate governance and leadership the world over, for the moral core is germane no matter what the ties to international entities.

The newly elected dean of the Harvard School of Business, Nitan Nohria, the first non-Western-born business dean, has written and spoken articulately about the new century. "If the 20th century was the American Century for Business, the 21st century is decidedly a Global Century and this (meaning Harvard) must be the place where the World's Best Thinking about Business and Management practices takes place. The world's best thinking must occur now, be embraced by business, and have leaders who have shared a vision for the value of human life, the necessity for a high moral ground in decision-making, and the political will to both articulate and transform this vision into reality. "[2] The world cannot wait!

Dean Nohria has most recently collaborated with Scott Snook and Rakesh Khurana, colleagues at Harvard, in writing about leadership and have coauthored and edited a text: *The Handbook on Teaching Leadership: What We Know: Knowing, Doing and Being* (© June 20, 2012). The text bravely makes a stab at collecting scholarly research on best practices in teaching leadership and lays out the text into three purposes: (a) Take Stock and Consolidate Progress (in teaching best practices in teaching leadership current today), (b) Establish a Foundational Reference for Teaching Leadership, (c) Build a Respected Community of Practice. This new book includes an impressive array of scholarship on leadership with some of the most renowned names in the field. This text is more in-line with how we need to proceed from this point, which is to compile what we know and take on the responsibility and accountability of teaching leadership in a more spiritual and meaningful way.

What is amazing is that from the shift to the idea that leadership could be taught, schools of business failed for years to change or to make much progress. It has not always been believed that you could teach leadership, just as character is believed to be so much a creation that comes from the fabric of the home. For too long, even the most prestigious schools of business were at best just a mirror for the practices of the business world. Rather than owning the responsibility for teaching and coaching men and women into becoming leaders and themselves (the schools of business) being the mirror for the world, schools of business have stayed with the case method and continued to teach from the academic model of classical leadership definitions and theory, and not much else. How can people who are strictly academics do much more? The truth is we can do more and the time has come to produce. When Jeffery Skilling (former CEO of Enron) was at Harvard, he wrote that the sole purpose of a corporation was to make a profit for the shareholders and to maybe operate within the law.

The truth is we can do more and the time has come to produce.

John Le Boutillier writes about Skilling at Harvard in his blog post from Harvard to Enron and describes the 1978 scenario in this manner: (directly quoted)

> "Productions and Operation Management was taught by Dr. Chip Bupp, a thoughtful and serious man. This was a course designed to study factory placement, assembly line management and plant facility problems. On this particular day the case in question for Section A involved a company that manufactured a product that may be, but wasn't definitively, harmful–even potentially fatal–to the consumer. If you were the CEO of this company what should you do in such an ambiguous–and potentially dangerous–situation?

Several students offered suggestions, none of which galvanized the class. Then a hand shot up from near the back row. Dr. Bupp called, "Jeff, what would you do?" Jeff was one of the brightest members of Section A.

With thinning blond hair and wire-rim spectacles, he had a mature persona to go with a slight Southern drawl. He often expressed disdain toward any government intervention. One of the natural leaders inside Section A, when he talked, as the commercial said, 'Everyone listened.'

Clearly, it is a global century.

'I'd keep making and selling the product,' Jeff said. 'My job as a businessman is to be a profit center and to maximize return to the shareholders. It's the government's job to step in if a product is dangerous.' Several heads nodded in agreement. Neither "Jeff" nor the others seemed to care about the potential effects of their cavalier attitude. What if this product harmed consumers? How about the company's employees? Were they in danger during the manufacture of this product? And what could happen to the company if the CEO made the wrong decision? Few in Section A that day dared to raise these questions. At HBS–and business schools nationwide–you were then–and still are–considered soft or a wuss if you dwell on morality or scruples."[3]

What Nitan Nohria and his cohorts understand is how pervasive and powerful this total lack of spiritual intelligence and accountability is for our charge as leaders and for teaching leadership. The discussion around the triple bottom-line, people, planet, and profit, begins to inform a new paradigm that the Harvard Business School and many schools of business now espouse.[4] It is a charge that is taken seriously, as in times past what we said or did in the classroom was purely academic. What is widely acknowledged currently is that what we say and do in the classroom should be the mirror by which society sees itself. The academic arena must model to the world of business ethics, corporate social responsibility, and leadership. We must say to a Jeffery Skilling that will not pass, not at Harvard, and not in a world to which you and we are accountable.

Clearly, it is a global century, as Nohria concludes, and we are one, and so closely intertwined that what happens in Greece today is as relevant—or even more so perhaps—as what is happening with Occupy Wall Street in New York and San Francisco. Note: Greece announced today (@ February 2012) that it will lay off 150,000 government workers by December.[5] Where will these people go and what will they do in a place and a space that is already overwhelmed with a population whom are not self-supporting?

I do hear some rather sophisticated chatter coming out of the World Economic Forum in Davos, Switzerland this month (© January 2012), and it comes not so much from the government figures present—governments use everything as a political platform—but from the likes of James Turley, CEO of Ernst and Young, and S. D. Shibulal, COO of Infosay.[6] They see the future in terms of business collaboration that, they subtly imply, will supersede what governments may or may not do. They have the clearer vision for the power of the corporate structure. What is missing is the expanded vision to go beyond their obvious solutions of business into spiritual business collaboration.

The Necessity for a Global Tomorrow

As we come, by choice or by force, to explore in cooperation with other countries how best to gather and distribute the planet's resources, we will need the spiritual core in the template.

As we transition from the current war over the world's resources and the desire to dominate into an understanding that there is enough to go around for everyone, we will advance all of civilization. I do not agree with the redistribution of wealth idea, which is so prized and panned at the same time. However, the reality is that the wealth is redistributed, as always, by choice, through the will of the corporation to take care of its own and of the wealthiest citizens in evolved countries (many of the top 25 philanthropists are in the United States)—by giving of their wealth to make the world whole. Just check out the list of the greatest philanthropists; their causes range from curing malaria, building freshwater wells, and aiding farmers in Africa, to curing AIDS, educating children, and being their brother's keeper by giving to causes that support education and human rights. These people understand that if it happens to the least of these people, it happens to us all!

As we come, by choice or by force, to explore in cooperation with other countries how best to gather and distribute the planet's resources, we will need the spiritual core in the template.

This is obvious to many, I think, and power rests with the corporation—in this case, with the large world corporations in energy, technology, health care, and possibly social media—that take a longer look and do the things we know must be done. The major consumers of energy—America, Europe, India, China, and Russia—must shift their dependence away from outside sources and become more self-reliant, both in use and in demand. As idealistic as this sounds, it is the way, and if we do not self-select, the way is about to be made for us.

World events are shaping up to demand a more civilized course of action, even for the oldest of cultures. Why do you suppose that the oil from the former Persian Empire—Iran, Turkey, parts of Central Asia, Pakistan, Thrace, Macedonia, much of the Black Sea coastal regions, Afghanistan, Iraq, northern Saudi Arabia, Jordan, Israel, Lebanon, Syria, and all significant population centers of ancient Egypt as far west as Libya—that is so desired by the world is so sweet and so precious? It is because it comes from a civilization whose history is fascinating and great at so many levels, and the sheer age of the land alone has made what is in the ground valuable.

The error or sin committed by corporations and countries in relation to oil, on which so much of the world is dependent, is that it was easy to take and use without regard to any price other than the monetary reward. The model for its use was easy to engineer, and oil has been profitable for the world for such a long time; it has been so sweet! It has always been just a process of the mind and body template, though, without any inclusion of the spiritual questions that should accompany the quest for or use of natural resources. The United States has an even greater supply of oil and other sources of energy such as natural gas than other countries of the world;[7] this coupled with the fascinating idea that between the northern borders of Canada to the southern border of Mexico lie three contiguous countries on one huge land mass. We could change the hold that the Organization of the Petroleum Exporting Countries (OPEC) has over not only the United States but others as well. We simply have not wanted to do the hard work of refining and paying the price for the development of these industries. It has always been easier to get oil from OPEC. Until now, that is. One strong voice that has explained for years the need to become energy independent is of T. Boone Pickens; it is worth the time to view his website, and while not without controversy, his data are convincing.[8] We must be better and smarter stewards of the world's resources, and we must not allow ourselves to be held hostage by un-evolved countries or industries that are propelled by the greed for immediate gain!

No one doubts that we are experiencing a crisis at many levels; this sense exists at the level of reality and at an existential level as well. While countries and civilizations have teetered on such a precipice before, we have the capacity to pull back from the path of destruction that we are on, recalculate, and look with that third eye and find the spiritual core! The major users of fossil fuel energy—have allowed the crisis in energy to reach catastrophic proportions in terms of the cost to human life. We are fighting wars over oil!

We must take the longer view. If the OPEC counties, on which we rely so heavily for the very sweet oil, were to ask for their payment in something other than dollars, we would be in yet another kind of crisis. All of the current world crises are linked together in an inexorable chain. The OPEC was born in Baghdad, Iraq, when five countries signed an agreement in September 1960. (OPEC: Brief History) The founding members were Iran, Iraq, Kuwait, Saudi Arabia, and Venezuela. These countries were later joined by Qatar (© 1961), Indonesia (© 1962), Libya (© 1962), the United Arab Emirates (© 1967), Algeria (© 1969), Nigeria (© 1971), Ecuador (© 1973), Gabon (© 1975), and Angola (© 2007). Currently, the Organization has 12 member countries since Ecuador, Gabon, and Indonesia have opted out. OPEC members have also come to rely solely on their oil as their source of survival, hence their use of the oil to blackmail the world and to keep their own people bound to their one world order. We cannot wait, and this is at more than one level: the world not only has to end its war over the use and distribution of natural resources, but also has to rethink its future interdependence.

We are one!

Along with the energy crisis, the world currency crisis threatens to destroy the fabric of our lives as well. We have done the same thing with the currency crisis as we have with the energy crisis. As of this writing, the truth about the international exposure to the sovereign debt in the countries of the euro zone is being concealed as a result of a lack of depth of financial knowledge in organizations such as the Securities and Exchange Commission (SEC); the revelation would cause world-wide panic, which would destroy financial markets overnight; it could wreak political upheaval, as any world leader on whose watch this occurs will be removed from office! The head of the International Monetary Fund (IMF), Christine LeGuard, is overseeing the supposed international outreach of monies to countries such as Greece, Italy, Spain, and Portugal; the outcome is still unclear (@ February 2012), but the consequences are surely influencing financial markets the world over. The IMF's Global Financial Stability report out October 9, 2012 from Tokyo says more of what the agency has been saying since the beginning of the problems with Greece and the euro zone. The global financial markets remain fragile and the risks have increased for all the players and specifically directing attention to the banking industry and the obligation of countries to act nationally to clean up the banking system, close the banks that are weak, and restructure and recapitalize the ones that are strong enough to profit from assistance. As a result of the crisis with the euro zone, investors, who have little or no trust, have fled to Japan and the United States as safe havens for money and thus long-term interest rates in these countries remain low, which is the not so good news, unless policy makers act now to capitalize on the rates. The report by the IMF is, of course, much studied and carefully intended to provide guidance, but not to instill panic into a world market that is already in panic.[9]

Even considering the unprecedented measures that the Federal Reserve has instituted and the 17-euro zone policy makers' measures to shore up the failed economies of the zone members, confidence is not restored. All the monetary intervention by the Federal Reserve's Ben Bernanke and the European Central Bank President Mario Draghi is only that, an intervention that has bought time. This recurring process of kicking the can down the road may be over in view of the immediate European sovereign debt challenge and the world economic crisis. I think what we are looking at now is a challenge that could call for a standardization in currency that will ultimately lead to a push for a one-world order over time and at some levels. This is certainly not desirable for any world power to obtain, but such a Spector seems more real now than in the past. Many world economists told us that the euro crisis of today was predictable, even from the time of the EU's inception in January 1999. For one thing, only 17 of the 27 countries in Europe are on the euro. More importantly, while there was a monetary agreement between the countries of the euro zone, there was no real fiscal policy.[10] In other words, like the dollar, there is agreement on the value of the euro and things such as interest rates, but unlike the dollar, there is no agreement on fiscal policy that dictates things like government expenditure and taxation across the euro zone's 17 members. On the eve of one of the more important meetings on the euro crisis (☉ July 30, 2012), Britain stands marginalized by its nationalistic insistence on holding on to the pound and with a weak voice in the euro issue. Tim Geithner, US Secretary of the Treasury, is running around Europe, China, and Japan, telling everyone to please make it work and the only real power the United States has is our dominance of the IMF, to which we are the major contributor. The IMF can be used to bail out the likes of Greece, Italy, Spain, and Portugal. I do not see Geithner—nor the United States, in general—having much power here, since a big part of the problem in this crisis is not only that US banks had exposure to foreign debt, but also that European countries, Germany in particular, were the fool in the room when it came to buying US-backed securities, derivatives, etc. Americans are the best sales people in the world! This is a world crisis, not simply a matter of euro zone problems.

Americans are the best sales people in the world!

Without question, the need to establish fiscal policy in the euro zone is a crisis right now for the EU; it is so much about nationalism, and the disparate European Union members seem so undisciplined— with the notable exception of Germany, Sweden, and Finland—that it is hard to sort out the solution here. The European Central Bank seems the player most likely to become the Federal Reserve of the EU, which will create and enforce fiscal policy. The catch is that everyone has to agree, and this is the hard part, of course, because we have dilatant players such as Greece, Italy, and Spain, and keeping them in the fold has a huge price tag (The European Central Bank).

The Germans are opposed to any kind of quick fix, and for good reason. A major scholar on German economics is Albrecht Ritschl, professor of economic history at the London School of Economics and a member of the advisory board to the German ministry of economics. He has researched and written extensively on the history of the German economy and while his works drill in at levels that reach far beyond the scope of this book, some of the messages on the economy can be summed up in the words of George Santayana: "Those who cannot remember the past are condemned to repeat it."[11]

In a 2012 paper; "Reparations, Deficits, and Debt Default: the Great Depression in Germany"[12] he draws parallels between Germany's debt crisis in 1931 and the current Southern European debt crisis. For those who say that Germany should feel obligated to take on the sovereign debt of other Eurozone nations in light of the reparation extended to Germany through the Marshall Plan, Ritschl is quick to point out that at the inner core of the Marshall Plan was an agenda much bigger than its outer shell. What began as a bipartisan American program to assist in rebuilding the German economy after World War II as a means to stave off the spread of communism and avoid the post-World War I debt crisis, set the stage for the distortion of exchange rates; the creation of an alternative currency (the Deutschmark); and questionable standards for valuing the economy.[13]

To create fiscal policy and have an enforcer of the policy means changing treaties, a process that can take 2 or more years; it is clear to everyone, though, that the clock is out on this as a plausible timetable. An example is the solution proposed by the president of the European Council and the euro zone, Herman Van Rompuy. He has suggested a change in the protocol of the treaty, not the treaties themselves—like an amendment. The protocol would mandate that countries would have to write into their law that they would go through the Central Bank and the European Parliament to reach a balanced budget and prove that they are maintaining a balanced budget over the economic cycle. There would be some built-in automatic reductions in expenses along with increases in taxes or both if a balanced budget were not attained.[14]

To create fiscal policy and have an enforcer of the policy means changing treaties, a process that can take 2 or more years.

However, the idea that the Euro-zone countries could just disband and everyone go their own way and revert to separate currencies would/will challenge the world order as we know it. As the crisis began to hit the street and talk was of the euro zone breaking up, Ireland was discovered on the Internet trying to buy printing presses, as it becomes clear that countries in the euro zone could be returning to their own currencies (② December 2011).[15]

In another episode of the continuing saga of the European sovereign debt challenge, Germany proposed that they set up courts to oversee the austerity measures and the spending cuts they have imposed in the countries that have been bailed out. This would snatch away whatever national sovereignty is left in the countries that are now in financial crisis. There is likelihood that the court idea will not fly, but other ideas are swarming over this crisis. Somehow, the spectator of a German court is not getting traction.[16]

The drama continues around the euro and its stability. As the head of the European Central Bank (ECB), Mario Draghi, takes on more characteristics of the US Federal Reserve's Chair, Ben Bernanke, the race to world inflation speeds up. In late ② July 2012, Draghi spoke to a group of London investors and, reportedly at the last minute, made the decision to make every effort to impress and reassure markets with his promise that the ECB would do whatever needed to be done.[17] This turn of events sets the stage for the printing of money; something the ECB has avoided based on solid historical and economic data. Let it be understood that no amount of monetary easing by the ECB or the Fed will cure the real systemic problems of loss of faith in the people who should lead us. Remember that since the currencies themselves no longer have any real value other than the power of the market (and even less since the announcement in July by Draghi), the only way that there is value in any of them is if goods move. It is just about the market, and the crisis now is that goods are not moving because of a lack of trust and faith in the future. In the end, it is not so much about the facts, but how we, as individuals, corporations, and countries feel about the future; and life and money are more about feelings than facts. So many seem fearful of the future, and the current spirit reminds me of other times in history when we were called to think and reason in a more clear and ethical way.

So many seem fearful of the future

Nouriel Roubini, Stern College of Business Professor at NYU, has been called both the Dr. of Doom and the Dr. of Realism. He predicted the housing market devastation. In an interview (@ October 2011), after he had painted a really bleak picture of Wall Street's future, WSJ anchor Simon Constable asked him where one should put their money if Wall Street was history? Roubini replied without a flinch, "cash."[18] Roubini also now says that we have something of a quite before the storm in the Euro Zone now as Angela Merkel, who is the central figure in the zone, awaits reelection (fall 2013). In other words, somehow the juggling act will continue until after the election, when all hell may break loose in this part of the world and bring the house down (December 17, 2012).

The Need for Global-Minded Leadership

I am not totally pessimistic, but I do see a real lack of leadership across the board and no simple answers. Of the three major currencies—the Dollar, Yuan, and Euro—as hard as it might be to believe, the dollar even in its weakened condition, is the least dirty. However, that position will not last forever unless we have some fundamental changes in the spirit of fear that now grips countries around the globe. The euro zone is most likely headed for a breakup; even with some agreements coming out of the meetings in Brussels and Berlin, and even with the ECB promising to print money, it is almost too late. The debt is too large to manage, and the breakup may well be disorganized and messy, which may trigger worldwide recession. The banks, domestic and foreign, have massive exposure in this debt, and the reason they are not lending is that they know they will have to absorb this debt. Knowing they will be unable to absorb it, they fear insolvency; hence, a world banking crisis becomes part of this picture. Therefore, it follows with the thesis that corporations, other than banks, must function as the entities that have the necessary money, jobs, and materials for civilization to continue. Again, the global corporation, not government, is the only hope of salvation here!

The idea that Germany would be able to solve its problem if the Africans went home is as naïve as Elias's, Catherine's friend from Greece (see International Insight Chapter 1), belief that if the Albanians went home, the Greeks would be just fine! The assimilation of the Africans into German society has not really failed; it is just in progress—a process that cannot be rushed and must be provided for, a process that the Germans do not like, at the moment.

We have something of the same mental block in the United States in that there is one contiguous land mass from the north border of Canada to the southern border of Mexico. A fence is not the answer in Mexico; really now! Such foolish talk of fences! When have we ever been able to fence anything in or out. If you could have contained a thing, person, or idea in the past, you will not be able to do that going forward in the new age of communication.

A fence is not the answer in Mexico; really now!

We must shift our thinking about how we work with our neighbors. Cleaning up the drug cartels and bringing the rule of law to that part of the continent is the answer for the United States. It is vital that the United States—and all evolved countries as well—remain the leaders of the pack, maintaining a high regard for human life. It is not just Mexico's problem; it is the world's problem. The border problem has to be taken out of such a political context, and we have to go to the core of the problem. The rule of law as defined by the World Justice Project, which was initiated in 2006 and became a 501(c)(3) on its website defines the Rule of Law as a system in which the following four universal principles are upheld: (quoted directly)

1. The government and its officials and agents are accountable under the law.
2. The laws are clear, publicized, stable and fair, and protect fundamental rights, including the security of persons and property.
3. The process by which the laws are enacted, administered, and enforced is accessible, efficient, and fair.
4. Justice is delivered by competent, ethical, and independent representatives and neutrals who are of sufficient number, have adequate resources, and reflect the makeup of the communities they serve.[19]

It is the position of the WJP that until we have universality of the rule of law, we will not progress as a civilization, and while this may seem to be the exclusive function of government, it well becomes the purvey of corporations who must fill the gaps where government and other nongovernment agencies cannot or have not functioned.

One reason the worldview of the EU is changing is business, and the power of corporations who see most clearly that what we have is one big marketplace that must be whole and united. It must also be protected, free, stable, healthy, and productive. You cannot cut off one part of the body and expect the remaining functionality to give you what you want. Government is powerless to fix this problem. Many multinational corporations have budgets bigger than that of entire sovereign countries. So, again, we have arrived at the place where the strongest functioning entity in our midst must take over, and that can only be the world's corporations.

The world over, we must begin to connect the dots and be so much smarter than we are at this moment, and the smarts will come when the corporations of the world embrace spirituality. Too often, when we speak of the quest for the spiritual, we interpret it as the pursuit of a fanatical belief or a falling into something weak. The opposite is true: when we connect the three parts of the individual again—body, mind, and soul—and identify it as the pattern that must be the new corporate structure, we will be stronger than at any time since the 18th century, when we left off the soul as an essential part of the whole of man.[20] The corporation alone has the organizational structure and ability to use information and innovation, which are our greatest commodities. It is when that information is used by the soul, which is where we find real wisdom, that we have the fabric that can save us. We must wake up to our inner world, and make the transformation now.

We must begin to connect the dots.

Never before has the emphasis been so strong on the operative word "NOW"! However, the dream of a United States of Europe has failed, and as I am writing this, if the collapse of the euro occurs sooner than late (© October 2012), this will hasten the need for the corporations to take charge. However, they will not be highly functional for this crisis without awakening and acknowledgment of the spiritual. In an interview with *Newsweek*, Prime Minister David Cameron of the United Kingdom (UK) was quoted as saying: "My vision is of a Europe that stretches from the Atlantic to the Urals, that includes Turkey, that is a vital, thriving single market of Innovation and invention … a continent of great political will, … but it wouldn't be a federal state. It wouldn't be a country called Europe."[21]

While he is a young, articulate leader on the world stage, it remains to be seen if his vision can become a reality without the UK being part of the euro zone or a currency that replaces the euro and the pound.

What we continue to see and feel are the results of the long time invested in the mind and body duo and an almost complete avoidance of the spiritual nature of mankind. Many people the world over attend church, synagogue, mosque, or ashram regularly. That is one way to connect to the spiritual, if it is more than just habit. However, the mindset seems to be that the spiritual practice is something that is just added on and not integrated into the whole of life. We compartmentalize our lives and the integration of the spiritual is ignored. In no way does attendance at sacred temples constitute or signal the integration.

We must have wisdom, and the only source and home for wisdom is the soul.

We currently have a great deal of research data from which we have acquired useful information, and from that information, we have created categories of knowledge to run our lives and our universe. The organization and utilization of information are the source of our intelligence, which we have plenty of today. However, as we enter the new era, the knowledge that has formed our intelligence will not be enough. We must have wisdom, and the only source and home for wisdom is the soul. It is wisdom that is conspicuously lacking from the current paradigm of the human condition. There is a sense among many, I think, that something is happening that will force us to shift the focus of the journey rather than continuing on the path where the mind has taken us. It is as though some are seeing with their third eye and know that a major shift has occurred to which we will voluntarily respond or be forced to create a new way of living. Bill Gates, in a talk called *Keeping America Great* he gave with Warren Buffet at Columbia in November 2009, said that one or two or may be three times in a professional life of 40 years, one knows that something major has changed, has sifted and that things will not be the same going forward. Obviously, I am not the only one that gets it. Gates and Buffet are friends and men of character whose leadership has shaped the last part of the 20th century and the first part of the 21st century and whose legacies may well be a touchstone for moving the world forward.[22]

Much of the religious heritage from early US history was very un-evolved, to put it mildly. Like so many primitive religious practices, it was fraught with superstition and a forced literal interpretation of sacred text. The faith was unenlightened and with a limited and skewed worldview. The controlling principle for human conduct was fear of a literal hell, which would be the fate of anyone who broke the narrow rules. This type of religious practice, very much like some of the ideology of the Catholic Church, has nothing to do with the spiritual part of the human condition. It does not serve the evolution of the soul, and in fact, retards that real spiritual part of man that is innovative and constantly questioning. Our lives are richer because of how significantly the sacred texts (often not the churches) wrestle with the human condition and offer patterns of thought and behavior that lead to a higher order of thinking. It is exactly this higher-order thinking that is called for now.

We are here and we must work with what is on the table. Much of organized religion does not provide any substance by way of a power or force that we can use now. This has disappointed and left us with many failed hopes. However, inasmuch as churches are corporations with a structure of ingathering and distribution, the church, not so much the theology, can be a way to rekindle the soul—once it finds its own way. This evaluation is a generalization, as there are enlightened churches with a theology that teaches that the greatest commandment is to love our fellow man. Now, that is progress.

We need to stop looking outside ourselves for the answer; we must stop looking for that savior

In our present state, more bad things are bound to happen; the center is not holding, and we see this reality in our nightly news and daily headlines. Also, there is a sense of being overwhelmed, and as individuals, we feel powerless.

We need to stop looking outside ourselves for the answer; we must stop looking for that savior. With this comes the intuition that with all we know of the current state of, say, the economy, or world conflict, there is more we do not know that has the potential to destroy our way of life. This is not restricted to a Western perspective, but includes a larger sense of the unfolding of the future held by many peoples throughout the world. We can blame no one else for where we are individually or collectively. We have done it to ourselves due to the lack of a will to rise up and challenge leaders when they are not doing the right thing. The tendency to blame some other entity is always heightened in times of economic crisis, and we are submerged in that right now. It has the power to destroy us and change the face of the world as we know it! We have no trust and are bereft of hope. We are violently fighting among ourselves; historically, this has been the path of destruction.

We are consumed by a poverty mentality—that there is not enough land, air space, market share, money, food, pleasure, recognition, and jobs to go around and we must thus grab for everything. In reality, we do have an abundance of life, here and now. Without question, we are challenged; however, to meet the higher order of thinking, it is imperative that we rescue ourselves in the only way possible, which is by rediscovering that spiritual part of who we are and embracing it.

We can clone life in a tube, send space ships to the moon and calculate their landing time with precision, and operate on a fetus while in the womb to correct a malformed lip. However, until we know, understand, and feel what all this means, we have only our minds to worship. What we must worship, acknowledge, and regrow from its dwarfed state is a sense of connectivity to the spiritual. The soul is that part of a human that connects inherently with the environment and wants to protect it; the part that always works in the best interest of the greatest number of people; that follows the golden rule in thought, word, and deed; that practices for war but prays for peace; that creates rather than destroys; that shares a sense of prosperity in all things and believes in the innate goodness of humankind; and that is strongest when it is giving to make the world a better place, in small ways or in big.

Without the soul, all the mind has brought forth does not satisfy us, bring us peace, or end our anxiety. The scientific method is a tool and the Enlightenment, a freedom of thought, but not an end in itself. It can tell us the what, but not the why or even the how; that is, not the why that brings clarity of vision and peace with moral certainty. The how is the domain of the universe, and we are only people who ask, seek, and knock.

Without the soul, all the mind has brought forth does not satisfy us, bring us peace, or end our anxiety.

The place to begin is within, from the place in which we find ourselves. The future may seem like a scary place at many levels, but if we are integrated as a people, as a country, and as a corporation, with focused and enlightened leadership, we will prevail, not just endure!

International Insight | Why Is It Time-Sensitive: We Must Name It

Caroline Myss is a medical intuitive with a strong background in both religion and history. Her current focus is educating people as to the personal control they have over their health and healing citing a lack of personal responsibility for the dramatic rise in health issues, especially mental health. In her book, *Why People Don't Heal and How They Can*, 1997, she explores illness from a spiritual perspective. Myss cites a phenomenon she refers to as "wound-ology," a term she uses to describe the human condition where one defines themselves in terms of the negative and traumatic experiences of the past. In a matter of minutes after meeting someone either personally or professionally, people tend to define themselves in terms of being a victim. Incest survivor, cancer survivor, recovering alcoholic, recovering Catholic, widow, divorcee, and a myriad of other past events form the core of a person's current self-worth. In the words of Myss, these experiences become "social currency" and can quickly be used as a manipulation and an excuse for special treatment. With a pay-off of clout and excuses, healing becomes a liability. Why would people want to heal when they are rewarded so generously for such challenges?[23]

From a human perspective, wound-ology fosters illness and dependence, but the same can be said of a society. At this point in time, it could be said that we are suffering from collective wound-ology. The United States has been at war for over 10 years, the economy is teetering, there is epic under- and un-employment, and we are strapped with massive personal and national debt. Many have lost confidence in what James Truslow Adams, in his book *The Epic of America* written in 1931, called the American Dream. Adams defined the term: "that dream of a land in which life should be better and richer and fuller for everyone, with opportunity for each according to ability or achievement. It is a difficult dream for the European upper classes to interpret adequately, and too many of us ourselves have grown weary and mistrustful of it. It is not a dream of motor cars and high wages merely, but a dream of social order in which each man and each woman shall be able to attain to the fullest stature of which they are innately capable, and be recognized by others for what they are, regardless of the fortuitous circumstances of birth or position" (p. 214–215). This "American Dream" rather became the World Dream after World War II.

Regardless of one's political leanings, it is hard to deny that there is now a clear incentive to rely on entitlements and labels than there is to succeed in spite of such circumstances. We as a culture have assigned a label to everyone and everything. Title IX, the Equal Opportunity Commission, gay and lesbian rights and woman's rights are just a few examples of well-intentioned programs, which at the time were solutions to much needed social change. Unfortunately, most of these altruistic solutions have since been hijacked by special interest-seeking power, further luring individuals into a poverty mentality. Just as people, who define themselves in terms of their losses, become ill, countries, communities, corporations, and society as a whole can tend to fester this sense of wound-ology. The result is a lack of incentive or optimism with respect to economic recovery, sustainability, and prosperity worldwide. Today, high school graduates question the value of a college education, focusing only on its short-term return on investment. Globally, the United States is falling behind other countries with respect to education. Some go as far to say, that the United States has gone from being the leader on the world's stage keeping the skies open and the seas free to the economy of a Third World country where our only option is to be bailed out by countries with emerging economies.

This mindset is infectious. From a global perspective, the United States is not the only country to have fallen into such a pattern. To move forward, our societal, collective wound-ology must transform into a spirit of collective optimism with respect to the future. To do so, we must look to history and reflect on its cyclical nature. Our collective world eyes should be looking forward, not behind us and we must accept difficult times as valuable tools with which we can chart a path into the future. Just look at the economic prosperity that is following great depressions.

Just as individuals can take cues from successful business practices in their personal lives, individuals can be a power of example to corporations. For example, take note of the story of Patricia Tracey, currently sitting for her CPA exams (May 2011) after graduating from an expensive private university with a 4.0 GPA. Unlike most of her classmates, she did not come from a privileged background; in fact, her personal history would make a college education quite unlikely. Courageously, she overcame a childhood of homelessness and poverty. Her mother was an alcoholic with no ability to provide any type of security for her children. She was alone, on the streets and homeless by 17, often scrounging for food. Despite this chaotic existence and personal circumstances setting the stage for a textbook case of "wound-ology" she joined the Navy, which enabled her to attend college on the GI bill supplemented with academic scholarships. As a student, her leadership skills were recognized by her professors and peers alike. In the words of one of her professor, "She pays it forward, and it's beautiful to watch." Ms. Tracey's message is as follows: "There's lots I can't control, but the things I can't control will change over time, and the things I can control, I must, so I can move forward and enjoy a successful future." In the end, you have to have hope for the future and in the meantime a strong sense of perseverance, focusing on the present and having faith in the future."[24]

Discussion Questions

- What are the identifiable paradigm cultural shifts that historic or contemporary thought leaders point us too?
- Can leadership be taught? If so, where and how can it be taught?
- What are the consequences of action and inaction in view of the world crisis? Can we just sit it out?
- Is there scientific evidence or historical precedent that is requiring course correction?

Exercise I Innovation I Is It Faster Than We Can Assimilate?

Identify a new trend, innovation, or invention introduced to the market within the past 15 years. List its contributions to society as well as the social challenges created. Address each social challenge; explain how it could have been avoided as well as whether or not society would have been better without the advancement and what alternatives could have eliminated some or all of the challenges.

A Case for Oversight | The United Nations
Compact and Beyond

Ethics oversight is not as easy as it may sound, especially on a global level. Oversight can become a moving target that requires both an understanding of history, an eye on emerging trends, and technological advances. It also requires a keen awareness of cultural differences almost from an anthropological level. While enforcement clearly requires adherence to stated universally accepted and incorporated principles, there must also be sufficient flexibility that the outcome is a sustainable protocol. The goal is to promote ethical practices, not to catch the noncompliant. The mindset should be one for a proactive creation as opposed to enforcement. We must accept that ethical lapses will occur for a myriad of reasons and the sheer size of the operation, not being the least of these. This fact should not allow us to be any less accountable or excuse any behavior that undermines the adherence to moral behavior that makes us strong and peaceful.

In an October 15, 2012 blog entry entitled: The Test of Time-Part-I-Proactive Ethics Oversight, Susan Liautaud made some keen observations about ethical lapses. These realities must be considered in the development and administration of any type of oversight, be it internal, national, or global. Consider the following:

- Ethical breeches become fodder for lawsuits, criminal proceedings, and increased regulations, all of which drive up the cost of business.
- Seemingly, minor breeches can surface at a future time for a number of reasons some deliberate others inadvertently.
- Time magnifies the consequences of even the slightest transgressions.
- Ethical lapses often set precedent or become normalized.
- Ethics affects the quality of decision making and risk management at all levels of an organization all the time.
- The catalytic implications of social media and technology expedite and magnify the consequences of unethical behavior.
- Unintended harm can be just as damaging as premeditated acts.

- Unethical behavior is contagious.

- Reputational, internal, and regulatory repair generally take much more time than the decision or transgression that gave rise to an incident.[25]

Corporations are the power and force that can really save us now. Communities are filled with people who work in corporations and countries are fueled and funded by corporations. All the streams of our lives run down to the Corporate Rivers and the Sea is not full.

Recognizing the far-reaching impact of ethical breeches, as well as the challenges faced by even the most ethical of corporations, it is important to craft oversight in a manner that serves as an incentive to engage in ethical business practices.

A Global Solution

Sébastien Bazin, managing director Europe and CEO of Colony Capital SAS, was interviewed by Susan Liautaud for her October Blog (2012), and Bazin makes the following observations with respect to ethical standards from a global perspective: "Global ethics standards should be universally possible and desirable, but in today's reality they are impossible to enforce. Ideally, there should be global standards, and then each organization or person either complies or explains with full transparency why and how they are not complying. In France, a secular country with a 'liberty, equality, fraternity' motto, there is no cultural reason for the highest international standards of ethics not to apply. However, this cannot happen globally in today's world, particularly in developing countries. It seems that some parts of Africa, of Asia, and ex-Soviet Union's members are mainly driven by profit-centered motivations and with individual wealth creation being the driving agenda for too many political leaders. It will be a long time before US and European standards of ethics percolate meaningfully into those regions."[26] While I believe this is an accurate evaluation at some levels, I am hopeful and see that many current initiatives are making major strides in pushing for the embracing of the rule of law, world over; we are not there yet, but some of the following initiatives are worthy of note.

We must, however, examine corporate governance and leadership the world over, for the moral core is germane no matter what the ties to international entities.

 ## United Nations Global Compact

The Joint Inspection Unit (JIU) is an independent external evaluation body of the UN, based in Geneva. The JIU in a report states: "On the whole, the Global Compact has been successful in legitimatizing the progressive and generalized engagement of the United Nations with the private sector, and promoting new partnerships whose effectiveness is yet to be proved. However, it has been less successful in making business participants translate their commitment into real policy change," the JIU says bluntly in a report. "The lack of company monitoring is the initiative's 'Achilles' heel,"[27] stresses the report. Nongovernment organizations such as Amnesty International, Greenpeace, Action Aid, and the Berne Declaration have long criticized the Compact for lacking teeth because of the lack of verification of compliance self-assessment.[28]

Bart Slob of the Amsterdam based Ethics at Work and The Centre for Research on Multinational Corporations (SOMO), an independent, nonprofit research and network organization working on social, ecological, and economic issues related to sustainable development said "If the U.N. is unwilling to take rigorous reform measures, it would be better to consider an alternative course of action, like establishing a code of conduct for large companies, as was suggested by the U.N. in the 1970s. An idea that unfortunately never materialized."[29] Note: SOMO is an NGO, which was set up in 2007 as a voice of concern and criticism of the UN Global Compact and often accuses the compact of "blue-washing," which references companies that use the blue laurel leaf logo to show their affiliation with the Global Compact. Even in view of the "blue-washing" criticism, the UN Global Compact is a model that can work, if enough partners join and maintain the principles.[30]

The Organization For Economic Co-Operation and Development (OECD), a forum where the governments of 30 democracies work together to address the economic, social, and environmental challenges of globalization, has released OECD Guidelines for Multinational Enterprises. The OECD member countries are: Australia, Austria, Belgium, Canada, the Czech Republic, Denmark, Finland, France, Germany, Greece, Hungary, Iceland, Ireland, Italy, Japan, Korea, Luxembourg, Mexico, the Netherlands, New Zealand, Norway, Poland, Portugal, the Slovak Republic, Spain, Sweden, Switzerland, Turkey, the United Kingdom, and the United States.[31]

The organization has published the *OECD Guidelines for Multinational Enterprises* in which they outline an infrastructure for sustaining ethical standards of operation, which are a balance of a commitment of political leadership and sufficient public involvement and scrutiny. More specifically, there is a Legislative Framework as well as accountability and oversight. Guidance comes in the form of Codes of Conduct and management comes in the form of a combination of the managing body and Public Service Conditions. The OECD also publishes a Reference Checklist, which sets forth questions such as:

- Are the principles and standards clear?
- Are ethical principles being practiced?
- Is the accountability and oversight adequate?
- What are the procedures and sanctions for wrongdoing?

They also provide guidance with respect to factors leading to trust in government, which is an essential component of sustaining ethical standards. Without trust in government, regulations and legislation are viewed as a determent to an organization's sustainability. Keys to restoring faith in governmental oversight include:

- Defining a clear public service mission.
- Safeguarding values while adapting to change.
- Empowering public servants and citizens to report misconduct.
- Integrating integrity measures to overall management.[32]

The Clinton Global Initiative

Established in 2005 by President Bill Clinton, the Clinton Global Initiative (CGI) convenes global leaders to create and implement innovative solutions to the world's most pressing challenges. CGI Annual Meetings have brought together more than 150 heads of state, 20 Nobel Prize laureates, and hundreds of leading CEOs, heads of foundations and NGOs, major philanthropists, and members of the media. To date, CGI members have made more than 2,100 commitments, which have already improved the lives of nearly 400 million people in more than 180 countries. When fully funded and implemented, these commitments will be valued at $69.2 billion.[33]

> *"The world's best thinking must occur now, be embraced by business, and have leaders who have shared a vision for the value of human life, the necessity for a high moral ground in decision-making, and the political will to both articulate and transform this vision into reality."[34] The world cannot wait!*

The defining feature of CGI is a call to action, which is a comprehensive plan for addressing significant global challenges. Commitments can be small or large and financial or nonmonetary in nature. Many commitments are the result of cross-sectorial partnerships, with CGI members combining efforts to expand their impact. To date, CGI members have made more than 2,300 Commitments to Action, which have improved the lives of over 400 million people in more than 180 countries. Regardless of the size or scope of a project, every CGI Commitment must meet three basic criteria:

1. A CGI commitment is a plan that presents a new idea or approach to a major challenge. While preexisting work is not eligible,

an expansion of a successful program also qualifies as a valid Commitment to Action. Additionally, participants can become partners on other CGI commitments, for example, by providing in-kind support or technical expertise.

2. A CGI commitment must outline a specific approach to a problem, have clear and feasible objectives to be accomplished within a defined period of time, and articulate the desired outcome of the effort.

3. A CGI commitment must have specific quantitative or qualitative goals that can be monitored by the commitment-maker to evaluate progress over time. As each commitment is implemented, annual progress is reported to CGI to show the extent of its impact.[35]

Private Sector Solutions

Oftentimes, there is the hope or belief that if a problem or challenge in any area of our lives is committed to the intervention of the private sector, then the results will come fast and the solutions will be implemented at a faster and more efficient rate. This is often the case as in the superior and efficient performance of private companies such as UPS or FedEx, which so outperform the US Post Office, which as we speak is bankrupt. However, what happens all too often is that the void is filled by the private sector, which merely hijacks the movement, capitalizes on the urgency for implementation, and is driven more by profit than a defined and strict focus on or passion for the real subject matter.[36]

One example of this is Corpedia, founded by Alex Brigham in Phoenix, Arizona in 1998. Brigham had been thinking about ethics and corporate governance for a long time providing the service to corporations of creating their mission statements and a code of conduct. Initially, he not only had to sell his product, he had to explain why a company needed more than what was currently in place. It was an educational process to convince a company to pay an outside vendor to review their operation and make recommendations on mission, vision, and compliance with ethical standards or create them anew. Most companies at the time would be only interested in superficial statements or what we today call "green wash." When companies such as Enron, World Com, Tyco, and MCI, and others made the nightly news for their guess what….lack of corporate governance and failed moral conduct, Brigham was now in vogue. Corporations were forced into a path of compliance, both by the public and by government regulation.[37]

Rather than owning the responsibility for teaching and coaching men and women into becoming leaders and themselves {the schools of business} being the mirror for the world, schools of business have stayed with the case method and continued to teach from the academic model of classical leadership definitions and theory, and not much else. How can people who are strictly academics do much more?

NYSSE Euronext bought Corpedia in 2011; this purchase, by the philanthropic arm of the NYSE, signals a serious understanding that the commercial world has no choice but to take the corporate social responsibility to the next level. The question remains are we doing the right things for the wrong reason and how do we get our hands around oversight.[38]

Brigham now takes over Ethisphere Institute, which is a company he created as an arm of Corpedia in 2007 and calls itself a think tank for ethical issues. Ethisphere is an organization that represents the best ideas around as a way to measure corporate social responsibility and presents the kind of "good housekeeping" seal of approval for leaders and corporations, who can prove they are applying best practices to the requirements of corporate social responsibility in areas such as governance and risk. Ethisphere provides seminars and conferences for education and offers consulting services for all the needs of a corporation in terms of compliance training. The company promotes their selections for the most ethical companies in social media and other media outlets. To be selected by Ethisphere as an ethical company is a coveted title. It is like the good housekeeping seal of approval, only more people know about this seal. The idea is that if your corporation receives the "blessing" of a company such as Ethisphere for putting into place best practices for social responsibility, your stock goes up, literally.[39]

The discussion around the triple bottom-line, people, planet, and profit begins to inform a new paradigm that the Harvard Business

School and many schools of business now espouse. (Scott, 2012) It is
a charge that is taken seriously, as in times past what we said or did
in the classroom was purely academic. What is widely acknowledged
currently is that what we say and do in the classroom should be the
mirror by which society sees itself.

Francesca Rheannon, in her blog for *CSRwireTalkBack,* simply titles
her review of Brigham's move to Ethisphere as *It Pays To Be Ethical: A*
Conversation With Corpedia Founder Alex Brigham. The title alone says
it all, Brigham cashed in when Corpedia was sold, which is the way capitalism works. However, this leads directly to the oversight question, the
private sector may operate, as Brigham does, with an attempt to bring
some standardization to the process, but the obvious hazards exist. Who
pays for it...all of it? Well, in this case, the corporations who are vying
for the good housekeeping seal of approval. However, Bingham contends, they do not pay much. So what is much? Also, note that the
offices of Ethisphere are still housed with Corpedia, and while Bingham
contends, an arm's length distance is maintained over conflict of interest
potential, the reality is evident.[40]

Will Evans' article, of March 2012 titled, *It's All Good: Beware the*
corporate consulting firms offering awards for corporate ethics is worth noting and ruminates on the issue that is so painfully obvious. The idea
that all companies want to be on "the list," whether it is the list for best
companies to work for or most friendly to working mothers, or Ethisphere's yearly list of World's Most Ethical Companies, is clearly
defined by how much we observe these lists and make decisions on
what the lists imply. Evans' investigation of some individuals, who are
listed as committee members who helped to define the methods used,
and well-known ethicists, revealed they were not connected to the organization and for some, did not know their name was attached. In addition, the information that is collected is, by in large, self-reported by the
corporation. Ethisphere does ask for documentation from the survey
information that is collected. While Evans notes, as a consensus, that
these awards may be useful to stir dialogue, the opposite can be equally
powerful. He recounts a previous conversation: "Last year, while working on another story, I was interviewing a corporate spokesman about

allegations of fraud against his company and government fines for a radioactive waste spill. He sent me a press release trumpeting the news that Ethisphere had named his engineering and construction firm, CH2M Hill, one of the 'World's Most Ethical.' It 'speaks for itself,' he said. If only he knew".[41] This is not to say that companies like Ethisphere are not providing a service; however, the ability of a private sector enterprise to monitor itself is improbable at best and unlikely at worst, and the rest of that story is that public agencies are often vagrant to politics and skewed public opinion.

As we come, by choice or by force, to explore in cooperation with other countries how best to gather and distribute the planet's resources, we will need the spiritual core in the template.

Important to note, and a most likely model for what needs to manifest to move the social justice we so desire in the world, stands The World Justice Project (WSJ), founded by former Microsoft attorney and president of the American Bar Association, William Nukom, in 2006. WSJ has as its mission statement: "To lead a global movement to strengthen the rule of law for the development of communities of opportunity and equity." The 501 (c)(3) stakeholders are from around the world and the list of corporate partnerships are growing (see the website http://worldjusticeproject.org/). The WJP on its website describes itself as: (quoted directly)

"an independent, non-profit organization, develops communities of opportunity and equity by advancing the rule of law worldwide. The rule of law helps people and communities thrive. Effective rule of law helps reduce corruption, improve public health, enhance education, lift people from poverty and protect them from injustices and dangers large and small. The World Justice Project is one of the world's foremost resources on the importance of the rule of law. The World Justice Project engages leaders in countries across the globe and from all work disciplines to advance the rule of law. Through its three complementary and mutually reinforcing

The World Justice Project

program areas of Research and Scholarship, Rule of Law Index, and Mainstreaming. The WJP seeks to stimulate government reforms that enhance the rule of law, develop practical programs in support of the rule of law at the community level, and increase public awareness about the concept and practice of the rule of law worldwide."[42]

The error or sin committed by corporations and countries in relation to oil, on which so much of the world is dependent, is that it was easy to take and use without regard to any price other than the monetary reward.

The most significant thing that the WSJ brings to the table and what sets it apart from other organizations promoting social justice is measurability with the rule of law index. The WSJ defines the rule of law index as: (quoted directly)

"The WJP Rule of Law Index® is an innovative quantitative assessment tool designed by the World Justice Project offering a detailed and comprehensive picture of the extent to which countries adhere to the rule of law in practice. It provides original data regarding a variety of dimensions of the rule of law, enabling the assessment of a nation's adherence to the rule of law in practice, identify a nation's strengths and weaknesses in comparison to similarly situated countries, and track changes over time."[43]

Note that the United States ranks 17 out of the countries of the world accessed according to this index. The index itself makes a strong statement as to comparisons among countries, and the value system in place in the countries. Note: While it may be that China is not fully prepared to be a country operating under the rule of law, at a conference celebrating the 30th anniversary of the constitution of China, January 8, 2012, Meng Jianzhu, head of the CPC Political and Legal Affairs Commission, declared that China embraces the rule of law. This public declaration indicates that the political leadership of China the value of the rule of law and shows a bowing to the will of business and the public.[44]

This is obvious to many, I think, and power rests with the corporation—in this case, with the large world corporations in energy, technology, health care, and possibly social media—that take a longer look and do the things we know must be done.

Supplemental Reading

The following are scholarly and peer-reviewed journal articles, conference proceedings, and dissertations on the concepts discussed in this chapter.

- *Thinking with Your Soul: Spiritual Intelligence and Why It Matters*, Richard Wolman, Harmony Books March 13, 2001
- The Seven Dimensions of Spiritual Intelligence: An Ecumenical, Grounded Theory, Yosi Amram, Institute of Transpersonal Psychology, Palo Alto, CA, Paper Session on 8/19/07, Presented at the 115th Annual Conference of the American Psychological Association
- How to Bounce Back from Adversity, Joshua D. Margolis and Paul G. Stoltz, *Harvard Business Review*, January 2010.[45]

Postscript | How I Know This Is So!

As individuals, we are simply microcosms of the macrocosm, and in order for the larger ship to right itself, we must put our personal house in order. How can the body heal itself if the head or the hands are not whole? I must say that I like reading about the new dean at Harvard, Nitan Nohria; possibly, it is his cultural sense of deference when he speaks that makes his messages so compelling. He speaks of being awed by his own position as dean of possibly the most highly regarded business school in the world, and how sacredly he holds this trust. He pointedly says that a major shift for the business school is the recognition that it is the responsibility of the school to create ethical leaders. In August 2011, Harvard business school made a complete overhaul of its curriculum, putting ethics at the core of the overhaul, along with entrepreneurship and leadership. When asked how one teaches character building, Dr. Nohria explained the tension between the understanding of one's responsibilities as business leaders and the capacity to live up to those, when faced with pressure and temptation, has to be explored. It is necessary, he asserts, to cultivate a moral humility to know that your moral compass might fail you, and if it does, to recognize it and be prepared with a plan on how to handle the test. He mitigates the assumption that moral character building is only a product of the early home life; he sees it as a life-long process. The Dean says that the test is not to see what leaders do in the face of adversity; rather, it is to see what they do with absolute power.[46]

Life is lessons and the lessons are intended for the soul or spirit. Thus, the message to all of us is that as individuals, we must find our moral humility, be realistic about who we are, and know that with this acknowledgement of our human frailty, a way can be made. If we are prepared when we do have absolute power with the strength of the mind, body, and the spirit, we have a chance. In the same manner, the corporation has the same absolute power over people, planet, and profit. The large multinational corporations have the opportunity to build on their strength and use their absolute power wisely.

Life is lessons and the lessons are intended for the soul or spirit.

People tend to try to delay the inevitable or run away from a situation, rather than face it and resolve to do the right thing. Remember, we are talking about "fixing" us as individuals and leaders in positions of power and influence first, as the way to "fix" the corporation world over.

The experiences we have on the journey are intended for the soul or spirit to grow and to move in the direction of light. Light is empathy, love, truth, wisdom, courage, and a sense of prosperity about life.

The rest of this story is that we cannot escape the lessons, and the lessons are the same no matter the social level; in other words, it matters not whether we are butcher, baker, or candlestick maker. The lessons are the same and are for the same purpose: to develop the spirit and move us along. In our vanity, we often try to skip the lessons. We think if we change careers, companions, houses, or geographies, or run off to a desert island, we can escape our lesson. Not so! Like the man listening to the witness in the dream about meeting death at the West Gate, we cannot use our minds to avoid, change, or escape our lessons. Life will keep coming at us until we learn the lesson; we will continue to repeat the lesson until we get it right, individually or collectively. Like Bill Murray in that old movie, *Groundhog's Day*,[47] which I think is the most secular, spiritual movie of all time, we will wake every morning and repeat the same pattern until we solve the mystery. The mystery is in being awake to the lesson and embracing our accountability in what happens to us. We create our own reality as we go along, and the light only comes when we acknowledge the spiritual and use this as the lens through which to see our choices and assume responsibility.

Closing Thoughts

We must have faith in ourselves, faith in the future, and faith that once we rebuild ourselves and our corporations with spiritual values, and unite the trinity of the mind, body, and soul, our focus will be clear and our path, more productive. The restoration of the soul will not be an overnight process, and the culture for this transformation must come from the top. Only we can save ourselves. Challenges will not go away and lessons will remain part of the human condition, but we will view them through this new lens. We must see that our leaders are not just doing things right to produce stockholder rewards, but that they become real leaders who are always, and in all things, doing the right thing.

The restoration of the soul will not be an overnight process, and the culture for this transformation must come from the top.

Once we transform our thinking at the individual level, we are ready to be part of the collective conscious of the corporation that defines and embraces its spiritual core. We split the trinity, and the outcome has created a productivity that we can rightfully be proud of and a pattern that worked, if not always ethically, at least we had the rule of law at the end, through most of the 20th century. The old phrase "if it ain't broke, don't fix it" has kept us mesmerized and fixated, but we have allowed many things to go unchecked. Most of all, we have ignored the missing piece: the soul. Leaders must first identify within themselves the spiritual core.[48] Remember the words that Jung put over the door of his house in the country (also placed on his tombstone): "Called or not, God is present".[49]

Once and for all, it is not about the money; we merely think it is. Money is just a code word with a universality to it that allows it to be bandied about as if we could all agree on something. The perfect storm has arrived; we have a serious depletion of natural resources, a world financial collapse, a huge gap between the haves and have-nots world over, the disease and poverty of the Third World countries that will surely come to developed countries, the political instability of the Arab world, impending war in more than one place, and a world ennui that far surpasses any historical knowledge of such a state. It is now (© the end of 2012), and I think Israel may bomb Iran. War!

We are afraid to talk about the spiritual life because we fear being branded as not being open minded or being nonintellectual and weak.

There are signs of attempted course correction:

- the embracing of the concept of corporate social responsibility
- the green movement for sustainability

- shareholders who are directly involved with the operation of a company, some companies that are employee-owned
- boards who are exercising their fiduciary and moral responsibility to the employees
- a few emerging leaders who take the long view and care more about the company than themselves or immediate profit
- leaders and world corporations that understand and embrace the principle of steady and secure growth.

These course corrections, while an acknowledgment that it is time for action, are not to critical mass; they are coming so late in the game and are not the total or singular answer. The missing piece is the acknowledgment by the most powerful entity in our world, the corporation, of that spiritual part of man that has been very much left behind. We are afraid to talk about the spiritual life because we fear being branded as not being open-minded or being nonintellectual and weak. We are so afraid of this; in fact, it is as if we are afraid not of our failure, but of our success. To acknowledge the spirit does not dictate the embracing of a specific religion in any form, and I think this presents the challenge. How do we seek the soul without the patterns and stories of the varied practiced faiths? The answer: we do not have to. The religious practices and stories present universal truths and offer guidance for the care and keeping of the soul. They may be embraced literally or metaphorically, and by either way, the patterns are clear, graphic in detail, and strong. Sacred texts and all great literature, art, and music have grappled significantly with the human condition and offer clarity on the spiritual core of our humanness. This holds true as long as we are not looking for forces outside ourselves to save us.

It is time for us to connect the dots and bring together our traditions, history, science, and cultural codes and beliefs to make one picture for civilization.

Barbara Kellerman in her new book, *The End of Leadership*,[50] discusses her 40-year journey in teaching and watching leadership, and she is worried, and so am I. When leadership is seen as a path to money and fame, as is the case for so many students in MBA and EMBA programs in the most prestigious business schools in the country, something is wrong with the plan. When we have been at this business of teaching leadership, which is now an industry with all manners of people teaching and training leaders, and as Kellerman points out, it has not gotten better and in fact, it is worse, there is reason for a paradigm shift. I know that with the democratization of the workforce a new breed of leader has and is emerging; however, it will not be enough for someone who leads to become a strong team player. Rather, leadership will require a soul where wisdom, a strong moral compass, and a sense of humanitarian purpose reside. It is time for us to connect the dots and bring together our traditions, history, science, and cultural codes and beliefs to make one picture for civilization. These are desperate times and desperate times call for men and women who possibly have not thought of assuming leadership roles, to step up to the plate; and for those who are currently destined to assume the reigns of leadership to seize this moment and find the courage to be spiritually, as well as physically and mentally prepared. To the men and women who are in leadership and power places today, the game is over and the peasants revolt. Not just in the United States, but also across the world order, current leadership is challenged, and we will not know peace until we have quelled the demons spawned by a two-dimensional view of life and the world, as the mind and the body. The spirit must have its day.

The crucible for corporations and leaders will be transparent, and the fire of our collective experience will have burned the dross and will demand the journey to sustainability for the planet. It is time. I believe that the strongest power to make this happen resides in our collective conscious and can be reached through prayer or meditation that focuses on the vision of the unity of mind, body, and spirit. However, the real instrument to make this a reality is the resurgence of the soul in the global corporate consciousness—the soul that produces real moral leaders who are more concerned about their people than their product, and the soul where wisdom resides and guides all members of the corporate family to a place of real power that will serve the greatest good for the greatest number of people. We must move to a global consciousness that is aware of its own humanity and the spiritual oneness with our fellow travelers. A simple acknowledgment of the power of a divine nature within us all would be an amazing first start!

The crucible for corporations and leaders will be transparent, and the fire of our collective experience will have burned the dross and will demand the journey to corporate wellness. It is time!

Date Stamp @ July 12, 2012

Today's news (@ July 12, 2012) is yet another date stamp we cannot ignore. On this date the Freeh Report was released stating that there was sufficient evidence that the leadership of Penn State University, including Head Football Coach, the legendary Joe Paterno had knowledge of and engaged in covering up evidence with respect to Jerry Sandusky's ongoing sexual abuse of young boys. It was clear that the leadership of Penn State for years elected to put their football program above the welfare and protection of countless children who were sexually abused over a period of at least 10 years. The real cost of the Penn State tragedy may never be entirely measured. No matter what the courts do or what punishment is meted out, it will not in any way compensate for the evil that was given permission to exist or restore the reputation of the University. Who could ever again go to a football game at Penn State's "Happy Valley" and not feel nauseated or horrified. The scandal is forever now part of the collective consciousness of Penn State that marks the worst of the human condition, which allows profit to overshadow every element of morality and human dignity. In his Thursday press conference (@ July 12, 2012), Freeh mentioned the Penn State janitors who saw Sandusky molesting a boy in the shower. One, a Korean War veteran, called the scene "the worst thing I ever saw." Nevertheless, he and the other janitors decided not to report it. They didn't want to get fired. "If that's the culture on the bottom," Freeh said, "God help the culture on the top." Yes. A thousand times, yes. And God help the channel-changing culture in the middle, too.

This scandal and the associated fallout has already become the topic of academic papers. (@ September 16, 2012), Dr. Bill George, professor of Management Practice, Henry B. Arthur Fellow of Ethics, at Harvard Business School says "Many leaders strive for such a high degree of perfection that they are unwilling to admit mistakes." He goes on to point out that when leaders bow to external pressure to be perfect, they often create a problem that is much larger in scope and that in this viral world, the truth cannot be hidden for long. Dr. George feels strongly that authenticity is a critical component of effective leadership.[51]

The list is long now of putting profit above people and of failed leadership to tell the truth and own responsibility for actions: ....the Catholic Church, Enron, Madoff, the Japanese Government, and Wall Street, Penn State, Political Parties. If we are to have a sustainable future then leaders must come forward who create, lead, and model a culture that emanates from a place of truth and integrity. The crucible for corporations and leaders will be transparent, and the fire of our collective experience will have burned the dross and will demand that only leaders present who have the vision of a world united by the need to manage world resources, care for all people, and the planet as they make profit. It is time!

A Leader's Guide to Fostering Spirituality in the Workplace | Seven Steps

- **Know your story**. I ran from my story for many years. Covering up for what seemed a crazy background, and full of dysfunction. It was not until I was in my late twenties and on a real path to higher education that I was able to come to terms with my personal story. Things, to which I had attached no value, in my story became clear as essential experiences that brought me to a clear understanding of who I was, and what I needed to be doing, and why. I realized that my story was a significant one and that it had brought me, in some unbelievable ways, to a powerful place of influence. Before one can become what it is their soul's destiny to be, it is essential that the inward journey is made with a specific purpose to know yourself. Socrates said: "The unexamined life is not worth living." For persons who dine to lead, it is a pre-requisite.

- **Face your fear**. The greatest fear that an individual faces is, of course, the fear of failure (or of great success) or of failing in the eyes of another person. Interestingly, we are not so much concerned with reality, just the perception that others hold. Get into the dark with yourself and have the conversation. If you know you own demons, no one can ever use them against you.

- **Know where you are in the Cycle.** Life and business are a cycle and the need to know and surround yourself with people who are connected at many levels to what is happening in the world is essential. You must also have the talent to interpret what these things mean for you, your people, and the greater commitment, to all the stakeholders, including the planet as well as the profit. Keeping your people safe for the short and long term has to be part of your plan.

- **Know your corporate DNA.** Leaders fail so often because they become myopic and do not read the signs of impending disaster from without or opposition from within. Leaders simply become too busy and stop walking around: Old idea, but one that has a new imperative today because of the loss of trust in leaders, and the fears about the economy. Too frequently, the leader begins to take the people for granted and cannot see what is so obvious to others. Know the history of your company, literally and from an emotional level develop an understanding beyond the superficial. As the leader, you are in charge of creating the culture, but you cannot create without the consent of the created.

- **Consult outside models and look for solutions worldwide.** The leader, who stays with such an internal view of just the company or even of the industry in the world today, is at best foolish, and at the worst, lost. World events impact and influence at the local level and even in our homes. Leaders must connect the dots, look, and listen for the larger patterns that forecast or warn or tell of a coming shift.

- **Take the long view, always.** Seeking short-term profit or forming short-term strategy to maneuver through a crisis is the formula for disaster. The leader must act as though the company is his/hers for a 100 years and with this attitude make decisions and plans for the way forward. A company is a commitment not a short course in cause and effect.

- **Now the global is the local.** A leader who is not thinking and going global is going bankrupt. Travel just briefly to the major cities of Europe, Japan, the Middle East, India, Russia, Brazil, or China and the reality of this becomes obvious. We are so connected and integrated that we must understand the world as our market place. This is not to be entered into lightly or without cultural awareness and understanding, both of yours and of your new neighbors. Leaders can no longer merely benchmark against their own sphere.

APPENDIX

Where We Go From Here

Additional Thoughts on the attributes, the ways of being, and the state of mind required for Leadership in the 21st century and how to acquire the attributes, develop the ways of being, and how to create and sustain the requisite state of mind:

On Becoming a Leader: The Berry Rules!

- A business today that is not thinking global will be out of business soon.
- To lead people well, you must first understand yourself.
- If you do not like some of the things you see on your interior journey, take them out, put them on the table, and speak to them.
- Be in control of the self-talk in your head; you are the only one who controls this message.
- If you are always chasing your own demons, you have little time to live into the vision you have of yourself as a leader. Leader, heal thyself.
- Throughout the organization and across the board, people need to believe they are important and that their opinion matters…really. People also need to believe that the leader has strong convictions and a steadfast moral compass.
- We create our own reality, and then we live in it. Honoring the power of our own minds to create is the first step in acquiring the power to lead.
- Involve yourself in something other than what you consider your profession; find a passion, and let that become your identity along with your official title.
- Leaders must have some kind of physicality in their daily routine.

- If you look disheveled and not put together, how can I trust you? Optics are everything. Whether it is a dress suit or a wet suit, you must look strong. The world needs strong.
- The ability to articulate your vision in language that can be heard is mandatory. To have the idea in your head is one thing; to put it in into the heads of those you lead is another.
- Securing social justice may not be possible, considering the general human condition; but if I do not sense that you believe it is what should be a reality, I will not follow you.
- Make sure you want to lead and are willing to make the tough calls. Wearing the mantel of power can be a heavy weight.
- Leaders are born, not made. They are men and women who then are shaped by the crucible of experience, and in whom the ability to lead connects with the willingness to make the commitment to be not your own.
- It takes real guts to say the buck stops here, when it originates somewhere else. If you cannot take responsibility for all of it, you should not try to assume leadership for any of it.
- You must value truth over everything; and you must select to surround yourself with people who are committed to truth above their jobs.
- There is no substitute for doing your own homework. When you rely on others, you give away your power.
- If you still believe in the command and control model, try the servant–leader model on for size.
- If you cannot name it for your company and for yourself, you cannot have it for yourself or your company. Naming it has power in and of itself.

On Becoming a Leader: Some Berry Tips!

- Keep music playing in the background of your office that helps to set the tone for your day.
- Make sure the art on the wall is strong; no flowers please. Colors set the tone for conversation and should be selected for what makes you "feel" good.

- Make sure that the people to whom you give the most access in a day are strong critical thinkers and problem solvers; you can watch your own back. No "yes" people need apply.
- Decide what kind of access you want people to have to you. Consider your own personality and the culture you are creating. For example, look at the major shift in leadership style between Steve Jobs and Tim Cook. Your door is always open, or it is not. Be clear.
- If you are not happy, pleased, and satisfied no one will be happy, pleased, satisfied; be happy! Your body language is everything; learn to talk with your body, and remember if you walk, you talk. It is a commitment to be self-aware at all times. The self-awareness must be natural, so if you are not self-aware, you must practice.
- You will only receive what you give. Understand that you are a mirror and that what you are receiving is what people see in you.
- The daily routine should not be a routine.
- Be consistent in your dress; people like to know what is coming in the door every day. Consistence is mandatory in business. Having a tailor is mandatory and someone who dresses you, if you do not have time or taste. Do not ask advice of your spouse or significant other.
- Be as careful and thoughtful with casual clothes as with the formal attire. Clothes always make the man or the woman. This never changes.
- Business etiquette is essential knowledge for doing business. International rules need to be understood and practiced. To be ignorant or naïve is irresponsible business.
- If you believe that you must separate your personal life from your professional life, you do not understand business life. There is only one life.
- You must be precise about what you want—even the food you order.
- Use both high-level intuition and sensing in every decision you make.
- Always be complimenting and speaking well of others. Gossip is not an option.

- Personal relationships should be eclectic and varied. Homogeneous grouping is not healthy.
- Always be on time....for everything.
- If you are not always genuinely and authentically busy, you should be.
- If others trust you, you have arrived.
- Be soft spoken and talk slowly and articulately.
- Be generous with your time and money; you will have more than you think.
- If you are not highly credentialed, start now. Harvard seminars or workshops on leadership are a place to begin.
- Only speak to something if you know the facts; never speculate.

There will be more to come on *Leadership Best Practices* for the 21st century.

Notes

Preface

1. O'Connor (2002).
2. Friedman (1970).
3. Malerba (2010).
4. Malerba (2010).
5. Pew Forum on Religion & Public Life (2012), p. 9.
6. Pew Forum on Religion & Public Life (2012).
7. Genesis, 4:9, KJV.
8. Donne (1624).
9. National Commission on Terrorist Attacks Upon the United States (2004).
10. Warren Commission (1964)
11. Personal communication, World Affairs Council, UNF (March 6, 2010).
12. Schurz (2009); Freedom (2009).
13. Joints Chief of Staff (2012).
14. Markoe (2012).
15. Romans, 12:21, KJV.
16. Aaron Goldstein on 9.11.12 @ 1:32PM American Spectator Blog; Goldstein (2012).
17. Iran Chamber Society (2012).
18. Rinke (2011).
19. Krugman (2012).
20. Blair (2010).
21. Kagan (2012).
22. Buchanan (1999).
23. Gladstone (2012).
24. Boot (2012).
25. Asseburg (2012).
26. Auslin (2012).
27. Walt (2012).
28. Higgins (2012).
29. Zakaria (2012).
30. Kagan (2012).
31. World Bank (2012).
32. Xuetong (2006).
33. Kagan (2012).

34. Kaplan (2012).
35. White (2011).

Chapter 1

1. Zakaria, The Post-American World (2008).
2. Shapiro (2009).
3. National Information Center (2012).
4. The Economist (2011).
5. Genesis, 19:26, KJV.
6. US Bureau of Labor Statistics (2012).
7. Anderson (2011).
8. Barakat (2012).
9. Schultz (2009).
10. Piereson (2005).
11. US Geology Survey (2012).
12. Leland & Oboroceanu (2010).
13. Smithstonian Institute.
14. Hemingway (2003).
15. Hayoun (2012).
16. Friedman (2011).
17. Harvard (2011).
18. Rogers (2012).
19. Hemingway (2003).
20. Aboy (2010).
21. Selig (2011).
22. Earle (2009).
23. Kermis (2009).
24. Margolis (2010).
25. Walt (2012).
26. Pierog (2011).
27. Touryalai (2012).
28. Boje (2002).
29. Romano (2005).
30. Mercatus Center George Mason University (2012).
31. KJV Ecclesiastes (2:11).
32. Guanzhong (1300–1400).
33. World Economic Forum (2012).
34. Axton (1969).
35. Bryant (2010).
36. Hernandez (June 16, 2011).

37. KJV Isaiah (53:6).
38. Myss Defy Gravity (2009).
39. KoranAn-Naba (78:31–34).
40. Genesis, KJV.
41. Rhodes (2006).
42. Bellah (2004).
43. Rhodes (2006).
44. Mc Laughlin (2009).
45. Oppenheimer (2012).
46. Hellenic International Studies in the Arts (2012).
47. Vervaeck (2011).
48. Cunningham (2012).
49. Clark Matthew (2010).
50. Google (2012).
51. Google (2012).
52. World Economic Forum (2012).
53. Google (2012).
54. Patagonia (2012).
55. Leone (2010).
56. Hoover's (2012).
57. Patagonia (2012).
58. Patagonia (2012).
59. Patagonia (2012).
60. Patagonia (2012).
61. Patagonia (2012).
62. Patagonia (2012).
63. Storm (1996).
64. Patagonia (2012).
65. Chouinard (2011).
66. Elliot (1964).
67. Working Mother (2012).
68. Chouinard (2011).

Chapter 2

1. Allen (2007).
2. Allen (2007).
3. Edwards (2012).
4. Thornbury (2003).
5. Clough (2011).
6. Newton (1934).
7. Kant (1784).

8. Sorrow (2011).
9. Zakaria (2008), p. 258.
10. Brokaw (1998).
11. Jefferson (2011).
12. Exodus 23:10, KJV.
13. Proverbs 14:23 KJV.
14. Quran, 9:34.
15. Easwaran (1985).
16. Bhagavad Gita, 16:21.
17. Tao Te Ching (46).
18. New York Times (2012).
19. Ford Motor Company (2007).
20. Saturday Evening Post (1925).
21. Ford Motor Company (2012).
22. Cavanaugh (2006).
23. Ford.Media.com (2006).
24. Ford Motor Company (2007).
25. Ford Motor Company (2011/2012).
26. Motor Trend (2008).
27. Strategos, Inc. (2012).
28. Ford Motor Company (2012).
29. Ford Motor Company (2012).
30. UN Global Compact.
31. Ford Motor Company.
32. Ford Motor Company (2012).
33. Environmental Protection Agency (2012).
34. Ford Motor Company (2012).
35. Leggett (1999).
36. Bowman (2004).
37. Garcia-Zamor (2003).
38. Moore (2008).

Chapter 3

1. Zunz (2012).
2. Starke (2012); World Bank (2012).
3. Damast (2010).
4. Bray (2012).
5. Schectman (2011).
6. Berrett (2010).
7. Robertson (2010).

8. Fortune, (2012).
9. Grey (1918).
10. Hanhimäki (2008).
11. The Better World Campaign (2012).
12. The Economic Times (2011).
13. Plett (2012).
14. Unger (2012).
15. Till (2011).
16. The Journal of Turkish Weekly (2012).
17. Petersmann (2002).
18. United Nations (2011).
19. Perez-Batres (2011).
20. Knudsen (2011).
21. Waddell (2011).
22. Schwartz (2011).
23. Thomson Reuters (2010).
24. Carr (2012).
25. Smith (2011).
26. Kagan, (2003).
27. UN Global Compact, (2012).
28. Accenture (2012).
29. Accenture (2010).
30. United Nations (2012).
31. United Nations (2012).
32. United Nation (2010).
33. Accenture release findings of largest CEO study on corporate sustainability (2010).
34. personal communication (November 20, 2012).
35. Accenture (2010).
36. Waddell, (2011).
37. Perez-Batres (2011).
38. Knudsen (2011).

Chapter 4

1. Bennis (1989).
2. Securities and Exchange Commission (2012).
3. The Financial Crisis Inquiry Commission (2011).
4. Isaacson (2011).
5. Pappu (2011).
6. Pappu (2011).

7. Nohria (2012).
8. Kaku (1997).
9. Kaku (1997).
10. Kaku (1997).
11. Winslow (2012).
12. Ignatova (2012).
13. Bair (2012).
14. Rand (1957).
15. Business Mode Institute (2012).
16. Goldman (2012).
17. Empower Network (2012).
18. Wilson (2010).
19. Longman (2006).
20. Collins Good to Great (2001).
21. Collins Great by Choice (2011).
22. Raice (2012).
23. Collins Great by Choice (2011).
24. Hyatt (2009).
25. Brown (2006).
26. Bush (2010).
27. Lewis (2006).
28. Champion (2011).
29. Hamilton (1942).
30. Do One Thing (2012).
31. Cyclinglim (2012).
32. Golluoglu (2012).
33. Suu (1990).
34. Friedman (2012).
35. Kaku (1997).

Chapter 5

1. Mayo (2011).
2. Lucchetti (2012).
3. Mayo (2011).
4. Weber (2008).
5. Fourth Sector (2012).
6. Strom (2007).
7. Clift (2010).
8. Collins (2011).
9. Clinton Global Initiative (2012).

10. Financial Freedom Inspiration (2012).
11. World Health Organization (2009).
12. Oseni (2012).
13. Ashoka (2007).
14. Financial Freedom Inspiration (2012).
15. Ashoka (2007).

Chapter 6

1. Jung (1961).
2. Franklin (2011).
3. Benedict (2007).
4. Covey (1989).
5. Sacirbey (2011).
6. Tyson Foods, Inc. (2010).
7. Ethisphere (2008).
8. Tyson Foods, Inc. (2012).
9. United States *v.* Tyson Foods, Inc. (1998).
10. Copeland (2001).
11. Stewart (2011).
12. Vinjamuri (2012) para 3.
13. Vinjamuri (2012).
14. Tyson Food, Inc. (2012).
15. National Information Center (2012).

Chapter 7

1. Shakespeare (1928).
2. Nohria (2012).
3. Le Boutillier (January 10, 2002).
4. Scott (2012)
5. Boston, William (2012).
6. World Economic Forum (2012).
7. Rosenthal (2012).
8. Pickins (2012).
9. International Monetary Fund (2012).
10. Bibow (2009).
11. Santayana (1905).
12. Ritschl (2012).
13. Ritschl (2012).

14. Van Rompuy (2012).
15. O' Carroll (2011).
16. Burgis (2012).
17. European Central Bank (2012).
18. Roubini (August 11, 2011).
19. World Justice Project (2012).
20. Berg (2003).
21. Fergus (2012).
22. CNBC (2009).
23. Myss (1997).
24. Soergel (2012).
25. Liautaud (2012).
26. Liautaud (2012).
27. Joint Inspection Unit (2010).
28. Agazzi (2011).
29. Agazzi (2011).
30. Agazzi (2011).
31. OECD (2008).
32. Armstrong (2003).
33. Clinton Global Iniatitive (2012).
34. Nohria, (2012).
35. Clinton Global Iniatitive (2012).
36. Stephenson (2012).
37. Rheannon (2012).
38. NYSE Euronext to Acquire Corpedia Corporation (2012).
39. Evans (2010).
40. Rheannon (2012).
41. Evans (2010).
42. World Justice Project (2012).
43. World Justice Project (2012).
44. Global Times (2013).
45. Margolis (2010).
46. Nohria (2012).
47. Ramis (1993).
48. Lehman (2012).
49. Associated Press (1961).
50. Kellerman (2012).
51. George (2012).

References

Aboy, M. (2010, August 15). *Are Derivatives 'Financial Weapons of Mass Destruction'? An Explanation of Why Derivatives are Controversial and Often Considered High Risk*. Retrieved October 10, 2012, from Social Science Research Network: http://www.researchgate.net/publication/228205429_Are _Derivatives_Financial_Weapons_of_Mass_Destruction_An_Explanation_of _Why_Derivatives_are_Controversial_and_Often_Considered_High_Risk

Adams, J. T. (1931) *The Epic of America*. New York. Blue Ribbon Books (pp. 214–215)

Ali Ahmad, Z. (2012). *Initiating the Incremental Impact by Shared Values: UNDP Pushes into High-Gear with Syria's Private Sector*. Retrieved from Business UN: http://business.un.org/en/documents/8872

Alighieri, D. (12th Century). *Dante's Inferno*. Italy.

Allen, J. T. (2007). *The Separation of Church and State: Myths, Mantras, Mandates*. Retrieved from Forum on Public Policy: http://forumonpublicpolicy. com/archivesum07/allen.tim.pdf

Amram, Y. (2007, August 19). *The Seven Dimensions of Spiritual Intelligence: An Ecumenical, Grounded Theory*. Retrieved October 11, 2012, from Yosi Amram: http://www.yosiamram.net/docs/7_Dimensions_APA_Accepted _Yosi_Amram.pdf

Anderson, L. (2011, June). Demystifying the Arab Spring. *Foreign Affairs*. Retrieved January 8, 2013, from Foreign Affairs http://www.foreignaffairs .com/articles/67693/lisa-anderson/demystifying-the-arab-spring

Anheuser Busch. (n.d.). Retrieved January 8, 2013 from http Anheuser Busch: http://anheuser-busch.com/index.php/our-heritage/history/

Asseburg, M. (2012). Protest, Revolt and Regime Change in the Arab World. Retrieved January 8, 2013 from *Stiftung Wissenschaft und Politik German Institute for International and Security Affairs*, 1–71.

Associated Press. (1961, June 7). *On This Day*. Retrieved October 11, 2012, from The New York Times: http://www.nytimes.com/learning/general/ onthisday/bday/0726.html

Auslin, M. (2012, September 19). *How Close are Japan and China to War?* Retrieved October 11, 2012, from National Review: http://www .nationalreview.com/corner/327794/how-close-are-japan-and-china-war -michael-auslin

Axton, H. (Composer). (1969). Joy to the World. [T. D. Night, Performer] Dunhill ABC Records.

Bair, S. (2012, September 25). *Sheila Bair on the Financial Crisis.* Retrieved October 10, 2012, from Economist View: http://economistsview.typepad .com/economistsview/financial_system/

Baker, L. (2011, November 16). *EU risks reopening Pandora's Box.* Taiwan: Retrieved January 8, 2013, from Reuters: http://www.reuters.com/article /2011/11/16/us-eu-treaty-idUSTRE7AF1BM20111116

Barakat, N. G. (2012, April 10). *Is Libya Entering a New Era of Violence or Peace?* Retrieved October 10, 2012, from The Tripoli Post: http://www .tripolipost.com/articledetail.asp?c=5&i=9254

Barrios-Choplin, B., Mccraty, R., Cryer, B. (1997, July) An Inner Quality Approach to Reducing Stress and Improving Physical and Emotional Well-being at Work, *Stress Medicine 13*(3), pl193–201.

Bellah, R. (2004). An interview published in *Tricycle: The Buddhist Review.* August, (New York, NY: The Tricycle Foundation).

Benedict, J. (2007). *The Mormon Way of Doing Business.* New York: Warner Business Books.

Bennis, W. (1989). *On Becoming a Leader.* Philadelphia: Basic Books.

Berg, R. P. (2003). *Taming Chaos: Harnessing the Power of Kabbalah to Make Sense of Our Lives (Technology for the Soul).* New York: Kabbalah Center.

Berrett, D. (2010, December 7). *Wharton, Rebooted.* Retrieved October 10, 2012, from Inside Higher Education: http://www.insidehighered.com /news/2010/12/07/wharton

Bibow, J. (2009, November). *The Euro and Its Guardian of Stability: The Euro and Its Guardian of Stability:* Retrieved October 10, 2012, from Bard College: http://www.levyinstitute.org/pubs/wp_583.pdf

Blair, T. (2010). *A Journey: My Political Life.* United States: Alfred A. Knopf.

Bloomberg, M. (2011, May). Mayor of New York City. (S. Pappu, Interviewer)

Boje, D. M. (2002, August 1). *Enron is Metatheatre.* Retrieved October 10, 2012, from New Mexico State University-College of Business: http://business .nmsu.edu/~dboje/enron/chronology.htm#actiIV

Boot, M. K. (2012, June 22). *Mr. Putin's Neighborhood.* Retrieved October 10, 2012, from Counsel on Foreign Relations: http://www.cfr.org/syria/mr -putins-neighborhood/p28837

Boston, William. (2012, January 28). Germany Calls for EU Control Over Greek Budget. Retrieved January 8, 2013 from *The Wall Street Journal* http://online .wsj.com/article/SB10001424052970204661604577188422134155212 .html

Bowman, T. (2004). Spirituality at Work: An Exploratory Sociological Investigation of the Ford Motor Company. (Thesis). Retrieved January 8, 2013 from Spirit at Work http://www.spiritatwork.org/library/bowman-tim-Spirituality %20at%20Work.pdf.

Bray, C. (2012, December 27). *Ex-Fund Manager Rajaratnam Resolves SEC Suit Over Gupta Tips*. Retrieved from The Wall Street Journal January 8, 2013: http://blogs.wsj.com/law/2012/12/27/ex-fund-manager-rajaratnam-resolves-sec-suit-over-gupta-tips/

Brokaw, T. (1998). *The Greatest Generation*. New York: Random House.

Brown, M. E., & Treviño, L. (2006). Ethical leadership: A review and future directions. *The Leadership Quarterly, 17* (2006) 595–616. Retrieved January 8, 2013 from https://elearn.wits.ac.za/usrfiles/context/padm5117/Leadership/Additional_Reading/Ethical_leadership_A_review_and_future_directions.pdf

Bryant, M., & Hunt, T. (2010, September/October). *BP and Public Issues (Mis) Management*. Retrieved January 8, 2013 from Ivey Business Journal: http://www.iveybusinessjournal.com/topics/leadership/bp-and-public-issues-mismanagement#.UITh0MXYE24

Buchanan, P. (1999). *A Republic, Not an Empire*. Washington, DC: Regency Publishing, Inc.

Burgis, T. (2012, September 12). *Eurozone live: German justice, Dutch election*. Retrieved January 8, 2013 from Financial Times: http://blogs.ft.com/the-world/2012/09/eurozone-live-german-justice/

Bush, G. (2010). *Decision Points*. New York: Random House.

Business Model Institute. (2012, October 6). *Blockbuster vs. Redbox Business Model*. Retrieved January 8, 2013 from Business Model Institute: http://businessmodelinstitute.com/what-is-a-business-model/

Canon. (2012, October 6). *Universal Design Guide*. Retrieved October 6, 2012, from Canon Global: http://www.canon.com/about/ud/guide/index.html

Carr, I. (2012, October 6). *Corruption in International Business*. Retrieved October 6, 2012, from IDEC, SA: http://idec.gr/iier/new/CORRUPTION%20CONFERENCE/Corruption%20in%20International%20Business-INDIRA%20CARR.pdf

Cavanaugh, G. F. (2006, November 13). *Ford Motor Company, Human Rights, and Environmental Integrity*. Retrieved from University of Notre Dame: http://www.nd.edu/~ethics/ethicsConference/presentations.shtml

Champion, D. R. (2011). White-Collar Crimes and Organizational Offending: An Integral Approach. *International Journal of Business, Humanities and Technology, 1*(3), 34–45.

Chan, A. T. Y. *Christ and Business Culture: Another Classification of Christians in Workplaces According to an Empirical Study in Hong Kong*. 2009. *Journal of Markets and Morality 12*: 91–111. (with Shu-kam Lee)

Clark, M. (2010, October 17). Germany's Angela Merkel: Multiculturalism has 'utterly failed'. *The Christian Science Monitor*.

Clift, D. (2010, February). *Networked Governance in the Global Financial Markets*. Retrieved October 10, 2012, from University of Bristol: http://www.cs.bris.ac.uk/home/dc/Foresight_NetGov_v2a.pdf

Clinton Global Initiative. (2012, October 1). *Clinton Global Initiative*. Retrieved October 1, 2012, from Clinton Global Initiative Commitments: http://www.clintonglobalinitiative.org/commitments/

Clough, G. W. (2011, October). *Secretary Clough on Jefferson's Bible*. Retrieved October 10, 2012, from Smithsonian: http://www.smithsonianmag.com/arts-culture/Jeffersons-Bible.html?onsite_source=relatedarticles&onsite_medium=internallink&onsite_campaign=SmithMag&onsite_content=Secretary%20Clough%20on%20Jefferson's%20Bible

CNBC. (2009, November 12). *CNBC Originals Warren Buffett and Bill Gates: Keeping America Great*. Retrieved October 11, 2012, from CNBC: http://video.cnbc.com/gallery/?video=1329393420

Collins, J. C. (2001). *Good to Great*. New York: Harper Business.

Collins, J. C. (2011). *Great by Choice*. New York: HarperCollins.

Coppedge, M., & Gerring J. (2011, June 3). *Conceptualizing and Measuring Democracy–A New Approach*. Retrieved October 10, 2012, from Boston University: http://people.bu.edu/jgerring/documents/MeasuringDemocracy.pdf

Covey, S. (1989). *The 7 Habits of Highly Effective People*. New York: Free Press.

Crossman, W. (2012, March). *From the Three Rs to the Four Cs: Radically Redesigning K-12 Education*. Retrieved October 10, 2012, from World Future Society: http://www.wfs.org/content/futurist/march-april-2012-vol-46-no-2/three-rs-four-cs-radically-redesigning-k-12-education

Cunningham, F. (2012, October 15). *Syria's Deadly Bomb Attack on Assad Cabinet: Is This 'The Price' Clinton Warned Of?* Retrieved from Transcend Media Service: http://www.transcend.org/tms/2012/07/syrias-deadly-bomb-attack-on-assad-cabinet-is-this-the-price-clinton-warned-of/

Damast, A. (2010, December 3). *Wharton Faculty Backs Curriculum Overhaul*. Retrieved October 10, 2012, from Bloomberg Businessweek: http://www.businessweek.com/bschools/content/dec2010/bs2010123_828086.htm

Degryse, H. D. (2011, November 13). *The Impact of Dark Trading and Visible Fragmentation on Market Quality*. Retrieved October 10, 2012, from Social Science Research Center: http://papers.ssrn.com/sol3/papers.cfm?abstract_id=1815025

Donne, J. (1624). *No Man Is An Island. Meditation 17, from Devotions Upon Emergent Occasions*. London.

Dungy, G. (2012, August 10). *Connecting and Collaborating to Further the Intellectual, Civic, and Moral Purposes of Higher Education*. Retrieved October 10, 2012, from Journal of College and Character: http://journals.naspa.org/jcc/vol13/iss3/3/

Earle, T. (2009). Trust, Confidence, and the 2008 Global Financial Crisis. *Risk Analysis, 29* (2009) 785–792.

Easwaran, E. (1985). *The Dhammapada.* Tomales: Blue Mountain Meditation Center.

Edwards, O. (2012, January). *How Thomas Jefferson Created His Own Bible.* Retrieved October 10, 2012, from Smithsonian: http://www.smithsonianmag.com/arts-culture/How-Thomas-Jefferson-Created-His-Own-Bible.html

Empower Network. (2012). *How A Lawnmower Can Change Your Life And Business!* Retrieved January 1, 2013 from Empower Network: http://www.empowernetwork.com/thomasspudic/blog/how-a-lawnmower-can-change-your-life-and-business/

Environmental Protection Agency. (2012). *2012 Climate Leadership Award Winners.* Retrieved January 8, 2013 from Environmental Protection Agency: http://www.epa.gov/climateleadership/awards/2012winners.html

European Central Bank. (2012, July 26). *Verbatim of the remarks made by Mario Draghi.* Retrieved October 10, 2012, from European Central Bank: http://www.ecb.int/press/key/date/2012/html/sp120726.en.html

Fagan, E. (2012, September 7). *Illicit Financial Flows Explained.* Retrieved October 7, 2012, from Global Financial Integrity: http://www.financialtaskforce.org/2012/09/07/illicit-financial-flows-explained-with-graphics-all-three-parts/

Fergus, N. (2012, March 12). *The British Prime Minister Is Coming to America.* Retrieved October 22, 2012, from Newsweek: http://www.thedailybeast.com/newsweek/2012/03/11/david-cameron-comes-to-america.html

Financial Freedom Inspiration. (2012). *Isaac Durojaiye – DMT Mobile Toilets.* Retrieved from Financial Freedom Inspiration: http://www.financialfreedominspiration.com/resources/success-stories/isaac-durojaiye-dmt-mobile-toilets/

Forman, J. (2007). Leaders as Storytellers: Finding Waldo. *Business Communication Quarterly, 70* n3, 369–374,

Fortune. (July 23, 2012). *Global 500.* Retrieved from CNN Money: http://money.cnn.com/magazines/fortune/global500/2012/snapshots/6388.html?iid=splwinners

FourthSector. (2012). *FourthSector.* Retrieved from http://www.fourthsector.net/

Freedom Challenge Awards, (2009, November 8). *Freedom Challenge Award.* Retrieved October 10, 2012, from Atlantic Counsel at 50: http://www.acus.org/event/freedoms-challenge-awards

Friedman, M. (1970, September 13). *The Social Responsibility of Business is to Increase its Profits.* Retrieved October 10, 2012, from Colorado University: http://www.colorado.edu/studentgroups/libertarians/issues/friedman-soc-resp-business.html

Friedman, T. L. (2011). *That Used To Be Us: How America Fell Behind in the World We Invented– and How We Can Come Back*. New York: Farrar, Straus & Giroux.

Friedman, T. L. (2012, September 22). *Hard Lines, Red Lines and Green Lines*. Retrieved October 10, 2012, from http://www.nytimes.com/2012/09/23 /opinion/sunday/friedman-hard-lines-red-lines-and-green-lines.html?_r=0

Garcia-Zamor, J.-C. (2003). Workplace Spirituality and Organizational Performance. *Public Administration Review*, 355–363.

General Electric. (2006, April 26). *Annual Shareholder Meeting*. Retrieved October 10, 2012, from General Electric: http://www.ge.com/pdf/investors /events/068/ge_annualshareownersmeeting_042606_en.pdf

George, W. (2012, July 18). *Penn State Lesson: Today's Cover-Up was Yesterday's Opportunity*. Retrieved October 10, 2012, from Harvard Business School: http://hbswk.hbs.edu/item/7051.html

Gladstone, R. (2012, February 4). *General Assembly Votes to Condemn Syrian Leader*. Retrieved January 8, 2013 from New York Times: http://www .nytimes.com/2012/02/17/world/middleeast/secretary-general-ban-ki-moon -castigates-syria-ahead-of-general-assembly-vote.html

Global Times. (2013, January 8). *Everyone is responsible for rule of law*. Retrieved January 9, 2013 from Global Times: http://www.globaltimes.cn /content/754390.shtml

Goleman, D., Boyatzis, R., & McKee, A. (2001, December). *Primal Leadership - The Hidden Driver of Great Performance*. Retrieved October 10, 2012, from Harvard Business School: http://hbswk.hbs.edu/item/7051.html

Goldstein, A. (2012, September 11). *Obama Still Does Not Get 9/11*. Retrieved October 2, 2012, from American Spector Blog: http://spectator.org/blog /2012/09/11/obama-still-doesnt-get-911

Google. (2012, October 2). *Ten things we know to be true*. Retrieved October 2, 2012, from Google: https://www.google.com/intl/en/about/company /philosophy/

Graham, F (2011, April 24). ABC News. (Amanpour, C., Interviewer). Retrieved January 9, 2013 from ABC News: http://abcnews.go.com/ThisWeek /video/interview-rev-franklin-graham-13446239

Grey, V. E. (1918). *The League of Nations*. London: Oxford University Press.

Guanzhong, L. (1300–1400). *Romance of the Three Kingdoms*. China.

Hamilton, E. (1942). *Mythology*. New York: Little, Brown & Co.

Hanhimäki, J. M. (2008). *The United Nations: A Very Short Introduction*. London: Oxford University Press.

Hayoun, M. (2012, August 15). *Understanding China's One Child Policy*. Retrieved September 23, 2012, from The National Interest: http://nationalinterest.org /commentary/understanding-chinas-one-child-policy-7330

Hellenic International Studies in the Arts. (2012). *Hellenic International Studies in the Arts*. Retrieved from Hellenic International Studies in the Arts: http://www.hellenicinternational.org/

Hemingway, Sean A. (grandson) (2003). *Hemingway on War*. New York: Scribner.

Hernandez, R. (2011, June 16). *Weiner Resigns in Chaotic Final Scene*. Retrieved January 9, 2013 from The New York Times: http://www.nytimes.com/2011/06/17/nyregion/anthony-d-weiner-tells-friends-he-will-resign.html?pagewanted=all

Hicks, D. A. (2003). *Religion and the Workplace, Pluralism, Spirituality, Leadership*. Cambridge: The Press Syndicate of the University of Cambridge.

Higgins, A. (2012, February 13). For Xi Jinping, set to become China's next leader, father's past is sensitive. Retrieved January 8, 2013 from The Washington Post: http://articles.washingtonpost.com/2012–02-13/world/35445774_1_xi-zhongxun-communist-party-official-biography

Hyatt, M. (2012, November 6). *8 Things Leaders Can Learn from Symphony Conductors*. Retrieved January 8, 2013 from Michael Hyatt, Intentional Leadership: http://michaelhyatt.com/8-things-leaders-can-learn-from-symphony-conductors.html

Ignatova, M. (2012, September 20). Gen. Colin Powell and GE's Jeff Immelt Talk About Leadership. Retrieved January 8, 2013 Salesforce Blog: http://blogs.salesforce.com/company/2012/09/gen-colin-powell-and-ges-jeff-immelt-talk-about-leadership-and-the-economy.html.

International Monetary Fund. (2012, October). *Global Financial Stability Report*. Retrieved October 11, 2012, from International Monetary Fund: http://www.imf.org/external/pubs/ft/gfsr/2012/02/index.htm

Iran Chamber Society. (2012). *History of Iran*. Retrieved January 8, 2013 from Iran Chamber Society: http://www.iranchamber.com/history/cyrus/cyrus.php

Isaacson, W. (2011). *Steve Jobs*. New York: Simon & Schuster.

Jefferson, T. (2011). *The Jefferson Bible, Smithsonian Edition: The Life and Morals of Jesus of Nazareth*. Washington, DC: Smithsonian. Not published during Jefferson's lifetime. First published by the National Museum in Washington, 1895.

General Martin E. Dempsey Chairman, Joints Chief of Staff. (2012, October 5). *Joint Chiefs of Staff*. Retrieved October 11, 2012, from Joint Chiefs of Staff: http://www.jcs.mil/biography.aspx?ID=135

Jung, C. (1961). *Memories, Dreams, Reflections*. New York: Random House.

Kagan, R. (2012). *The World America Made*. New York, New York: Knopf Doubleday Publishing Group.

Kaku, R. (1997, July). *The Path of Kyosei*. Retrieved October 10, 2012, from Harvard Business Review: http://hbr.org/1997/07/the-path-of-kyosei/ar/1

Hassall, P. (1997, August). What is Enlightenment? Retrieved January 8, 2013 from Modern History Sourcebook: http://www.fordham.edu/halsall/mod/kant-whatis.asp

Kaplan, R. D. (2012). *The Revenge of Geography: What the Map Tells Us About Coming Conflicts and the Battle Against Fate*. New York: Random House.

Kaufmann, D. (2009, January 27). *Corruption And The Global Financial Crisis*. Retrieved October 8, 2012, from Forbes: http://www.forbes.com/2009/01/27/corruption-financial-crisis-business-corruption09_0127corruption.html

Kellerman, B. (2012). *The End of Leadership*. New York: Harper Collins.

Kermis, G. F. (2009). Model for the Transition from Ethical Deficit to a Transparent Corporate Culture: A Response to the Financial Meltdown. *Journal of Academic and Business Ethics, 2*, 1–11.

Kiviat, B. (2008, September 23). *How Much is the SEC's Cox to Blame?* Retrieved October 10, 2012, from Time business: http://www.time.com/time/business/article/0,8599,1843519,00.html

Klein, A. (2012, October 1). *How the Government Failed to Fix Wall Street*. Retrieved October 10, 2012, from The Daily Beast: http://www.thedailybeast.com/articles/2012/10/01/how-the-government-failed-to-fix-wall-street.html

Klein, J. (2011, June). *The Failure of American Schools*. Retrieved October 10, 2012, from The Atlantic: http://www.theatlantic.com/magazine/archive/2011/06/the-failure-of-american-schools/308497/#

Knudsen, J. (2011). Company Delistings from the UN Global Compact: Limited Business Demand or Domestic Governance Failure? *Journal of Business Ethics*, 331–349.

Lehman, J. J. (2012). *Chardin and Jung's Influence on Today's Society*. Retrieved January 8, 2013 from The Society of Clerks Secular of Saint Basil: http://www.reu.org/public/theological/text-15.txt

Leland, A., & Oboroceanu, M.-J. (2010, February 26). *American War and Military Operations Casualties: Lists and Statistics*. Retrieved October 10, 2012, from Federation of American Scientist: http://www.fas.org/sgp/crs/natsec/RL32492.pdf

LeRoy, M. (Director). (1962). *Gypsy* [Motion Picture].

Lewis, M. (2006). *The Blind Side: Evolution of a Game*. New York: W. W. Norton & Company.

Longman, R. (2006). *Pfizer's Change Management: Unfamiliar Faces*. Retrieved January 8, 2013 from Elsevier Business Intelligence: http://www.elsevierbi.com/publications/in-vivo/24/8/pfizers-change-management-unfamiliar-faces

Lucchetti, A. (2012, September 12). *Corzine Meets with MF Global Investigators*. Retrieved October 10, 2012, from Wall Street Journal: http://online.wsj.com/article/SB10000872396390443884104577648004211274044.html

Malerba, L. (2010). *Green Medicine: Challenging the Assumptions of Conventional Health Care.* New York: Random House.

Margolis, J. D., & Stoltz P.G. (2010, January). *How to Bounce Back from Adversity.* Retrieved September 20, 2012, from Harvard Business Review: http://unitus.org/FULL/HBR_Bounce%20Back%20from%20Adversity.pdf

Markoe, L. (2012, September 5). *Democrats under fire for removing 'God' from party platform.* Retrieved October 11, 2012, from The Washington Post: http://www.washingtonpost.com/national/on-faith/democrats-under-fire-for-removing-god-from-party-platform/2012/09/05/61b3459a-f79e-11e1-a93b-7185e3f88849_story.html

Mayo, M. (2011). *Exile on Wall Street: One Analyst's Fight to Save the Big Banks from Themselves.* Hoboken: John Wiley & Son's, Inc.

Mayo, M. (2011, November 8). Why Wall Street Can't Handle the Truth. Retrieved January 8, 2013 from *The Wall Street Journal:* http://online.wsj.com/article/SB10001424052970203804204577016160354571908.html

McLaughlin, C. (2009). *Spirituality and Ethics in Business.* Retrieved October 10, 2012, from The Center for Visionary Leadership: http://www.visionarylead.org/articles/spbus.htm

Mercatus Center George Mason University. (2012, October 6). *Mercatus Scholars Comment on the Dodd-Frank Financial Reform Bill.* Retrieved October 6, 2012, from Mercatus Center George Mason University: http://mercatus.org/features/mercatus-scholars-comment-dodd-frank-financial-reform-bill

Miller, D. W., & Ewest, T. (2011, January 11). The Present State of Workplace Spirituality. Retrieved January 8, 2013 from Princeton Faith and Work Initiative: http://www.princeton.edu/faithandwork/tib/research/aom-litreview

Moore, T. W. (2008) Individual Differences and Workplace Spirituality: The Homogenization of the Corporate Culture. *Journal of Management and Marketing Research,* 1 Dec, 79–93.

Motor Trend. (2008, November 19). *GM, Ford, Chrysler, Bankruptcy and Bailout.* Retrieved January 8, 2013 from Motor Trend: http://blogs.motortrend.com/gm-ford-chrysler-bankruptcy-and-bailout-2129.html#axzz2H8ikwOBx

Moukheiber, Z. (2011, March 30). *President Assad And The Syrian Business Elite.* Retrieved September 23, 2012, from Forbes: http://www.forbes.com/sites/zinamoukheiber/2011/03/30/president-assad-and-the-syrian-business-elite/

Myss, C. (1997). *Why People Don't Heal and How They Can.* New York: Random House – Three Rivers Press.

Myss, C. (2009). *Defy Gravity.* San Diego: Hay House.

National Commission on Terrorist Attacks Upon the United States. (2004). *The 9/11 Commission Report.* Washington DC: Government Printing Office.

National Information Center. (2012). *National Information Center.* Retrieved January 8, 2013 from http://www.ffiec.gov/nicpubweb/nicweb/NicHome.aspx

Newton, I. (1934). *Mathematical Principles of Natural Philosophy (Motte's Translation from Latin)*. Berkeley: University of California Press.

Norman, W., & McDonald, C. (April 2004). Getting to the Bottom of the Triple Bottom Line. *Business Ethics Quarterly, 12* 243–262 (2004) Retrieved from Business Ethics Quarterly: http://www.businessethics.ca /3bl/triple-bottom-line.pdf

O'Carroll, L. (2011, September 26). *What if Ireland pulls out of the euro and prints punts?* Retrieved from The Guardian: http://www.guardian.co.uk /business/ireland-business-blog-with-lisa-ocarroll/2011/sep/26/eurozone-crisis -ireland-euro-punt?INTCMP=SRCH

O'Connor, E. (2002). Storied Business: Typology, Intertextuality, and Traffic in Entrepreneurial Narrative. *Journal of Business Communication, 39* (1) 36–54.

OPEC, *OPEC: Brief History*. Retrieved January 8, 2013 from OPEC: http:// www.opec.org/opec_web/en/about_us/24.htm

Oppenheimer, M. (2012, August 23). *The Rise of the Corporate Chaplain*. Retrieved October 10, 2012, from Businessweek: http://www.businessweek .com/articles/2012–08-23/the-rise-of-the-corporate-chaplain

Pappu, S. (2011, August 8). *What's Next For Michael Bloomberg*. Retrieved October 10, 2012, from Fast Company: http://www.fastcompany.com /1769004/whats-next-michael-bloomberg

Perez-Batres, L. A., Miller, V. V., & Pisani, M. J. (2011). Institutionalizing sustainability: An empirical study of corporate registration and commitment to the United Nations Global Compact guidelines. *Journal of Cleaner Production, 19*, 843–851.

Petersmann, E.-U. (2002). Time for a United Nations Global Compact for Integrating Human Rights into the Laws of Worldwide Organizations-Lessons from European Integration. *Oxford Journal, 621–650*. Retrieved January 8, 2013 from Oxford Journal: http://ejil.oxfordjournals.org/content /13/3/621.full.pdf

Pew Forum on Religion & Public Life. (2012). *"Nones on the Rise"*. Washington, DC: Pew Research Center. Retrieved January 8, 2013 from Pew Forum: http://www.pewforum.org/uploadedFiles/Topics/Religious_Affiliation /Unaffiliated/NonesOnTheRise-full.pdf

Pickens, T. B. (2012). *T. Boone Pickens – His Life, His Legacy*. Retrieved January 8, 2013 from T. Boone Pickens Website: http://www.boonepickens.com

Piereson, J. (2005, November 3). *The New Criterion*. Retrieved October 10, 2012, from ArmaVirumque: http://www.newcriterion.com/posts.cfm/lyndon -johnson-and-cult-of-4082

Pierog, K. (2011, November 30). Michigan governor approves state takeover of Flint. Retrieved January 8, 2013 from *Reuters*: http://www.reuters.com/article /2011/11/29/us-flint-michigan-emergency-idUSTRE7AS2YN20111129

Plett, B. (2012, August 12). *Syria crisis: Kofi Annan quits as UN-Arab League envoy.* Retrieved January 8, 2013 from BBC New-Middle East: http://www.bbc.co.uk/news/world-middle-east-19099676

Raice, S. (2012). *SEC Probes Groupon.* Retrieved January 8, 2013 from Wall Street Journal: http://online.wsj.com/article/SB1000142405270230 3816504577319870715221322.html

Ramis, H. (Director). (1993). *Groundhog Day.* Motion Picture.

Rand, A. (1957). *Atlas Shrugged.* New York: Penguin Books.

Reich, H. (2010, August). *A Qualitative Study of Heart-Mind Coherence Techniques for Stress Relief and Mental and Emotional Self-management. California Institute Of Integral Studies*, 2010, 139 pages.

Reiser, D. B. (2009). For Profit Philanthropy. *Fordham Law Review 77*(5) Retrieved October 10, 2012, from Fordham Law Review: http://ir.lawnet.fordham.edu/cgi/viewcontent.cgi?article=4445&context=flr

Rhodes, K. (2006). Six Components of a Model for Workplace Spirituality. *Graziadio Business Review* (6) 2 (2006) Retrieved October 10, 2012, from Graziadio Business Review: http://gbr.pepperdine.edu/2010/08/six-components-of-a-model-for-workplace-spirituality/

Rinke, B. M. (2011, November 9). Italy at Breaking Point; Fears Grow of Euro Zone Split. Rome, Italy. Retrieved January 8, 2012 from Reuters: http://www.reuters.com/article/2011/11/09/us-eurozone-idUSTRE7A8315 20111109

Ritschl. A. (2012, June). CEP Discussion Paper No 1149 Reparations, Deficits, and Debt Default: the Great Depression in Germany. Retrieved January 8, 2013 from Centre for Economic Performance: http://cep.lse.ac.uk/pubs/download/dp1149.pdf   http://cep.lse.ac.uk/pubs/download/dp1149.pdf

Ritschl. A. (2012, June 15). *Germany, Greece and the Marshall Plan.* Retrieved January 9, 2013 from The Economist: http://www.economist.com/blogs/freeexchange/2012/06/economic-history

Ritschl. A. (2012, June 21). *Germany, Greece and the Marshall Plan, riposte.* Retrieved January 9, 2013 from The Economist: http://www.economist.com/blogs/freeexchange/2012/06/economic-history-2

Ritschl, A. (2012, June 25).*Germany, Greece and the Marshall Plan, another riposte.* Retrieved January 9, 2013 from The Economist

Robertson, T. A. (2010, October 18). *Global Business Leaders Can Help Drive Positive Social Outcomes.* Retrieved October 10, 2012, from The Huffington Post: http://www.huffingtonpost.com/thomas-robertson/global-business-leaders-c_b_766714.html

Robicheau, J. W. (2011, December 27). Ethical leadership: what is it really? *AASA Journal of Scholarship & Practice, 8*(1), 34–42.

Rogers, P. (2012, September 11). *Coastal Cleanup Day this Saturday: Will volunteers find Japanese tsunami debris?* Retrieved October 10, 2012, from Santa Cruz Sentinel: http://www.santacruzsentinel.com /nationalbreaking/ci_21519894/coastal-cleanup-day-this-saturday-will -volunteers-find

Romano, R. (2005, May 3). The Sarbanes-Oxley Act and the Making of Quack Corporate Governance. *The Yale Law Journal, 114*, 1523–1611.

Rosenthal, E. (November 12, 2012). U.S. to Be World's Top Oil Producer in 5 Years, Report Says, Retrieved January 8, 2013 from New York Times: http://www.nytimes.com/2012/11/13/business/energy-environment/report - sees-us-as-top-oil-producer-in-5-years.html?_r=0

Roubini, N (2012, December 17). The Eurozone's Delayed Reckoning, Retrieved January 8, 2013 from Project Syndicate: http://www.project -syndicate.org/commentary/the-inevitable-return-of-europe-s-crisis-by-nouriel -roubini

Roubini, N. (2011, August 11). Stern College of Business Professor New York University. (S. W. Constable, Interviewer) Retrieved January 9, 2013 from Wall Street Journal: http://live.wsj.com/video/roubini-warns-of-global -recession-risk/C036B113–6D5F-4524-A5AF-DF2F3E2F8735.html#! C036B113–6D5F-4524-A5AF-DF2F3E2F8735

Russell, G. (2012, October 8). *UN-sponsored group in Syria included Assad kin cited as corrupt by US, documents show.* Retrieved October 8, 2012, from Fox New: http://www.foxnews.com/world/2012/10/08/un-sponsored -group-in-syria-included-assad-kin-cited-as-corrupt-by-us-documents/ #ixzz290p005ir

Sacirbey, O. (2011, December 30). *For U.S. Muslims, Work-Time Prayer a Struggle*, Retrieved January 8, 2013 from Religious News Service http:// archives.religionnews.com/faith/doctrine-and-practice/worktime-prayer-a -struggle-for-u.s.-muslims

Santayana, G. (1905). *The Life of Reason; or, The Phases of Human Progress: Introduction, and Reason in common sense.* New York: Charles Scribner's Sons.

Schectman, J. (2011, May 15). *Wharton Grads: More Ethics Needed.* Retrieved October 10, 2012, from Poets & Quants: http://poetsandquants.com /2011/05/16/some-wharton-grads-say-more-ethics-training-needed/

Schnaubelt, A. (2012, October 10). *Fairness, Spiritual Maturity And Socio-Economic Theory.* Retrieved October 10, 2012, from Illuminate Me: http://www.illuminateme.org/politics/fairness-spiritual-maturity-and-socio -economic-theory.html

Schurz, C. (2009, November). *Atlantic Council Freedom's Challenge Dinner.* (Admiral. James Stavridis, Speaker/Award Recipient) Berlin, Germany.

Retrieved January 8, 2012, from Atlantic Council: http://www.acus.org /event/freedoms-challenge/video/stavridis

Schwartz, M. S. (2011). *Corporate Social Responsibility: An Ethical Approach (Broadview Guides to Business and Professional Ethics)*. Peterborough, ON: Broadview Press.

Scott, R. (2012, September 14). *The Bottom Line of Corporate Good*. Retrieved October 10, 2012, from Forbes: http://www.forbes.com/sites/causeintegration /2012/09/14/the-bottom-line-of-corporate-good/

Securities and Exchange Commission. (2012). *Securities and Exchange Commission*. Retrieved January 8, 2013 from Securities and Exchange Commission: http://www.sec.gov/about/whatwedo.shtml

Selig, K. (2011, August 8). *Greed, Negligence or System Failure, Credit Rating Agencies and the Financial Crisis*. Retrieved October 10, 2012, from Kenan Institute for Ethics at Duke University: http://kenan.ethics.duke.edu/wp -content/uploads/2012/07/Case-Study-Greed-and-Negligence.pdf

Shakespeare, W. (1928). *Macbeth*. New York: Houghton Mifflin Company.

Shapiro, M. (2009, October 21). *Securities and Exchange Commission-Speeches*. Retrieved January 8, 2013 from Securities and Exchange Commission: http://www.sec.gov/news/speech/2009/spch102109mls.htm

Smith, R. E. (2011, July 7). *Defining Corporate Social Responsibility: A Systems Approach For Socially Responsible*. Retrieved October 10, 2012, from University of Pennsylvania Scholarly Commons Capitalism: http://repository.upenn .edu/cgi/viewcontent.cgi?article=1009&context=od_theses_mp

Smithsonian Institute. (n.d.). *The Price of Freedom-Americans at War*. Retrieved January 8, 2013 from http://americanhistory.si.edu/militaryhistory/printable /index.asp

Soergel, M. (2012, May 6). *Once a homeless teen, she's now a JU grad with a perfect GPA*. Retrieved January 8, 2013 from Jacksonville.com: http:// jacksonville.com/news/metro/2012-05-04/story/once-homeless-teen-shes-now -ju-grad-perfect-gpa

Sorrow, K. M. (2011, May 5). *Morgan Stanley executive, Jacksonville native gives commencement address at JU*. Retrieved January 8, 2013 from Jacksonville Florida Times Union: http://m.jacksonville.com/community/southside/2011 -05-05/story/morgan-stanley-executive-jacksonville-native-gives-commencement

Starke, D. (2012, July 18). *Charitable Giving: It's in the Numbers*. Retrieved October 10, 2012, from Foundation News: http://www.givingusareports .org/news-and-events/news.aspx?NewsTypeId=3&NewsId=45

Strategos, Inc. (2012). *Ford Crises of 1920–1921*. Retrieved January 8, 2013 from Strategos: http://www.strategosinc.com/ford_crises.htm

Strom, S. (2007, May 6). Businesses Try to Make Money and Save the World. Retrieved January 8, 2013 from *The New York Times*.: http://www

.nytimes.com/2007/05/06/business/yourmoney/06fourth.html?pagewanted
=all&_r=0

Summers, L. H. (2012, January 20). *What You (Really) Need to Know.* Retrieved January 9, 2013 from *The New York Times*: http://www.nytimes.com/2012/01/22/education/edlife/the-21st-century-education.html?pagewanted=all

Swidler, L. (1997). *International Codes of Business Ethics.* Retrieved October 10, 2012, from Temple University: http://astro.temple.edu/~swidler/swidlerbooks/codes.htm

Syriatel. Retrieved October 10, 2012, from Syriatel: http://www.syriatel.sy/

Tax Policy Center. *The Bowles-Simpson "Chairmen's Mark" Deficit Reduction Plan.* Retrieved October 6, 2012, from Tax Topics: http://www.taxpolicycenter.org/taxtopics/Bowles_Simpson_Brief.cfm

The Better World Campaign. *The UN Budget Process.* Retrieved January 8, 2013 from The Better World Campaign: http://www.betterworldcampaign.org/issues/funding/the-un-budget-process.html

The Economic Times. (2011, December 28). *International Business.* Retrieved October 11, 2012, from Economic Times: http://articles.economictimes.indiatimes.com/2011-12-28/news/30565297_1_budget-agreement-financial-plan-second-time

The Economist. (2011, September 24). *A Game of Catch-up.* Retrieved October 11, 2012, from The Economist: http://www.economist.com/node/21528979

The European Central Bank. Retrieved January 8, 2013, from the European Central Bank http://www.ecb.int/home/html/index.en.html

The Financial Crisis Inquiry Commission. (2011). *The Financial Crisis Inquiry Report.* Washington DC: US Government Printing Office.

The Journal of Turkish Weekly. (2012, July). China Rejects US Criticism Involving Syria Conflict. *The Journal of Turkish Weekly.*

Thomas, P. (2012, September 5). *Fear of China Syndrome.* Retrieved October 10, 2012, from Economist View: http://economistsview.typepad.com/economistsview/2012/09/fear-of-china-syndrome.html

Thomas, C. W. (April, 2002). The Rise and Fall of Enron-When a company looks too good to be true, it usually is. *Journal of Accountancy*, 41–45, 47–48. Retrieved January 8, 2013 from University of Colorado: http://leeds-faculty.colorado.edu/durhamg/fnce3010/enron.pdf

Thomson Reuters. (2011, April). *Conference Call Transcript, GE–GE Annual Meeting of Shareowners.* Retrieved January 8, 2013 from General Electric: http://www.ge.com/pdf/investors/events/04272011/ge_annual_meeting_shareowners_transcript_04272011.pdf

Thornbury, G. A. (2003, January). *Thomas Jefferson's Anticlericalism, Church, and State. Kairos Journal.* Retrieved October 10, 2012, from: (January

2003)   http://www.perryville.org/2012/08/13/thomas-jefferson%E2%80%
99s-anticlericalism-church-and-state/reprinted with permission from the
Kairos Journal.

Till, B. (2011, December 25). *Could Revolution Come to Putin's Russia?* Retrieved
October 11, 2012, from The Atlantic: http://www.theatlantic.com/interna-
tional/archive/2011/12/could-revolution-come-to-putins-russia/250486/

Touryalai, H. (2012, December 19). *Libor Scandal Just Took A Nasty Turn,
Collusion Findings Should Make Banks Very Nervous.* Retrieved January 8,
2013 from Forbes: http://www.forbes.com/sites/halahtouryalai/2012/12
/19/libor-scandal-just-took-a-nasty-turn-collusion-findings-should-make-banks
-very-nervous/

UN Global Compact. Retrieved January 9, 2013 from Global Compact Lead:
http://www.unglobalcompact.org/HowToParticipate/Lead/index.html

UN Global Compact. (2012, October 10). *UN Global Compact.* Retrieved
October 10, 2012, from UN Global Compact–Syria: http://www
.unglobalcompactsyria.org/cgi-sys/suspendedpage.cgi

UN Global Compact. (n.d.). *UN Global Compact.* Retrieved January 8, 2013
from http://www.unglobalcompact.org

Unger, A. (2012, February 12). *Arutz Shiva.* Retrieved October 10, 2012, from
Israel National News: http://www.israelnationalnews.com/News/News.aspx
/152414#.UGM5to1lQ4k

United Nations. (2010). *UN-Business Focal Point Newsletter Issue 14.* Retrieved
January 8, 2013 from UN Business: http://business.un.org/en/documents
/9012

United Nations. (2011). *UN Global Compact.* New York: UN Global Compact
Office.

United Nations. (2012, October 10). *Initiating the Incremental Impact by
Shared Values: UNDP Pushes into High-Gear with Syria's Private Sector.*
Retrieved January 9, 2013 from UN Global Compact: http://business.un
.org/en/documents/8872

United Nations. (2012). *We Can End Poverty 2012.* Retrieved January 8, 2013
from Millennium Development Goals (MDGs): http://www.un.org
/millenniumgoals/

United Nations General Assembly. (2010, June 24). *United Nations.* Retrieved
October 10, 2012, from United Nations News: http://www.un.org/News
/Press/docs/2010/ga10955.doc.htm

US Bureau of Labor Statistics. (2012, December 11). *Economic News Release.*
Retrieved January 8, 2013 from US Bureau of Labor Statistics: http://
www.bls.gov/bls/newsrels.htm

US Geology Survey. (2012, October 6). What is a tectonic plate? Retrieved October
10, 2012 from USGS: http://pubs.usgs.gov/gip/dynamic/tectonic.html

US Census Bureau. (2012, May) *The Foreign Born Population in the United States.* Washington, DC. Retrieved January 9, 2012 from US Census Bureau: http://www.census.gov/prod/2012pubs/acs-19.pdf

Van Rompuy, H. (2012). *Towards a Genuine Economic and Monetary Union.* Brussels: European Counsel. Retrieved January 8, 2013 from Consillium: http://www.consilium.europa.eu/uedocs/cms_data/docs/pressdata/en/ec /132809.pdf

Verchick, R. (2012, February 22). *Mardi Gras, Check. BP "Trial of the Century" Here We Come.* Retrieved October 10, 2012, from Center for Progressive Reform: http://www.progressivereform.org/CPRBlog.cfm? idBlog=A567E577-A5C9–1E94–68C789455C641E35

Vervaeck, A. (2011, November). *New Insights into the October 2011 Van (Turkey) Earthquake–detailed analysis by the CEDIM Forensic Earthquake Analysis Group.* Retrieved January 8, 2013 from Earthquake Report: http:// earthquake-report.com

Waddell, S. (2011). *The Global Compact: An organizational innovation to realize UN Principles.* Retrieved October 10, 2012, from UN Global Compact: http://www.unglobalcompact.org/docs/news_events/9.1_news_archives/2011 _11_16/UNGC_Organizational_Innovation_Note.pdf

Walt, S. M. (2012, September 5). *Another Neocon 'Success Story'.* Retrieved October 10, 2012, from Foreign Policy: http://walt.foreignpolicy.com /posts/2012/09/05/another_neocon_success_story

Warren Commission. (1964). *National Archives.* Retrieved January 8, 2013 from The Warren Report: http://www.archives.gov/research/jfk/warren -commission-report/index.html

Weber, J. H. (2008). The Bell System Divestiture: Background, Implementation, and Outcome. *Federal Communications Law Journal,* 21–29.

Weisul, K. (2012, May 7). *Jim Collins: Good to Great in 10 Steps.* Retrieved October 10, 2012, from Inc.: http://www.inc.com/kimberly-weisul/jim -collins-good-to-great-in-ten-steps.html

White, G. (2011, February 1). *China Just Made A Huge Investment In The American Energy Source That Everyone Still Ignores.* Retrieved September 22, 2012, from Business Insider: http://www.businessinsider.com/china -cnooc-investment-niobrara-shale-2011–2#ixzz1CsT0IkQ4

Wilson, D. (2010, December 5). *Pfizer's Chairman and Chief Retires Unexpectedly.* Retrieved January 9, 2013 from The New York Times: http://www .nytimes.com/2010/12/06/business/06drug.html?_r=0

Winslow, L. (2012, October 10). *Michael Moore Dislikes Capitalism But Makes Money Trashing It – How Does That Work?* Retrieved October 10, 2012 from Capitalism: http://www.capitalism.co/welfare-capitalism/news

/michael-moore-dislikes-capitalism-but-makes-money-trashing-it-how-does
-that-work#.UGNqFY1lQ4l

Wolman, R. (2001). *Thinking with Your Soul: Spiritual Intelligence and Why It Matters*. New York: Harmony Books.

World Bank. (2012). *World Bank*. Retrieved January 8, 2013 from World Bank: http://data.worldbank.org/indicator/NY.GNP.PCAP.PP.CD

World Health Organization. (2009, August). *Fact sheet N°330*. Retrieved January 8, 2013 from World Health Organization: http://www.who.int/mediacentre/factsheets/fs330/en/index.html

World Justice Project. (2012). *The Rule of Law*. Retrieved January 8, 2013 from World Justice Project: http://worldjusticeproject.org/what-rule-law

Xuetong, Y. (2006). The Rise of China and its Power Status. *Chinese Journal of International Politics, 1*(1), 5–33.

Yeats, W. (n.d.). *The Academy of American Poets*. Retrieved January 8 from Poet.org: http://www.poets.org/viewmedia.php/prmMID/15527

Zakaria, F. (2008). *The Post-American World*. New York: W. W. Norton.

Zakaria, F. (2012, February 5). *GPS*. Retrieved October 10, 2012, from Global Public Square: www.google.com/search?oq=globalpublicsquare.&sugexp=chrome,mod=17&sourceid=chrome&ie=UTF-8&q=globalpublicsquare.

Zunz, O. (2012). Philanthropy in America: A History (Politics and Society in Twentieth-Century America). Princeton: Princeton University Press.

Works Cited | A Case for Sustainability Manifestation | Chapter 1 | Patagonia: A Model for a 21st Century Corporation

Chouinard, Y. (2011, October 1). *The sustainable economy*. Retrieved January 8, 2013 from Harvard Business Review: http://hbr.org/2011/10/the-sustainable-economy/ar/1

Elliot, T. (1964). *Murder in the cathedral*. New York: Harcourt, Brace Jovanovich/Harvest. Retrieved from The Television History Resource Site.

Hoover's. (2012, June). *Columbia Sportswear Company*. Retrieved January 8, 2013 from Hoover's: http://www.hoovers.com/company-information/cs/company-profile.Columbia_Sportswear_Company.3a52bcc2e2687b7e.html

Leone, M. (2010, October 1). *I hate CFOs who always say no*. Retrieved January 8, 2013 from CFO Magazine: http://www.cfo.com/article.cfm/14526627

Patagonia. (2012). *Common threads initiative*. Retrieved January 8, 2013 from Patagonia: http://www.patagonia.com/eu/enGB/common-threads

Patagonia. (2012). *Company information*. Retrieved January 8, 2013 from Patagonia: http://www.patagonia.com/us/patagonia.go?assetid=2047&ln=140

Patagonia. (2012). *Environmentalism*. Retrieved January 8, 2013 from Patagonia: http://www.patagonia.com/us/environmentalism

Patagonia. (2012). *Environmentalism/The footprint chronicles: Our supply chain*. Retrieved January 8, 2013 from Patagonia: http://www.patagonia.com/eu/enGB/footprint/

Patagonia. (2012). *Environmentalism: What we do*. Retrieved January 8, 2013 from Patagonia: http://www.patagonia.com/eu/enGB/patagonia.go?assetid=9159

Patagonia. (2012). *Fabric: Down insulation*. Retrieved January 8, 2013 from Patagonia: http://www.patagonia.com/eu/enGB/patagonia.go?assetid=58468

Patagonia. (2012). *The cleanest line*. Retrieved January 8, 2013 from The Cleanest Line: http://www.thecleanestline.com/

Patagonia. (2012). *Environmentalism: Our common waters*. Retrieved January 8, 2013 from Patagonia: http://www.patagonia.com/eu/enGB/patagonia.go?assetid=9163

Storm, S. (1996, June 27). *A sweetheart becomes suspect; Looking behind those Kathie Lee labels*. Retrieved January 8, 2013 from New York Times: http://www.nytimes.com/1996/06/27/business/a-sweetheart-becomes-suspect-looking-behind-those-kathie-lee-labels.html?pagewanted=all&src=pm

Working Mother. (2012). *2012 Working Mother 100 Best Companies*. Retrieved January 8, 2013 from Working Mother: http://www.workingmother.com/best-company-list/129110/1581

World Economic Forum. (2012). *World economic forum*. Retrieved from World Economic Forum: http://forumblog.org/event/annual-meeting-2012/

Works Cited | A Case for Being of the People and for the People: Ford Motor Company | Chapter 2

Cavanaugh, G. F. (2006, November 13). *Ford Motor Company, Human Rights, and Environmental Integrity*. Retrieved January 9, 2013 from University of Notre Dame: http://www.nd.edu/~ethics/ethicsConference/presentations.shtml

Ford Motor Company. (2007, November). *Code of Conduct Handbook*. Retrieved January 9, 2013 from Ford Motor Company: http://corporate.ford.com/doc/corporate_conduct_standards.pdf

Ford Motor Company. (2011/2012). *Climate Change and the Environment*. Retrieved January 9, 2013 from Ford Motor Company: http://corporate.ford.com/doc/sr11-environment.pdf

Ford Motor Company. (2012). *Model U Concept: A Model for Change.* Retrieved January 9, 2013 from Ford Motor Company: http://media.ford .com/article_display.cfm?article_id=14047

Ford Motor Company. (2012). *News Center.* Retrieved January 9, 2013 from Ford Motor Company: http://corporate.ford.com/news-center/press-releases -detail/677-5-dollar-a-day

Ford Motor Company. (2012). *Policy Letter No. 24: Code of Human Rights, Basic Working Conditions and Corporate Responsibility.* Retrieved January 8, 2013 from Ford Motor Company: http://corporate.ford.com/microsites /sustainability-report-2011–12/blueprint-governance-sustainability-policy-code

Ford Motor Company. (2012). *Sustainability.* Retrieved January 8, 2013 from Ford Motor Company: http://corporate.ford.com/our-company/sustainability

Ford Motor Company. (n.d.). *Ford Automotive Operations–Ford Exports.* Retrieved January 9, 2013 from Ford Motor Company: http://media.ford .com/article_display.cfm?article_id=51

Ford.Media.Com. (2006, January 23). *Ford Motor Company.* Retrieved Januaary 8, 2013 from FORD DECLARES RESURGENCE OF FORD MOTOR COMPANY: http://media.ford.com/article_display.cfm?article_id=22465

Leggett, C. (1999, Spring). *The Ford Pinto Case: The Valuation of Life as it Applies.* Retrieved January 8, 2013 from Wake Forest University: http:// www.wfu.edu/~palmitar/Law&Valuation/Papers/1999/Leggett-pinto.html

New York Times. (2012, October 30). *New York Times Business Day.* (V. Goel, Ed.) Retrieved January 8, 2013 from The New York Times: http://topics .nytimes.com/top/news/business/companies/ford_motor_company/index.html

Saturday Evening Post. (1925, January 24). *Ford Motor Company Ad. Saturday Evening Post*, p. 29. Retrieved January 9, 2013 from Ford Motor Company: http://corporate.ford.com/microsites/sustainability-report-2011–12 /financial

Strategos, Inc. (2012). *Ford Crises of 1920–1921.* Retrieved January 9, 2013 from Strategos: http://www.strategosinc.com/ford_crises.htm

UN Global Compact. (n.d.). Retrieved January 9, 2013 from Global Compact Lead: http://www.unglobalcompact.org/HowToParticipate/Lead/index.html

Works Cited A Case Study for Collaboration I Accenture and the UN Global Compact I Chapter 3

Accenture. *Accenture release findings of largest CEO study on corporate sustainability.* (2010, June 22). Retrieved January 9, 2013 from Ethical Performance: http://www.ethicalperformance.com/reports/alerts/Accenture -release-findings-of-largest-CEO-study-on-corporate-sustainability-506

Accenture. (2010, June). *A New Era of Sustainability–CEO Study*. Retrieved January 9, 2013 from Accenture: http://www.accenture.com/SiteCollection Documents/PDF/Accenture_A_New_Era_of_Sustainability_CEO_Study.pdf

Accenture. (2012). *About Accenture*. Retrieved January 9, 2013 from Accenture: http://www.accenture.com/us-en/company/Pages/index.aspx

United Nation. (2010). *UN Global Compact*. Retrieved January 9, 2013 from United Nations: http://www.unglobalcompact.org/news/42–06-22–2010

United Nations. (2012). *At A Glance*. Retrieved January 9, 2013 from United Nations: http://www.un.org/en/aboutun/index.shtml

United Nations. (2012). *Ban Ki-moon*. Retrieved January 9, 2013 from United Nations: http://www.un.org/sg/biography.shtml

Works Cited | A Case Study for Leadership | Aung San Suu Kyi | Democracy for Burma: A Beginning | Chapter 4

Cyclinglim. *Aung San Suu Kyi, The Whole World Salutes You!* Retrieved January 9, 2013 from Life is Really Beautiful: http://lifeisreallybeautiful.com/tag /sakharov-prize-for-freedom-of-thought-in-1990/

Do One Thing. (2012). *Heros – Daw Aung San Suu Kyi*. Retrieved January 9, 2013 from Do One Thing: http://www.doonething.org/heroes/pages-k/kyi-bio.htm

Friedman, T. L. (2012, September 22). *Hard Lines, Red Lines and Green Lines*. Retrieved January 9, 2013 from The New York Times: http://www .nytimes.com/2012/09/23/opinion/sunday/friedman-hard-lines-red-lines-and -green-lines.html?_r=0

Golluoglu, E. (2012, April 2). *Aung San Suu Kyi hails 'new era' for Burma after landslide victory*. Retrieved January 9, 2013 from The Guardian: http:// www.guardian.co.uk/world/2012/apr/02/aung-san-suu-kyi-new-era-burma

Suu, A. (1990). *Freedom from Fear Speech*. Retrieved January 9, 2013 from Third World Traveler: http://www.thirdworldtraveler.com/Burma /FreedomFromFearSpeech.html

Works Cited | A Case for For-Profit Philanthropy | DMT Mobile Toilets | Chapter 5

Ashoka. (2007). *Raising Health Standards by Answering Nature's Call*. Retrieved January 9, 2013 from Ashoka: http://www.citizenbase.org/node/2989

Financial Freedom Inspiration. (2012). *Isaac Durojaiye–DMT Mobile Toilets.* Retrieved January 9, 2013 from Financial Freedom Inspiration: http://www.financialfreedominspiration.com/resources/success-stories/isaac-durojaiye-dmt-mobile-toilets/

Oseni, A. L. (2012, April). *Mobile toilets set to pooh-pooh poverty.* Retrieved January 9, 2013 from West Africa Insight: http://westafricainsight.org/articles/PDF/168

World Health Organization. (2009, August). *Fact sheet N°330.* Retrieved January 9, 2013 from World Health Organization: http://www.who.int/mediacentre/factsheets/fs330/en/index.html

Works Cited | A Case for the Ethical Corporation | Tyson Foods | Chapter 6

Bold Faith in the Workplace | Gospel Ministries # 74, Retrieved from http://gospellightminute.wordpress.com/2012/09/30/john-h-tyson-bold-faith-in-the-workplace-gospel-light-minute-73/ Retrieved on October 2012.

United States v. Tyson Foods, Inc., 97–0506 (D.D.C. January 12, 1998).

Copeland, J. D. (2001, Winter). *The Tyson Story: Building an Effective Ethics and Compliance Program.* Drake Journal of Agricultural Law, p. 257.

Ethisphere. (2008). *Best Ethics Programs Overall.* Retrieved January 9, 2013 from Ethisphere: http://ethisphere.com/best-ethics-programs-overall-government-contractors/

National Hog Farmer. (2012, October 12). *Industry Experts Respond to Tyson Initiatives.* Retrieved January 9, 2013 from National Hog Farmer: http://nationalhogfarmer.com/animal-well-being/industry-experts-respond-tyson-initiatives

Souza, K. (2012, April 30). *Business Ethics Muted in Mexican relations.* Retrieved January 9, 2013 from The City Wire: http://www.thecitywire.com/node/21692#.ULKYPYfXYj4

Stewart, J. B. (2011, June 24). *Bribery, but Nobody Was Charged.* Retrieved January 9, 2013 from The New York Times: http://www.nytimes.com/2011/06/25/business/25stewart.html?pagewanted=all

Tyson Foods, Inc. (2010). *Fact Book.* Springdale, Arkansas: Tyson Foods, Inc. Retrieved January 9, 2013 from Tyson Foods, Inc.

Tyson Foods, Inc. (2012, April 19). *Tyson Foods Ranked as 'Best Corporate Citizen' by Corporate Responsibility Magazine.* Retrieved January 9, 2013 from Tyson Foods, Inc.: http://www.tysonfoods.com/Media-Room/News-Releases/2012/04/Tyson-Foods-Ranked-as–Best-Corporate-Citizen–by-Corporate-Responsibility-Magazine.aspx

Tyson Foods, Inc. (2012, October 12). *Tyson Foods Announces New Audit Program to Help Ensure Responsible On-farm Treatment of Animals (press release)*. Retrieved January 9, 2013 from Reuters: http://www.reuters.com/article/2012/10/12/idUS148285+12-Oct-2012+GNW20121012

Vinjamuri, D. (2012, May 11). *Tyson Foods and Piglet Abuse: Is Ethical Behavior Profitable?* Retrieved January 9, 2013 from Forbes: http://www.forbes.com/sites/davidvinjamuri/2012/05/11/tyson-foods-and-piglet-abuse-is-ethical-behavior-profitable/

Works Cited in A Case for Oversight | The United Nations Compact and Beyond | Chapter 7

Agazzi, I. (2011, March 26). *Global Compact rejects independent panel's criticism*. Retrieved January 9, 2013 from Global Compact Critics: http://globalcompactcritics.blogspot.com/2011/03/global-compact-rejects-independent.html

Armstrong, E. (2003, September 29). *Establishing and Implementing Ethical Standards in the Public Service: the Role of the Un and the OECD*. Retrieved January 9, 2013 from United Nations Public Administration Network: http://unpan1.un.org/intradoc/groups/public/documents/un/unpan012359.pdf

Clinton Global Initiative. (2012). *About Us*. Retrieved January 9, 2013 from Clinton Global Initiative: http://www.clintonglobalinitiative.org/aboutus/

Clinton Global Initiative. (2012). *The CGI Model*. Retrieved January 9, 2013 from Clinton Global Initiative: http://www.clintonglobalinitiative.org/aboutus/the_cgi_model.asp

Evans, W. (2010, March 19). *It's All Good*. Retrieved January 9, 2013 from Slate: http://www.slate.com/articles/business/moneybox/2010/03/its_all_good.html

Joint Inspection Unit. (2010). *United Nations corporate partnerships: The role and functioning of the Global Compact*. New York: United Nations Joint Inspection Unit: https://www.unjiu.org/en/reports-notes/archive/United%20Nations%20corporate%20partnerships%20-The%20role%20and%20functioning%20of%20the%20Global%20Compact.pdf

Liautaud, S. (2012, October 15). *The Test of Time-Part-I-Proactive Ethics Oversight*. Retrieved January 9, 2013 from Susan Liautaud: http://susanliautaud.com/the-test-of-time-part-1-proactive-ethics-oversight/

New York Stock Exchange. *NYSE Euronext to Acquire Corpedia Corporation (press release)*. (2012, May 24). Retrieved January 9, 2013 from New York Stock Exchange: http://www.nyse.com/press/1337855267449.html

Nohria, N. (2012). *The Dean–Harvard Business School.* Retrieved January 9, 2013 from Harvard Business School: http://www.hbs.edu/dean/

OECD. (2008). *OECD Guidelines for Multinational Enterprises.* Retrieved January 9, 2013 from OECD Publishing. http://www.oecd.org/investment /guidelinesformultinationalenterprises/1922428.pdf

Rheannon, F. (2012, May 30). *It Pays to be Ethical.* Retrieved January 9, 2013 from CSRwire: http://www.csrwire.com/blog/posts/419-it-pays-to-be-ethical -a-conversation-with-corpedia-founder-alex-brigham

Stephenson, E. (2012, November 15). *U.S. Postal Service has record loss, may face cash shortfall.* Retrieved January 9, 2013 from Reuters: http://mobile .reuters.com/article/businessNews/idUSBRE8AE18Q20121115

World Justice Project. (2012). *What is the Rule of Law?* Retrieved January 9, 2013 from World Justice Project: http://worldjusticeproject.org/what-rule-law

World Justice Project. (2012). *Who We Are.* Retrieved January 9, 2013 from World Justice Project: http://worldjusticeproject.org/who-we-are-0

Zunz, O. (2012). Philanthropy in America: A History (Politics and Society in Twentieth-Century America)

Index

Lightning Source UK Ltd.
Milton Keynes UK
UKOW031223070613

211868UK00012B/382/P